"In *Fit to Compete*, Michael Beer provides leaders with an elegant framework for having unvarnished conversations about their organization's strengths, limitations, and needs. This is required reading for anyone looking to implement new strategic directions."

—**ROBERT I. GROSSMAN,** MD, Dean, NYU School of Medicine; CEO, NYU Langone Health

"Michael Beer shows you how to develop shared ownership for your organization's success. From courageous leadership at the top to speaking truth to power in the lower echelons, *Fit to Compete* will help you create trust, a higher-ambition culture, and sustainable performance."

—**KENNETH W. FREEMAN,** Dean Emeritus, Boston University Questrom School of Business; founder and former Chairman and CEO, Quest Diagnostics

"Michael Beer's strategic fitness process will help unlock the hidden wisdom and energy inside your company. I know this because I've had the privilege of leading an organization of twenty thousand people and seeing it work firsthand. The effort translated into a substantial increase in retention, revenue, and profit growth."

—**PETER DUNN,** cofounder and Principal, Activate Healthcare

"In *Fit to Compete*, Michael Beer provides incredible insights and proven tools for leaders to create a safe and encouraging environment to hear the truth from employees—what they like about the culture, what they dislike, what concerns them about the company's current direction, and how they believe they can help you win. If you want to improve the culture and purpose of your organization, this book should be your foundational text."

—**FRED LYNCH,** former President and CEO, Masonite

"Speed and adaptability are required in the digital age, and organizational trust is a crucial ingredient for both. In this very practical and timely guide, Michael Beer vividly shows how honest, collective, and public conversations are the best way to build those necessary levels of trust."

    —RAVI VENKATESAN, Special Representative for Young People & Innovation, UNICEF; former Chairman, Microsoft India; and former Chairman, Bank of Baroda

"In *Fit to Compete*, Michael Beer provides leaders with a detailed and instructive approach to conducting honest conversations inside companies. Filled with practical insights, case studies, and great research, this book belongs in every leader's library."

    —LOUIS CARTER, founder and CEO, Best Practice Institute; author, *In Great Company*

Fit
to
Compete

Fit
to
Compete

**Why Honest Conversations
about Your Company's Capabilities
Are the Key to a Winning Strategy**

MICHAEL BEER

HARVARD BUSINESS REVIEW PRESS · BOSTON, MASSACHUSETTS

HBR Press Quantity Sales Discounts

Harvard Business Review Press titles are available at significant quantity discounts when purchased in bulk for client gifts, sales promotions, and premiums. Special editions, including books with corporate logos, customized covers, and letters from the company or CEO printed in the front matter, as well as excerpts of existing books, can also be created in large quantities for special needs.

For details and discount information for both print and ebook formats, contact booksales@harvardbusiness.org, tel. 800-988-0886, or www.hbr.org/bulksales.

The web addresses referenced in this book were live and correct at the time of the book's publication but may be subject to change.

Library of Congress Cataloging-in-Publication Data

Names: Beer, Michael, author.
Title: Fit to compete : why honest conversations about your company's capabilities are the key to a winning strategy / by Michael Beer.
Description: [Boston, Massachusetts] : Harvard Business Review Press, [2019] | Includes index.
Identifiers: LCCN 2019024079 | ISBN 9781633692305 (hardcover)
Subjects: LCSH: Communication in management. | Organizational behavior. | Honesty. | Trust. | Organizational effectiveness.
Classification: LCC HD30.3 .B437 2019 | DDC 658.4/5–dc23
LC record available at https://lccn.loc.gov/2019024079
ISBN: 978-1-63369-230-5
eISBN: 978-1-63369-231-2

The paper used in this publication meets the requirements of the American National Standard for Permanence of Paper for Publications and Documents in Libraries and Archives Z39.48-1992.

In memory of Cynthia,
the love of my life

Contents

Author's Note

This book is a product of a deep collaboration with Russell Eisenstat, my colleague at the Harvard Business School in the 1990s and in several professional endeavors that have followed. While I wrote this book alone and am responsible for the ideas in it, Russ was a full partner in the development of the strategic fitness process (SFP), the method for enabling honest, collective, and public conversations in organizations and the subject of this book. Our collaboration gave rise to the insights I present here. We collaborated on the early applications of SFP and on several studies to evaluate its effectiveness. We also had many discussions to make sense of our research findings and observations as we helped managers lead honest conversations. In short, I am deeply grateful to Russ for the many contributions he made to the ideas in this book.

Preface

Every organization faces challenges in executing its strategy. Great companies know how to work through them.

Organizational agility is on everybody's mind these days. But you are much more likely to read about it than to see it. An astonishing number of businesses that try to respond to new circumstances with a new strategy find themselves stuck in neutral. If that sounds familiar, you are the audience I have in mind.

Corning's Electronic Products Division (EPD) was one of those stuck organizations. I was working for the company years ago, following my doctoral studies, as an internal management researcher and consultant and had founded Corning's Organizational Research and Development Department, itself an innovation at the time. Tom MacAvoy, vice president and general manager of EPD, came to me with his frustration and a request for help.

When he had been put in charge of the division two years earlier, it was already underperforming because of dramatic changes in the market and in the competitive landscape. He was expected to turn the division around and had done a good job cutting costs, but that wasn't enough. The market was becoming more competitive, morale was low, and he could not seem to resolve conflict between functional departments. The lack of coordination and mutual confidence was undermining EPD's ability to develop the new products it needed if it were to pull ahead.

MacAvoy knew perfectly well what EPD needed to do to succeed. In my experience, most CEOs and business-unit leaders do. But what they don't know—and often don't realize they don't know until they are stalled in neutral—is how to get the organization and its people to change and adapt to a new strategic vision.

EPD's story ends differently from most. A year later, at a dinner celebrating a glowing business review, MacAvoy presented me, as his consultant, with an oil can—one with a big spout used to oil machinery—labeled "Emotional Oil Can" and filled with good whiskey. The good news was the progress EPD had made on the very issues MacAvoy had outlined for me in our first meeting. As the division's ability to execute its own strategy improved dramatically, so had its health, culture, and performance.

MacAvoy, with my advisory help, had orchestrated a fundamental change in the whole system by which EPD's senior team organized, managed, and led. In short, everything changed, and it did so in a coordinated way so that the whole system would be aligned with—or fit—the strategy of developing new products. How such wide-ranging positive changes in organizational capabilities can be made so rapidly is the topic this book.

Years of research—much of it carried out along with consultation (a combination known as *action research*)—have shown me that systematic organizational change, carried out the way EPD did it, improves the organization's effectiveness and performance and dramatically changes its culture. There is more trust, more coordination and teamwork, and more commitment to executing the leaders' strategic aspirations. The "Emotional Oil Can" MacAvoy gave me reflected the transformation of EPD from a culture of anger and blaming to one of positive and productive relationships—a community of shared purpose with a system of organizing, managing, and leading now fit to compete.

MacAvoy's approach to getting unstuck—to carrying out his strategy—was different from most senior managers' approach. He did not try to lead top-down change by giving inspirational speeches to mobilize improved performance. He did not introduce financial incentives to motivate different behavior. Nor did he take further cost-cutting initiatives or launch a culture or leadership development program. In fact, his predecessor had launched a leadership development program, but it had made little difference.

Instead, MacAvoy led EPD's transformation from the bottom up. He and his senior team commissioned interviews with key people in the division about what was working and not working. Then there was honest dialogue about what those interviews had uncovered—the good, the bad, and the ugly. The senior team conducted a holistic diagnosis of why the organization was ineffective—taking into account the organization's anatomy, physiology, and psychology, so to speak. Just as a doctor or a surgeon needs a confident diagnosis before prescribing a treatment, these top managers wanted to be sure they really understood what was wrong before deciding what to do about it.

Once the team members arrived at a diagnosis and a plan for change, the whole team held one-day meetings in fifteen parts of the organization scattered across the country, including corporate functions. The team members explained their diagnosis and how they planned to reorganize EPD in response to feedback. They asked those below them for yet more reaction to their plan. MacAvoy himself did something quite unusual but powerful in these meetings. He shared publicly the feedback he had received about his own management style. Thus, EDP's surprisingly rapid and successful realignment with its new strategy emerged from open discussion and reflection, not simply from some other organization's or consultant's idea of a best practice.

MacAvoy and his team carried out an example of what I call an *honest, collective, and public* conversation, In everyday life, a conversation is often unstructured but often fails to be truly open. But the honest conversations I am talking about are quite structured and are based on years of research and experience by me, Russ Eisenstat, and our colleagues at TruePoint Partners, a research-based consultancy I cofounded with Russ. These open conversations work, despite the obvious concerns you probably had while reading the brief description above. In this book, you will learn much more about how to lead effective conversations to accelerate change and why these conversations work better than most conventional approaches to leading change.

In my experience, this collaborative, open approach transformed not only the company or business unit but sometimes also the careers of executives who led it. MacAvoy became president of Corning just four years later; he attributed his promotion partly to the dramatic turn-around he had initiated. As he well appreciated, one cause of the turn-around was the honest conversations he had led.

For years, I have had the privilege of sitting on the front line of trans-formations in many organizations and industries. Often, I function as an action researcher. While facilitating and advising, I also document cases and conduct rigorous research on why some transformations are more successful than others. My work has led me to an actionable the-ory of how to rapidly develop an organization *fit to compete*, that is, an or-ganization able to realign itself rapidly with ever-changing competitive demands. The approach I and my colleagues have developed—honest, collective, and public conversation—is, I freely admit, unconventional and counterintuitive. But it is successful. It asks much of everyone in-volved but delivers even more.

Why Your Strategy Needs an Honest Conversation

Management systems require knowledge of the interrelationships between all components within the system and of everybody that works in it.

—**W. Edwards Deming, presentation at Western Connecticut University, February 1990**

"Courage is the most important of all the virtues, because without courage you can't practice any other virtue consistently. You can practice any virtue erratically, but nothing consistently without courage."

—**Maya Angelou, as quoted in *Diversity: Leaders Not Labels*, by Stedman Graham**

In 2010, Ed Ludwig, CEO of global medical technology maker Becton Dickinson (BD), was a year away from his planned retirement but was by no means ready to coast. In fact, he and his designated successor, Vince Forlenza, intended to give their company a new strategic direction—and they had decided to do it the hard way.

BD had already been outperforming its competitors for a decade. Nevertheless, after many discussions, the senior team concluded that with the changing competitive landscape, the company's good performance wouldn't be good enough. BD had to transform itself from an excellent operating company that had succeeded through trustful customer relationships, ethical behavior, and incremental product improvement into a much more innovative company capable of delivering value-added solutions outside its "home court." As Gary Cohen, a member of the senior team, put it, BD was already a fine athlete, but now it had to become an "Olympian."[1]

Ludwig and Forlenza knew that company cultures don't change just because someone at the top wants them to. Instead, they knew that they would need to obtain commitment from BD's managers around the globe. Their new strategy would require the transformation of BD's entire system of organizing, managing, and leading.

For these reasons, the transformation they had in mind would depart dramatically from the conventional top-down change practiced by most top managements. Ludwig and Forlenza did not hire a consulting firm to recommend changes in BD's organization and processes so that top management would then sell these changes to lower levels to execute. Instead, they launched an organization-wide honest, collective, and public conversation about two things: which of BD's strengths had to be preserved for the new strategy to work and which barriers within the company would sabotage that strategy.

Honest, collective, and public conversation can take several forms, but in BD's case, it involved about 150 people. Most were the company's key employees in all its various units and functions. They were given a chance to safely express—to a chosen group of twelve managers trusted by both the senior team and the lower levels—their opinions about BD's capability to execute the new strategy. The other participants in the conversation were external stakeholders—investors, customers, thought leaders, and a few CEOs in the industry and partners—who offered their views of the company's strengths and barriers to executing the new strategy. The twelve managers then presented to the senior team—in person—what they had heard. The senior team members, in turn, shared with the rest of the company exactly what they had heard from the lower levels—however uncomplimentary some of it was to themselves—and what they planned to do about it. Nothing was hidden in a consultant's report or the minutes of a board meeting.

Let's consider how unusual a step Ludwig and Forlenza had taken. They already knew the strategy they wanted to pursue. Why, then, would they commit themselves to listen to, and act on, unvarnished opinions about barriers to the transformation from people over whom they had authority? Why not just tell people what was expected of them? Why would they commit themselves to communicate honestly to hundreds of people around the world the uncensored truths they had heard about those barriers to innovation and their plans for change? Wouldn't this signal to everyone that they were weak and indecisive? Wouldn't it slow down the transformation they so urgently wanted to make? Wouldn't it lead to a culture of complaints, endless debate, and inaction? And in any case, would people below the top have that much to contribute to high-level strategy?

In short, why go asking for trouble? Why not just lead?

Ludwig and Forlenza understood that "poor implementation will eat a good strategy for lunch." They had learned how hard it is to get their organization and their people to understand the new strategic direction and work together to transform the organization's capability to execute this change. And the challenge is growing for most companies because the competitive environment is becoming more brutal and changing ever more quickly. Your organization and you, its leader, may not survive and will certainly not prosper in the long run unless your organization learns to adapt and change continuously.

Why Most Transformations Fail

Nearly every organization—whether private, social, or governmental—is grappling with huge strategic challenges, often with a need to reimagine its very purpose, identity, strategy, business model, and structure. Most of these efforts to transform will fail.[2] And in most cases, they miss the mark not because the new strategy is flawed, but because the organization can't carry it out. Let's consider several examples.

Nokia: Poor collaboration and coordination

As the first company in the mobile phone industry to achieve commercial success, Nokia enjoyed a huge share of the global market.[3] But by 2010, its share was declining, with Apple's introduction of the iPhone. Surprisingly, years before the iPhone was introduced, Nokia leaders understood where the industry was going. The company had developed an early version of an internet-ready touchscreen handset with a large display and was working on improving it. How then can we account for this failure?

The story is complex. Nokia clearly faced huge headwinds—dramatic changes in the industry and in mobile technology. Senior management understood that it had to improve its proprietary operating system, Symbian. But several things kept getting in the way. One was an organizational context—a system of organizing, managing, and leading that did not fit the new strategy. Such an environment would enable not only differentiation (strong functional capabilities) but also integration, coordination, and cooperation within and between business segments.

The inadequacy of Nokia's matrix organization and the company's subsequent decision to decentralize complicated the coordination across departments or managerial levels required for rapid innovation. The design of the organization prompted infighting among managers with competing objectives and views. Moreover, those at the top never dealt with these tensions properly, because they never fully knew the depth of these problems. Nor did managers see how their own leadership contributed to the problems or realize that developing an organizational structure for effective decision making was their principal task. As a result, the organization failed to change and coordination remained stagnant.

British Petroleum: A failure to organize and lead effectively

The gigantic oil spill after the failure of a British Petroleum oil platform in the Gulf of Mexico in 2010 was, according to HR consultant Richard Lepsiger, an enormous execution failure: "Leading up to and after the oil spill BP violated almost all the guidelines of effective execution, including lacking an effective structure and lacking clear accountability." Moreover, "following the spill, BP was unable to get input from those who had the knowledge and experience to make the best decisions about how to handle it."[4] BP had failed to develop the leaders it needed in an emergency like that and had failed to develop a culture that empowered its people to use their best judgment and take appropriate action.

Johnson & Johnson: An erosion of values

Johnson & Johnson's McNeil Consumer Healthcare, a maker of over-the-counter drugs, has had eight product recalls since 2009. But as far back as 2005, employees were reporting a lack of alignment between managers' behavior and J&J's historical values of integrity, honesty, quality, and doing the right thing. CEO James Burke had exemplified and institutionalized these values in the 1980s, when, at great company expense, he pulled all Tylenol products off retail shelves and launched a costly initiative to develop tamper-proof bottle caps. The move was in response to the deaths of seven people after they took medication that had been tampered with after the bottles were on the retail shelf. The company's failure to sustain this culture of integrity demonstrates the importance of alignment between strategy and culture.

Toyota: Poor organization design

In 2010, millions of Toyota vehicles were recalled because of numerous defects, a surprising outcome for a company that had long been recognized for reliable quality. A decentralized structure that had worked in earlier years turned into a liability as the company grew exponentially and became the dominant player in the industry. Senior executives

believed that Toyota's worldwide functional structure required all customer complaints to go to Japan, rather than being dealt with in each
region, thereby undermining local responsibility, accountability, and
rapid response.

General Electric: Failure to listen

General Electric had prospered for over a hundred years when its celebrated CEO, Jack Welch, retired in 2002, the year GE stock hit a high
of $55. But by January 2019, the stock had fallen to $8. Welch's successor, Jeff Immelt, was an equally celebrated CEO with a magnetic and
optimistic personality, but he ran into strong headwinds in the business
environment, including a depressed energy sector—one of GE's biggest
markets—and the financial crisis of 2008–2009.

Immelt tried to rescue the company and his legacy by acquiring
Alstom, GE's chief competitor in the energy sector, despite wariness by
some board directors, senior executives, and advisers. Knowing that
Alstom had made bad deals, followed bad practices, and performed
poorly, executives in GE's energy and power sector cheered every time
the deal seemed about to collapse. But it was difficult for them to challenge what they considered Immelt's overoptimism; when executives
presented what they considered realistic plans, he was known to quip,
"Where is the guy I used to know?" They believed that he overrated
GE's capabilities and that he did not listen to subordinates who tried to
tell him so. The deal went through, but Alstom has not performed and
is one of the main reasons GE's stock price has collapsed and investors
have lost faith in the company.[5]

As a group, these failures illustrate the common root cause of organizational ineffectiveness: a flawed strategy or failure to align the organization and management processes with the strategy and values. Misalignment tends to produce the very symptoms we see in these five stories:
unclear or flawed strategy (GE); unclear values (J&J); poor coordination (Nokia, BP, Toyota); inadequate capacity for honest communication

(GE); inadequate leadership development (BP); and failure by leaders to listen and learn (GE). We will examine these and other common manifestations of misalignment—which I call the silent killers—in chapter 4, and trace them back to the failure of leaders to have an honest and productive organization-wide conversation.

Employees below senior management collectively know a lot about why their strategy or organization is not effective. They cannot, however, convey their understanding to senior management. Sometimes, it is clearly unsafe, careerwise, to be the bearer of bad news. Other times, management lets people complain but doesn't take the complaints seriously.

Organizationally lifesaving information cannot get where it needs to go when management has not institutionalized a disciplined way to receive it. This information needs to be delivered to leaders regularly, not only in sufficient detail but also with enough urgency and coherence to provoke action.

Ironically, these companies had established a disciplined total quality management process in their operations. Toyota had pioneered such methods, and the others had learned their lesson from Toyota and other Japanese companies: enabling frontline employees to communicate safely about quality problems and involving them in improving production can continually improve quality and reduce costs. Yet none of these companies had thought to apply such a process to continuously improve the quality of their own organizations, that is, the effectiveness of their own leadership. As I hope this book will convince you, honest, collective, and public conversation is total quality management for the organization as a whole.

The Strategic Fitness Process

If a company's organization, management, and leadership are to improve, the people affected by these elements have to feel involved. They must be encouraged to discover problems and to correct them. This sense of ownership can only come about if the people involved in the system feel involved in the process of improving it; that is, involved in discovering problems and correcting them. That can only come about if they trust both the intentions and the competence of their leaders. In such an open environment, honest conversations can thrive and the needed changes can take place. These conversations require senior leaders to have the courage to temporarily suspend their convictions and to cancel, as it were, their immunity to challenge so that less powerful people can speak truth to power.[6] In many organizations, people sense that none of this is possible.

A few decades ago, my colleague Russ Eisenstat and I joined forces with Ray Gilmartin, then CEO of Becton Dickinson, and his leadership team to pioneer a technique of rapidly improving the quality of BD's management. We jointly invented the strategic fitness process (SFP). This process enabled Gilmartin to learn about barriers to execution and to change how BD was organized, managed, and led. With those changes, BD became an organization that could—and did—carry out Gilmartin's strategy to grow BD's business in Europe.

SFP is a carefully designed platform that has proven successful in fostering otherwise difficult, honest, collective, and public conversations about an organization's effectiveness. It begins with the senior team's developing and writing down on two pages the business's strategic direction and then appointing a task force of eight of their best leaders below the top to interview a hundred people who have intimate knowledge of the challenges at hand. Task forces sometimes need to be larger than eight people, depending on circumstances, but eight has proven to work well. The leader describes the strategy to the task force members so that the members can explain it to the interviewees. The task force asks them for their frank feedback about the organizational strengths and weaknesses that will affect the execution of the strategy. In a face-to-face meeting, the task force presents the senior team with what they have learned. The senior team then develops an action plan for change. Next, they discuss the plan with the task force members: is it responsive

FIGURE I-1

Overview of the strategic fitness process

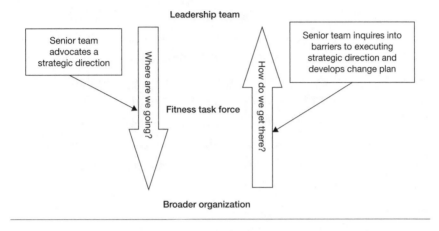

to the feedback, and do the members see barriers to executing it? The senior team then shares their findings with the larger organization: here's what we heard, and here's what we plan to change. Figure I-1 provides an overview of how SFP works. Chapter 1 will show you how to lead this process.

The process usually takes six to eight weeks. SFP is not a special program; it should not be presented as a program. It is essential management work to improve organization and leadership effectiveness. If SFP seems like something extra, then the process has probably never been done when it should have been.

Thirty years of facilitating and studying honest organization-wide conversations in culturally different regions around the world has provided my colleagues and me with many useful insights. We have seen the power of such conversations and the conditions that moderate this power.

SFP is not, however, a magic bullet. It does not always transform an organization rapidly or completely. The result depends on the leadership and the organizational context. Most important is the leadership's will to close a performance gap and the extent to which the leaders' values align with SFP's underlying values, namely, openness to learning and acting on the unvarnished truth. My research shows that implementation of SFP also transforms the environment. The process changes the nature of a system and how senior management leads—the leaders' effectiveness, human sensibilities, and willingness to continue learning through honest conversations. (Appendix B summarizes the research my colleagues and I have conducted to evaluate SFP.)

At first, SFP seemed somewhat risky to the leaders with whom we worked. Yet they instinctively knew that honest conversations would result in higher commitment and better performance. The leaders include the CEOs and business-unit leaders whose stories are told in this book as well as many others whose stories are not included here. We have worked with Ray Gilmartin at Becton Dickinson and later at Merck; Robert Grossman, dean and CEO of New York University Langone Medical Center; Ravi Venkatesan, chairman of Microsoft India; Patrick Decker, president and CEO of Xylem; and Fred Lynch, president and CEO of Masonite International; and many others who have implemented SFP.

The thirty-year journey in developing, applying, and researching SFP reflected in this book provides insights into what is possible when leaders have the courage and innovative spirt to apply an unconventional approach to strategic change. The most courageous people transformed not only their organizations but also themselves as leaders.

My and my colleagues' research demonstrates that SFP works, though there are many variations that can also do so.[7] Leaders need a disciplined and repeatable route toward honest conversations to transform their companies into high-quality systems of organizing, managing, and leading. SFP, a prototype of the missing strategic learning and governance process described later in the book, awaits further development by others.

However you conduct them, honest conversations must involve the exchange of two truths. First, senior management shares with lower levels the hard and sometimes inconvenient truths about what the firm must do to compete. These observations do not always go over well with those at lower levels. They may see themselves at the losing end or feel they are being made to pay for top management's mistakes. Or they may not trust senior management to even do what it says is necessary. Nor is the conversation likely to be pleasant for leaders; whatever trouble the company is in is bound to reflect on their own management.

Second, those below the top share their own experience of the organization's strengths and weaknesses in these conversations This assessment does not always go over well with senior management, which is often identified as one of the problems. And again, even if the managers are not the problem, any serious issue with how the company is run has to be a reflection on them. Consequently, outright critical honesty presents a challenge for the lower ranks; they can't help but wonder if there will be a price to pay for telling senior management its house is not entirely in order.

The purpose of SFP and other such methods of honest conversation is to make all honest conversations possible despite everyone's natural fear, reluctance, and embarrassment. Chapter 1 will describe how you can lead these conversations. When they do take place, they develop something priceless—the partnership needed between top management and their people to transform a company into a high-performance, high-commitment community of shared purpose.[8] These interchanges—not only what is said but the very fact that it *can* be said and that senior management wants it said—demonstrate senior leadership's authenticity, caring, humanity, and commitment to drive change. This mindset energizes stakeholders and accelerates organizational transformation as nothing else can.

The work that my colleagues and I have done with leaders who have taken this counterintuitive and unconventional approach to corporate transformation has demonstrated that honest conversations can simultaneously improve several areas of an organization. They develop a more effective and high-performing organization, increase its internal trust and commitment, and build its capacity to learn and change continuously—and keep making these improvements.

In too many transformations, rapid top-down change enhances performance in the short term but seriously undermines people's trust and commitment. Consequently, they neither take the initiative to speak up about barriers to strategy execution nor feel a commitment to help their leaders make necessary, immediate changes or help in the future. The organization's capability to adapt is seriously damaged, so that what it gains in the short run it more than loses in the long run.

The companies we have worked with and studied are part of an ever-larger circle of leading-edge, higher-ambition enterprises.[9] Paul Adler and Charles Heckscher call them collaborative communities: "By marrying a sense of common purpose to a supportive structure, these organizations are mobilizing knowledge workers' talents and expertise in flexible, highly manageable group-work efforts. The approach fosters not only innovation and agility but also efficiency and scalability."[10] Keep in mind that the knowledge production to which Adler and Heckscher refer is not just knowledge about new products or processes; it is inside knowledge about the company itself and how its management system is working. Honest conversation is therefore a way to take your organization to the next level, not just once but over and over again. My experience, and that of my colleagues, confirms that this is exactly what happens.

The Promise of Honest Dialogue

A disciplined and repeatable process for having honest conversations has several benefits. These conversations overcome, as I will explain, the distance, low trust, and low commitment created by differences in power. They reveal the whole truth; nothing is left out about organizational and management barriers to strategy execution. In this way, the whole system is thoroughly evaluated and can be transformed. And if the conversations are structured and made safe through a transformational leadership platform like SFP, they overcome people's reluctance to speak up about ineffectiveness found in most institutions.

Overcoming hierarchy

By this point, you might think that honest conversations would be anathema to a hierarchy. That's not at all true. Rather, these conversations recognize that a hierarchy, though essential for any organization, can sometimes be counterproductive. Through honest conversation, hierarchical organizations can overcome the weaknesses to which they are inherently vulnerable.

In particular, a top-down, command-and-control form of organization can cause as many problems as it solves in an environment of rapid and continuous change—and that's the environment we're all in now. It's not that top executives can't figure out what to do quickly enough. It's that they can't get the organization to change itself quickly enough— if at all. You can see the iceberg and give the command, but that doesn't mean a huge ocean liner loaded with passengers can change course in time. Honest conversation—and SFP in particular—makes transformation much more achievable because it releases the energy, innovation, commitment, and collaboration that the competitive situation requires. SFP is also much faster than the typical successive and unconnected initiatives, each targeting a specific barrier that top management thinks is important for strategy execution. In fact, honest conversation is arguably the best method of organizational transformation that can keep pace with today's competitive environment.

How exactly do differences in power thwart strategy execution? First, they promote self-interest and politics, which undermine teamwork. Second, the differences demand deference, which inhibits honest conversations about what is working and not working and consequently prevents the learning required to adapt to continual change. Lack of openness, in turn, produces cynicism and anemic levels of trust, engagement, and commitment below the top. People know there are problems, but management doesn't fix them. So why should management be trusted? Is it any surprise, then, that multiple studies have shown decades of decline in employee engagement and satisfaction and low trust in corporations and their CEOs?[11] Without trust, it's going to be hard to stimulate innovation and change, because these involve risk. All told, hierarchy can block its own arteries by erecting barriers to strategic alignment and change.

These drawbacks of hierarchy undoubtedly undermine organizational agility. The lack of agility is evident in the inability of most business organizations to sustain high performance levels over a long period. One study found that only 20 percent of the businesses in the sample consistently performed well. Some 60 percent swung between high and low performance. Of the businesses studied, 20 percent never broke out of the low-performance zone. The same study found that high-performing firms that avoided these swings were less hierarchical, more collaborative, and more open to the truth about their competitive and internal weaknesses.[12]

Transforming the whole system

Honest, collective, and public conversations enable leaders to change the whole system of organizing, managing, and leading.[13] For a transformation, whole-system change is a necessity, not an option. A transformation that isn't systemic will simply replace one imbalance with another. Whole-system change requires a collective effort to change multiple facets of the organization. People from different parts of the organization who know what is or is not working must be brought into the conversation. Making it public internally—that is, telling employees that the leadership team is launching an honest conversation to improve effectiveness and has committed to telling everyone in the organization honestly what was learned and will be changed—energizes the organization and legitimizes management's efforts to lead change. When, earlier in his career at Becton Dickinson, Ed Ludwig led an honest conversation about what was holding his unit back, he noted that "people were relieved to learn that we [the senior team] actually thought there was a problem."

Because most leaders fail to take on this type of holistic change, organizational transformations fail to achieve what was hoped for. Or if they do, it takes far too long. Partial transformations fail because when you change one facet of the organization without changing the others to re-inforce it, the change you want won't last—if it even occurs at all. Honest conversation lays a foundation for systemic transformation because the partnership it creates enables senior leaders to change how the whole place is organized. Normally, such multifaceted change would be re-sisted because it would present too many threats to too many people's status, competence, comfort, and power and they would have little faith that management would support or protect them.

Three forms of fitness. Leaders who want an organization that can realign itself rapidly with ever-changing competitive demands—one that is fit to compete—must make sure the organization is fit in three areas:

- **Fit to perform:** How the firm is organized and managed—its structure, leadership, processes, measurement system, IT system, and management policies and practices—has to align with the firm's strategy and values.[14] Alignment does not mean the elimi-nation of tensions required to innovate. An organization aligned to innovate will be designed to promote ambidexterity— the capability to exploit existing opportunities while also exploring radically new ones.

  A firm that is not fit to perform cannot carry out its strategy or live up to its values, even if the strategy or values are great. In an unaligned system, the components will just get in each other's way.

- **Fit for trust and commitment:** Management policies and practices must be consciously designed to enable employees to satisfy their enduring needs for meaning, bonding, learning, justice, and voice.[15] For example, performance evaluation of leaders must consider not only their results but also their capacity to engage their people. Practices that allow lower levels to speak up must be embedded in the company culture, and jobs must be designed to be meaningful. A firm that is not fit for trust and commitment cannot take a new direction in strategy, values, or cultural aspirations, because people will mistrust management's motives and protect themselves rather than take the risks required to change successfully.

- **Fitness to adapt:** The organization must have the capabilities and culture that support honest, collective, and public conversations about how well it is adapting to changing competitive or social realities and how well it upholds the values espoused by senior management. A firm that is not fit to adapt will be left behind— dead or alive.

A firm must reach all three levels of fitness to survive and prosper in the long run. Such an organization is fit to compete. Honest and collective conversations are uniquely suited to achieve all three outcomes simultaneously.

The fallacy of programmatic change. Research my colleagues and I conducted in the late 1980s showed the importance of the systems approach to change.[16] At that time, companies were trying to transform their capability to develop high-quality products in response to Japanese competitors. Many companies launched top-down programs to teach people by the thousands about Japanese methods and teamwork. Some firms introduced matrix structures to facilitate coordination. Others introduced training and education programs. Seeing that these top-down programs generally failed, Russ Eisenstat, Bert Spector, and I wrote a *Harvard Business Review* article on the topic: "Why Change Programs Do Not Produce Change."[17]

Those programs targeted only one facet of an entire system. They were driven by functional staff groups such as HR or Quality; top management failed to assign unit leaders the task of deciding when and how to use the new ideas in their own strategic agendas and priorities. Unit leaders passively complied but failed to actively lead change. Successive initiatives thus became notorious as passing fads. With regard to training—the most frequent initiative—we found that regardless of how well trained and motivated individuals were, they could not overcome a system that wasn't comprehensively aligned with the desired changes. And when it comes to systems, if they're not for you, they're against you.[18]

The most successful transformations in those studies used a unit-by-unit approach.[19] The implication is clear: to change a large and complex company, an honest conversation and the learning process it enables ideally occur within each major unit (whether corporate, business, functional, regional, or operating), and each unit is a system with its own culture. The unit's collective behavior—collaborative or uncooperative—is shaped by how well the leadership team organizes and manages the unit.[20] Thus, each unit faces as many potential leadership and organization barriers as corporate level. Recall that Johnson & Johnson's product recalls began four years after employees reported in a corporate survey that their operating units and leaders were not aligned with the firm's historic values of integrity and quality. What if an honest conversation had occurred in the first year?

Emotions matter. To understand transformation failures—which are much more common than transformation successes—we must also recognize that organizations are *socioemotional systems*. What happens inside them—or fails to happen—is very much the product of how people feel and how they behave with each other. Both these factors depend not just on the individuals but also on the culture and other circumstances.

By definition, change involves loss by some (others may feel they have won). This win-lose element of change brings to the fore the emotions of employees at every level.[21] My colleagues and I have observed both positive and negative emotions in the honest conversations we have facilitated. For example, people felt pride in their company and its ethical standards at the same time that they felt frustration and anger at its shortcomings. These conversations revealed the leadership's deeply held assumptions about how the business should be led. Sometimes those assumptions were no longer valid because of new competitive and social realities and were therefore explicitly threatened by the changes being discussed. The conversations also revealed emotions normally not shared, such as frustration with the organization's ineffectiveness, disillusionment with its values, lack of confidence in its leadership, pessimism about whether improvement was even possible, and—hovering over everything—considerable fear of speaking truth to power about these matters.

Senior management was often just as frustrated with the employees. It blamed performance problems on their lack of ability and commitment. Blaming people rather than the situation in which people find themselves—the organizational context or system—is an established principle in psychology. Called the *fundamental attribution error*, it is supported by many studies.[22] Senior managers that were worried about arousing defensiveness and anger were reluctant to have honest conversations about the system, because they feared that the open discussion would make things worse. The result was less trust and commitment and therefore less chance of fixing whatever needed to be fixed. Their response to these problems was more top-down command and control, which accomplished exactly what they were so worried about: even more defensiveness and less trust and effectiveness. But the successful leaders I describe in this book had the courage to go in the opposite direction. They opened up a safe, honest conversation that would eventually change the system and at the same time replace the fear of speaking up. This fear would be supplanted with both hope that the company could actually change and with commitment, the desire to help with the transformation by saying what needed to be said.

But without honest conversation, fear can undermine this commitment, even among people who had trusted each other before new competitive challenges made their system ineffective. Consider how a member of Hewlett-Packard's Santa Rosa Systems Division described the impediments to change in his business unit: "I think people did not know how to break through to it . . . You read about these bad marriages, where the wife and the husband both know what's wrong. They just can't find a way to talk to each other about it. And I think that's what was going on. We all knew the problems were there, and I think we could not find a way to discuss it with each other in a constructive way" (see chapter 4).[23]

Consider, too, how failure to have an honest conversation about deeper emotional issues contributed to Nokia's failure to execute its strategy and sabotaged its transformation, as described earlier. Top managers' fears of failure led them to exert pressure on middle managers, making those managers too afraid to let top management know how little progress was actually being made. This omission misled senior management into being overly optimistic, so they underresourced change initiatives and promised too much to investors. The executives failed to properly manage these strategic initiatives by prioritizing better or making the long-term investment needed to compete with Apple.[24]

This and similar unhealthy organizational dynamics were frequently reported in the many honest conversations I have observed. They reflect leaders' failure to create the right balance between: (1) short-term pressures for immediate nonsystemic improvements and longer-term systemic strategic change and (2) "harder" tangible issues (e.g., structure, processes, IT, and incentives) and "deeper socioemotional issues (figure I-2).[25] Emphasis on the short-term, tangible, and surface issues is in the comfort zone of most managers and becomes their go-to position under pressure. It prevents people from looking at the long-term, deeper, and less tangible changes required for sustained change. As you will see, honest conversations help leaders achieve the right balance.

Confronting the softer and deeper socioemotional issues is well outside the comfort zone of most people, but corporate leaders *should* be an exception—it is more and more a requirement of the job. In this regard, executives shouldn't have ordinary personalities any more than pro football players should have ordinary physiques. The stakes are simply too high. Unfortunately, short-term pressure for fast improvement causes many leaders to go straight for their comfort zones and focus on the numbers, the equipment, the supply chain, the org chart. Fundamental transformations require the step-out courage that the leaders at Becton Dickinson demonstrated when they decided to use SFP to hold

FIGURE I-2

Why transformations fail to change the system

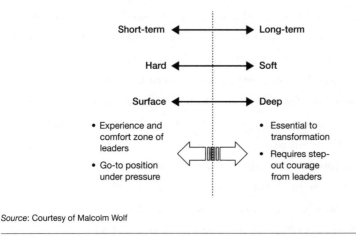

Source: Courtesy of Malcolm Wolf

an honest, collective, and public conversation about BD's strengths and about its barriers to innovation and faster growth. Because such a conversation is wide open (though not without boundaries), it can address *all* the elements of the system that need to be changed. The leadership platform of SFP also helps leaders move safely and productively through a conversation they see as risky, thereby learning that open discussion isn't as uncomfortable as they thought.

Banishing silence

Hierarchy leads to organizational defensive routines, as management scholar Chris Argyris called them, and they preserve the status quo.[26] People at the top do not seek feedback from lower levels, and the deference of those at lower levels prevents them from giving it. But there is a way around this impasse. Suspending the hierarchy temporarily—so a safe, productive, and honest conversation about the state of the enterprise can take place—overcomes these defensive routines. It is a way to avoid being stuck in a pattern of management that once produced superior performance but no longer does. That is what Becton Dickinson and the other organizations described in this book were able to do.

Even senior leaders who embraced honest conversations enthusiastically did not fully understand how their management conspired to create emotions and collective behavior that blocked success. In effect, organizations are like icebergs. Only the tip of the iceberg is visible to all; the rest is underwater and not fully known or understood. As management scholar Barry Oshry has shown, no one in the organization, including senior leaders, can see the whole system and act to change it.[27] Too often we blame others—top management blames the bottom, and the bottom blames the top or one function blames another—instead of engaging in a fact-based conversation that reveals the truth about what is going on and why. To develop a healthy, collaborative system that spurs high performance and commitment, leaders need valid data—the whole truth about the system.[28] The "whole truth" very much includes people's feelings; these, too, have consequences.

Leaders can usually sense when something is wrong in their organization. But that's not the same as knowing *what* is wrong any more than feeling unwell tells you what is wrong with your body. Even leaders who think they know what the problem is don't know what is really going on underneath the surface. Nor do they even have a way to discover that they don't. They lack the tools to create an honest conversation about a problem, as in the bad marriage mentioned earlier. This book shows you how to make the truth discussable—safely and constructively. This *dynamic capability* enables organizations to adapt to the ever-changing competitive landscape and the new strategies it requires.[29]

The absence of this capability has a name, too—*organizational silence*—and has been identified as a major barrier to organizational transformation.[30] Organizational silence is not just a problem in bad companies with bad leaders. Consider the comment from a manager in an innovative and high-performing global company led by a CEO who wanted to learn the truth but never could: "People don't go to management with the options because they are afraid. They try to second-guess what management wants instead of what management really needs to know, and so problems build up."[31]

Organizational silence is a pervasive condition because, as discussed above, organizations are hierarchical and the people in them are human. It's human to avoid troublesome truths about ourselves or the organization we are leading. At lower levels, people feel a combination of courtesy and fear. They know how painful it can be to hear disconfirming information and don't want to hurt their leaders. But they are also afraid to speak truth to power because they know they might be repaid with defensiveness, resentment, and even anger—or worse.

My colleagues and I, along with many other researchers, have found that with few exceptions, employees at lower levels feel that the risk of speaking truth to power is too great. They have often heard individuals labeled as poor team players or seen them passed over for promotion or even fired after challenging senior executives. On the rare occasions when people do speak up, even if it is directly to senior management, they seldom learn whether their feedback resulted in meaningful change, so they are little inclined to risk it again. As Jim Detert and Amy Edmondson have shown, employees at all levels develop an "implicit theory"—a deeply rooted assumption—that speaking truth to power is both dangerous and useless, even when their leaders have explicitly asked for it.[32] When the pervasive belief that "this organization cannot change" takes hold, transformation, of course, becomes all that much harder.

Problems become taboo for discussion, and this taboo is itself taboo, since that would reveal that the organization is not as open to frank dialogue as management proclaims. This unintended cover-up, as Argyris called it, prevents the continuous improvement that an always-changing competitive environment demands.[33]

Pervasive silence prevents senior teams from learning about the silent killers. (Earlier in the introduction, we saw examples of silent killers at Nokia, British Petroleum, Johnson & Johnson, Toyota, and General Electric.) Like cholesterol in the human body, they clog organizational arteries. As I will show later in the book, these barriers create the organizational friction that impedes realignment and sustained improvement within organizations. But I will also show that honest conversations can transform these silent barriers into the organizational strengths needed to respond to the brutal competitive environment you face as a leader.

The exceptional leaders with whom we worked broke the spell of silence. They saw the value of honest conversation about the fitness of their organizations to respond to unforgiving competitive realities.

Successful transformations have to engage leaders and their people emotionally through constructive dialogue. In the chapters that follow, I will show the power of this engagement. Leaders and employees must discover truths about their enterprise and themselves *together* so they can change individually and collectively. Dan Heath and Chip Heath call this "tripping over the truth."[34] The truth about what is and is not working in an organization cannot be fully revealed or made believable through speeches, training, or consultants. It must be personally discovered. That is what honest, collective, and public conversations made possible at Becton Dickinson and in hundreds of other organizations around the globe.

In movies and plays, the truth strikes like lightning. One moment, Luke Skywalker has no idea who his father is; the next moment, he knows it's Darth Vader. But in the complicated real life of an organization, the truth reveals itself over time and is absorbed and believed over time. The evidence isn't available all at once. People know parts of the truth, and the parts don't fit together instantaneously. Most importantly, people who think they have been doing something right for years don't suddenly just change their minds. One aspect of the wisdom of the leaders of the 1960s civil rights movement is that, although they believed that white America could change, they understood that it would take time and devised their strategy accordingly. Honest, collective, public conversation is a bit like nonviolent resistance. It is a way of confronting what is wrong and setting a systemic agenda for change over time without poisoning the well with too much anger and defensiveness so that the people who need to change their ideas and attitudes have the psychological leeway to do so.

The best leaders we worked with were inclined to engage people in honest conversation but did not know how to orchestrate it so that those at lower levels could do so safely. Even in the healthiest and most effective organizations we studied, key people below the senior management typically displayed anxiety about putting the truth on the table for discussion. Everyone needed a structured process that reduced their anxiety, particularly if the organization had never done anything like this before.

Leaders can be as defensive as the rest of us—sometimes verbally and sometimes in their body language. One business-unit leader, presented by an employee task force with feedback he didn't agree with, responded, "That's not true." Possibly it wasn't as he saw it, but the truth was less likely to come out, thanks to a response like that. We improved the SFP to discourage this sort of defensive behavior, precisely because it cuts the truth-finding process off prematurely. Because honest conversation is difficult—in a sense, an unnatural act in most organizations—it requires a disciplined platform, a structured guided process, such as SFP, that guarantees a safe and constructive dialogue for both the top and the lower levels. From this platform, people can learn together about the causes of their company's ineffectiveness and become committed to change.

Most importantly, the capacity to talk honestly about what is really going on in the organization demonstrates leadership's authenticity. It is the only way all the stakeholders inside and outside the company can believe that its leaders will truly implement the values that appear in company marketing pieces, be they documents or speeches or material displayed at headquarters or on the corporate website. Honest dialogue is the best way to develop the collaborative community needed to implement strategy and values. Without the truth, cynicism and mistrust begin to erode commitment. Bill George, former CEO of Medtronic and now my colleague at Harvard Business School, put it best in describing why he made transparency and truth the cornerstone of his successful run as CEO:

Values begin with telling the truth, internally and externally. Integrity must run deep in the fabric of an organization's culture. It

guides the everyday actions of employees and is central to its business conduct. Transparency is an integral part of integrity. The
truth, both successes and failures, must be shared openly with the
outside world . . . Such organizations are characterized by a spirit of
inquiry, the constant desire to understand the issues in their fullest
breadth—and to use it on the job every day.[35]

Summing Up

Organizations in all spheres—business, nonprofit, government, and
nongovernment organizations—face major challenges in executing
their evolving strategies in response to ever-changing markets, technology, customer preferences, and social norms. Many top managers are
failing to transform their organizations *effectively* and rapidly, incurring
significant economic, social, and human cost.

Two interrelated reasons explain these well-documented failures.
First, the whole system of organizing, managing, and leading has to be
transformed if organizational behaviors and underlying mindsets are
to be changed. But—the second reason—hierarchy discourages knowledgeable people at lower levels from sharing their vital information
with senior leaders So leadership is left unaware of critical aspects of
the systemic change it needs to make.

Honest organization-wide conversations between top management
teams and employees who know why their organization is foundering
have proven to be a powerful way to transform an organization. But
these conversations are difficult to lead, given people's fears about revealing the truth.

The strategic fitness process, or SFP—one of several possible forms
of honest conversation—is a safe, respectful, and powerful leadership
platform that courageous leaders in many organizations have used to
accelerate change. The remainder of the book will show you why and
how to use the strategic fitness process or a method of your own choosing that conforms to its underlying principles in your organization.

The Power of Honest Conversations

PART ONE

Chapter 1

How to Lead Honest Conversations

The SFP informed the basis of the CEO's agenda for several years and became the focus of key [senior team] members. Perhaps it was not completely obvious at the time, but the SFP was instrumental to many of the changes at BD.

—**Ed Ludwig, former CEO, Becton Dickinson**

ynne Camp knew her new strategy was stuck in neutral. As vice president and general manager of the Systems Generation and Delivery Unit (SGDU) at Agilent Technologies, Camp had been charged with creating a single global company from a fragmented set of businesses in Asia, Europe, and the United States. To gain control over product decisions being made by the regional teams she had inherited, Camp and her senior team had originally adopted a functional structure. This configuration enabled them to exit many marginal local businesses and focus on the most promising opportunities from a global perspective. It also allowed them to introduce shared processes that were more efficient.[1]

That functional structure fit Camp's short-term strategy but not SGDU's long-term strategy of innovation and growth. Predictably, problems began to emerge. The functional departments didn't give the new businesses the attention they needed. The staffs of the regional field organizations were in a funk; they thought their customer perspective was being overlooked. Conflict between the functions, the businesses, and the field organizations was growing. The senior team was slow to make decisions and no one took responsibility for the performance of the developing businesses.

Camp surveyed the problems and concluded that the best way to increase accountability and speed up decision making—and thus to support the strategy of focusing on a few promising businesses—was to switch to a matrix structure she had seen work in a sister business unit. But members of her senior team were doubtful, and, besides, they were already too overloaded to undertake another major reorganization. Camp could have imposed her solution unilaterally, but she knew that if she did, she would undermine the senior team's commitment, which was critical to making a complex global matrix work. She needed to find a different way out of this impasse.

Camp also began to suspect (correctly) that people throughout the unit were talking about difficulties they were having in executing her new strategy—and that plenty of managers a couple of layers down had insights that she needed to hear. But these conversations largely took place behind closed doors. Private conversations, by their nature, cannot mobilize an organization to address the gaps between its business strategy and its structure, capabilities, and competitive environment.

In our experience, the challenge Camp faced—the unit's collective inability to talk openly about its problems—is all too common. In the introduction, I referred to this inability as organizational silence. This lack of openness lies behind many failures to implement strategy. My experience in many organizations and that of scholars who study organizational change suggests that the most powerful way for leaders to realign their organization is to publicly confront the truth about the barriers blocking strategy implementation. Barriers can then be overcome through changes in how the system is organized, managed, and led. As a consequence, responsibilities and decision rights of various parts of the business change, and people's behavior at all levels changes quickly.

Public, organization-wide conversations about such fundamental issues are difficult and likely to be painful. But pain contributes to an organism's survival by triggering learning and adaptation; it can have the same benefit for an organization. Businesses and the people inside them don't learn to change unless they have the courage to confront difficult truths. Confronting the truth collectively allows an organization to accept radical change, as I will show in this and later chapters.

Because most initiatives fail to uncover the truth, they lead to only superficial change. Employee surveys, 360-degree feedback, interviews by external consultants, and even relatively honest one-on-one conversations between a key manager and the CEO seldom move the organization forward. Many Americans remember the courageous discussion Sharon Watkins, Enron's vice president of corporate development, had with CEO Kenneth Lay about the company's major business and ethical problems. That private discussion did not change anything, and we all know what happened to Enron.

The fallacy of all such initiatives is that they do nothing to convince employees that management wants to know the truth and is ready to act on it. Quite the reverse, such methods often lead to cynicism, which is the enemy of commitment to change. In one highly regarded company we studied, a task force of respected managers rebelled when asked by senior management to conduct and analyze a worldwide employee survey. They refused to get involved in what they presumed was yet another hopeless exercise. Meanwhile, senior managers fully (but wrongly) believed that they had acted on past feedback.

After many years of observing leaders use SFP successfully—and observing many failures in companies where honest conversation never took place—I have found that the evidence is clear. Organization-wide honest, collective, and public conversations are essential. The strategic fitness process was designed, in partnership with senior executives, to enhance a company's capacity to implement strategy quickly and effectively. It accomplishes this by fitting the organization to the strategy and by increasing its capacity to learn and change, in sum, by increasing its fitness. SFP has been used effectively in the retail, hospitality, high technology, banking, and pharmaceutical industries.

Crafting a Conversation That Matters

After nearly thirty years of implementing SFP and researching its consequences, my colleagues and I have identified several overriding lessons. We believe these are relevant to any organization-wide conversation aimed at transforming the system of organizing, managing, and leading, whether or not leaders use our particular process.

Move back and forth between advocacy and inquiry

Most failures in organizations start when top management advocates a new direction and begins to develop programs for change without finding out what influential people in various parts of the organization think of the new focus. They thereby set themselves up to be blindsided by concerns that emerge much later. A few well-intentioned leaders make the opposite mistake. They do not advocate at all. Instead, in the name of participation and involvement, they depend entirely on inquiry—assembling a large group of managers and asking them to define a direction. The result is often widespread frustration. Managers and employees look to leaders to articulate a point of view about where the business is going—a point of view to which they can respond. Leaders need to advocate, then inquire, then repeat as needed.

Tackle the issues that matter the most

To energize the organization, the conversation must be focused on the most important issues: the company's strengths and the obstacles to performance. It's all too easy for senior managers to become swamped in the operational details of managing a business. What gets crowded out are tough and honest conversations about the fundamental issues that will determine long-term success: Do we have a distinctive business strategy that key managers believe in? Do we have the capabilities to execute that strategy? Is our leadership effective? Are our employees on board with the leadership and its strategy?

Make sure the conversation is collective and public

Realigning an organization with a new strategic direction almost always requires simultaneously changing the worldviews and behaviors of a whole set of interdependent players: the CEO, the senior leadership team, and managers all down the line. This turnaround won't happen without a collective public conversation. By *collective*, I mean that several levels of management across important functions and value-chain activities have to be engaged. By *public*, I mean that senior managers need to make sure that everyone below them is informed about what has been learned and what changes are planned in response. And when those changes are made, senior management has to make clear that these changes emerged from the iterations of advocacy and inquiry.

Allow employees to be honest without them risking their jobs

In most of the companies we've studied, managers talked about strategic problems with one or two people they trusted but pulled their punches in more public settings. In Agilent's SGDU, for example, everyone knew about the tensions between the regional entities and the functional departments. Everyone was aware that the senior team wasn't managing effectively, and many managers doubted Camp's ability to lead the organization out of the morass. But for two reasons, none of these issues was discussed publicly. First, managers feared that honesty would hurt their careers or even endanger their jobs. Second, they were afraid that Camp and her senior team would feel so hurt and defensive that the conversation would not lead to change and might even set back the organization.

Be sure to structure the conversation

When people hear "honest," they tend to think "spontaneous." But public conversations in organizations are rarely spontaneous, because the stakes are so high. Lou Gerstner found this out when he took charge of IBM in 1993. He describes a strategic meeting at which managers sat at a large conference table with scores of assistants behind them, all listening to a PowerPoint presentation and engaging in little or no discussion. He was so frustrated by the lack of real dialogue that he turned off the overhead projector with what he calls "the click heard around the world." Gerstner learned, as we have in our work, that the "free-for-all of problem solving" so essential for high performance "does not work so easily in a large, hierarchically based organization." Paradoxically, to achieve honesty and full engagement in these organizations, you need to structure the conversation carefully.[2]

Driving Change, One Step at a Time

In the rest of this chapter, I'll outline the process that my colleague Russ Eisenstat and I developed to support productive, organization-wide conversations about barriers to performance. Figure 1-1 outlines nine steps in the process typically implemented sequentially in five separate meetings over six to eight weeks (see appendix A for details). Steps 5 and 6 are usually implemented in one three-day fitness meeting. The sequence is more important than the specific allocation of these steps to the five meetings. Numerous organizations have spread the nine steps over more meetings and a longer period. I'll focus on important points to remember as the honest conversation unfolds. These points—and the principles underlying them—hold true in any setting in which the senior team truly wants strategic change.

Businesses are designed with a built-in directional gyroscope: the senior team. Yet we consistently find that in many companies, these built-in gyroscopes are broken. So that's where the honest conversation needs to start. The individuals in the senior team oversee the parts of the organization that need to work together to implement business strategy. They need to set direction, resolve conflicting views about priorities, and create the context and culture that will enable the many other

FIGURE 1-1

The strategic fitness process

Senior team

1. Senior management launch meeting (1 day)

- The senior team develops a statement of strategic and organizational direction.

- The team selects a task force of eight of the best people in the organization.

Fitness task force

2. Task force training session (1 day)

- The task force is trained in interviewing.

- The task force identifies interviewees.

Broader organization

3. Data collection period (2–6 weeks)

- The task force interviews people throughout the organization.

Fitness task force

4. Task force data consolidation meeting (1 day)

- The task force identifies major themes in the interviews.

- The task force prepares feedback.

- The meeting is held immediately.

Fitness task force

5. Task force feedback discussion (1 day)

- The task force presents feedback to the senior team using the fishbowl format.

Senior team

6. Senior team feedback response (2 days)

- The senior team conducts an analysis of the root causes of the issues identified in the feedback and develops an integrated plan to address them.

Fitness task force

7. Task force plan critique (1 day)

- The senior team meets with the task force again to present its plan and receive feedback.

Broader organization

8. Implementation

- The senior team announces change plans to the "top 100" and initiates further dialogue.

- Changes are implemented throughout the organization.

Broader organization

9. Institutionalization

- The senior team periodically repeats the process and extends it into subunits.

individuals who make up the organization to deliver results. Yet in an extraordinary number of companies, the senior team is not fulfilling these obligations, allowing unclear strategy and conflicting priorities that obstruct performance. The cause, as perceived by people at lower levels and by members of the senior team themselves, is their own ineffectiveness. When these teams meet, they tend to review results, focus on specific problems, or discuss administrative matters. They do not dig into or resolve fundamental strategic issues.

All of this was true at SGDU. During senior team meetings, people tended to interrupt the conversation by advocating their own views and ignoring the views of others. Side conversations abounded, usually to obtain support for a leader's own position. Underlying differences in assumptions were never surfaced. As a result, the group had difficulty achieving consensus and making timely decisions, particularly about the politically charged issues of strategy and organizational design. Camp recalled: "I don't think I understood at the time how ineffective we really were as a team. We were very siloed. It was not obvious to me then how political it was, but, in retrospect, it was pretty darn political."

Honest conversation has to begin at the top because the responsibility for building an aligned organization cannot be delegated. The senior managers must work together to define the business strategy as well as the capabilities and values essential for long-term success.

SFP therefore starts with a one-day meeting of the senior team in which they develop the strategy and draft a statement of direction (strategy and values) that will later be used as the basis of their inquiry into the organization's strategic alignment. To promote an honest dialogue that uncovers differences among members of the senior team themselves, I ask each member to prepare his or her answers to six simple but profoundly important questions:

- What are the company's objectives and aspirations?

- What are the market threats and opportunities?

- What is the value proposition you are delivering?

- What are the most critical things the business must do to deliver on the value proposition and create or sustain competitive advantage?

- Which organizational capabilities are needed to implement the strategy?

- Which values should guide the organization?

At SGDU, the senior team's answers to these questions and their efforts to create a direction statement revealed to them that they were trying to straddle two very different strategies. The first was a reactive strategy: grow sales quickly by responding to immediate customer needs using existing technology. The second was a proactive, R&D-driven strategy of building distinctive, technology-based solutions platforms that competitors could not easily replicate. In creating the statement of direction, the senior team finally acknowledged and then resolved this conflict, clearly committing themselves—in writing—to a technology-based platform strategy. Camp later recalled: "What I had to accept was that my staff and I had been running so fast that we hadn't actually put the words to paper. When it came time to write down our strategy, we found out there were several areas where we weren't aligned. We spent a whole day discussing and debating our strategy and ended up with something that we all felt good about."

Draft your best managers to collect data and engage the organization in a conversation

The two conventional approaches to collecting data about strategic and organizational problems are to survey thousands of employees anonymously or to ask outsiders (consultants or HR specialists) to conduct interviews. The assumption is that only anonymous surveys and outsiders can elicit objective, truthful information. The problem is that, out of a desire for objective data, the senior team is distancing itself from the people who have seen and experienced problems. That distance enables executives to underestimate or even deny problems and to delay action. In many companies we have studied, the senior team had massive amounts of survey data but had taken little action on anything it had learned. The information failed to arouse the executives' empathy or horror: "Oh my God, how could this be going on in our organization?" If this imagined reaction sounds overly dramatic and undignified, you'll see that leaders sometimes do react this way, much to their own surprise, and that's what makes all the difference.

When a senior team appoints a task force of up to eight of its best managers to interview pivotal people in all parts of the organization, the team sends a clear message that it is serious about uncovering the truth and making changes. To ensure that the task force is seen as representing the interests of the entire organization, the team collectively selects the members. If anyone on the team expresses a concern about a proposed individual, that individual's name is stricken from the list. Camp and her team, like many other executive groups, hesitated to appoint their best managers because these were also the busiest managers. I have learned the hard way, however, that if you do not appoint your best people, the task force's feedback will have less credibility with the senior team and with the larger organization. It becomes all too easy to discount or explain away painful truths. Remember that the work of developing an aligned organization capable of executing its strategy is indispensable management work—a job for your *best* people, not those whose time you can most afford to waste.

But even with a credible task force collecting the data, there is likely to be skepticism among those from whom it is being collected. Managers are apt to remember previous information-collecting efforts that yielded few tangible results. The firm can allay this skepticism by having the task force, rather than the senior team, select the hundred or so people who are to be interviewed. This arrangement helps assure the organization that the task force members—not senior management—control this piece of the process. To be blunt, it has to be clear that the senior team isn't handpicking the interviewees to exercise control over the feedback it gets. The interviewees should be a representative sample of people—including managers—from the value-creating areas most responsible for implementing the strategy. Each interviewee is provided with the statement of strategic direction in advance of the interview.

The process rarely needs more than a hundred interviewees, even for a worldwide *Fortune* 50 corporation. If the organization is small, every employee can be interviewed by the task force (chapter 5 describes SFP for a small restaurant). So much the better. But because data collection focuses on three clear topics—the quality of the strategy, the organization's strengths to be preserved, and the barriers to the implementation of strategy—not on employee satisfaction and morale, the interviews can be limited in a larger organization to people in pivotal roles along the value chain.

You may wonder whether a task force handpicked by top management will confront the senior team with the truth. The answer, emphatically, is yes. Provided that certain safeguards are in place (I will describe these in a moment) and that task force members believe the leadership team is prepared to make changes, the task force quickly becomes a cohesive group, even when made up of people from warring factions of the organization. Moreover, the members come to feel a deep obligation to those they have interviewed. Many see the assignment as a once-in-a-lifetime opportunity to make things better—and therefore do not shy away from confronting the brutal facts. As one task force member at SGDU put it, "People had spilled their guts to me in the interviews and I owed it to them to really see this through."

To uncover the truth, protect the people in the conversation

In most organizations, lower-level managers are afraid to talk openly about problems that may be blocking effectiveness and performance. Several approaches help mitigate that fear. First, and most important, the confidentiality of interviews must be safeguarded. The task force members should report back general themes that come up in multiple conversations, not comments that can be attributed to any one person or that don't seem to reflect the experience of more than one person.

We have constructed a simple and rigorous method for doing this. People conducting the interviews are instructed to avoid mentioning any individual, except the head of the organization, by name. Negative feedback about a department signals leadership problems, and senior managers understand this. Finally, task force members should interview people outside their own parts of the organization. In this way, the interviewer is less likely to have an ax to grind and the interviewees less likely to feel intimidated.

The task force members have their own fears to deal with, of course. In going out to the organization on behalf of the senior management team, they risk their own reputations. As one task force member at SGDU pointed out, "We're going to put our careers on the line assuming the top team is going to follow through. If we do the interviews and nothing happens, then we'll look stupid." In addition, most members are fully aware of the political costs of speaking uncomfortable truths. Many task forces, especially in organizations that have a history of top-down management, are anxious about these risks (although our research shows that a disproportionate number of task force members are later promoted). In one instance, it took three hours to assure an anxious task force that its members were not being given a career-limiting opportunity. One team walked into the meeting with top management wearing buttons that said "Don't shoot the messenger," and more than one team said as much when presenting its findings.

The top manager must clarify his or her expectations for openness if these fears are to be addressed. Camp told the task force at the launch meeting, "I want the truth. Nothing should be sugarcoated . . . We have confidence in you and we are counting on you to help us identify and address the real issues." In addition, the task force members feel more obliged to speak the truth because they are representing the hundred people they have interviewed. We've also found that it helps if task force members can think of themselves as researchers with a job to do. They remind management of this reporter role by citing the number of people they interviewed and the general area in the company where they collected information (without, of course, revealing individual sources).

Ask a few fundamental questions

The conversation between task force members and the people they interview is kept focused but open-ended. Interviewees are asked simply, "Does this strategy make sense? What are the strengths to build on and the barriers to address in implementing this strategy?" Task force members will often find that respondents are eager to discuss strategic issues because this interview is often their first chance to talk to management honestly about the overall health and direction of the company. Task force members in our research have reported long, emotional interviews. Employees who are not scheduled to be interviewed have sometimes lined up outside conference room doors, hoping for the chance to speak.

The task force's next job is to extract from its hundreds of hours of rich and emotionally charged discussions the most important issues. The interviewers do this through a series of screens. At the end of each interview, the interviewee is asked to summarize the two or three most business-critical issues to be shared with senior management. Each task force member then reviews all of his or her interview notes and selects the three or four most commonly mentioned barriers to implementing business strategy and the major organizational strengths that need to be preserved. When members come together, they collate these themes. The most important ones form the basis for their presentation to the senior management team.

The task force should be careful to illustrate the themes with descriptions of specific events or projects; these rich stories provide the top team with an in-depth view of how the organization really functions. The stories, which resemble well-researched case studies, are vital to convincing senior management that the data is real and valid. Senior executives also respond powerfully to quotes from (unnamed) interviewees; these quotes tend to bring home the employees' deep commitment as well as their frustration.

Enable truth to speak to power

The task force's presentation to senior management is always a charged meeting. This stage of the process, perhaps more than any other, needs to be carefully managed. When we first developed SFP, the task force members would use slides. But we quickly learned that the members had great difficulty agreeing on a few words that would convey their rich findings. We also found that, for all the safeguards we thought were in place, the members were apprehensive about their individual parts of the presentation. They felt vulnerable because they could be individually identified with some portion of the bad news.

We now suggest that task force members present their findings in the form of a discussion. They sit around a table in the middle of a room, in what we call a fishbowl, while the senior team sits at tables around the outside of the fishbowl, observing (figure 1-2). No designated notetaker is allowed, but members of the senior team can take their own notes. For each major theme, the task force members discuss the perspectives that emerged from their interviews and the questions that the theme raised. They neither recommend solutions nor deliver a written report of any kind; the executives will develop far greater understanding and insight when they actively listen and take their own notes.

Certain ground rules are set at the beginning of these meetings to protect the task force members and to enable senior managers to hear

FIGURE 1-2

The fishbowl

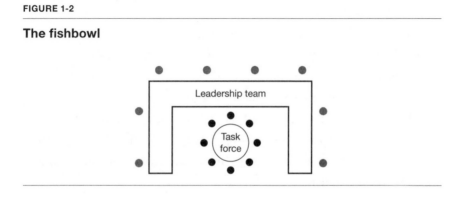

what's being said. The executives are not allowed to interrupt or challenge the task force; instead, at the end of each theme discussion, they are allowed to ask questions for clarification. As they listen, they're also encouraged to recognize that perceptions are facts that shape behavior and determine how well a strategy is implemented.

In every SFP that we've observed, the task force was able to speak the truth with a level of openness and richness that went well beyond the initial expectations of the managers involved. One senior manager described the task force as "operating much like a professional consulting firm, except unlike consultants, they were a part of the organization and knew it inside and out. I think they worked so well together because they believed in what they were doing."

As discussed later in the book, Joshua Duncan, CEO of American Diner (not the CEO's or company's real name), used SFP to transform his national restaurant chain.[3] He explained why enabling a task force of key people below the top to interview a hundred others and speak the whole truth to power works so well: "It is very difficult for someone to say, 'I think you, the emperor, has no clothes.' People have never done this, and that is why the story is a fairy tale. It is much more possible to say to the emperor, 'I have spoken with your subjects, and they say you have no clothes.' As a leader, it is important to know if you have no clothes."

This is not to say that the task force feedback sessions are easy or painless. After all, senior executives are learning about the business consequences of their own actions. At SGDU, Camp learned that she was perceived as an authentic leader whom people liked and trusted but that she was letting down the organization by not moving more quickly. "I think there was some question in the organization," Camp recalled, "about my effectiveness as a leader and whether I could really turn this thing around, given my lack of experience in the systems business and in leading a globally dispersed team."

Camp also learned about four major organizational problems she and her team had to resolve:

- **Slow decision making:** "Our functional organization is killing speed."

- **Lack of business focus:** "Lynne and her staff don't know the business well enough to ask the right questions."

- **Lack of accountability:** "Everyone reports to a function; no one is accountable."

- **Leadership ineffectiveness:** "Management has no track record in taking action. This is the last chance for Lynne and her staff to get it right."

Hard-charging leaders focused on delivering results seldom hear these types of truths. "Frankly, there was no real upward dialogue that was honest, transparent, and public," Camp told me. "I was very driven to deliver results, and, at the time, I don't think I had as open an ear for what was really going on at the ground floor as I should have."

The power of direct feedback from eight or so of the best people moves executives to bring about changes they have otherwise been reluctant to make. This happened at SGDU. As Camp explained to the task force, "You lit a fire under us. Thank you for the unvarnished truth . . . I take your feedback very seriously. It is my performance appraisal . . . If the organization is going to change, I must change." Camp pledged to do whatever it took to address the issues raised.

Diagnose the organization, and develop a plan for change

None of us would feel comfortable agreeing to surgery before a full diagnosis had been made. Yet on hearing about problems in their organization, managers often move too quickly to institute major changes without undertaking a rigorous diagnosis of the root causes. Why? Time pressures prevent reflection and in-depth diagnosis. Managers also lack an analytical framework for diagnosing the situation. One senior team created a forty-nine-item action list, one for each problem it had perceived. This overeager cataloguing enabled the general manager to avoid confronting the underlying issues, which included his own top-down style, his focus on the short term over the longer term, and a senior team unable to bridge functional silos.

To avoid such problems, the senior team should convene for a full three-day meeting—the fitness meeting—to engage in feedback, diagnosis, and action planning. A fitness meeting creates the discipline the team needs to go beyond symptoms and uncover root causes.

On the first day, the task force gives its feedback and the senior team gets an overnight assignment: to identify the organization's core strengths and weaknesses as they relate to its strategic objectives. The task force is done for now—they'll be back—but the senior team continues to meet for two more days. The next day, the team—using the results of its overnight assignment—diagnoses the organization. The executives decide as a group what the company's strengths and weaknesses are, which weaknesses will materially undermine the strategic goals, and what is causing the weaknesses. Possible causes include organization structure, the leadership team's effectiveness, corporate culture, management processes, reward systems, HR policies and practices, and people's roles, responsibilities, and decision rights. The best teams look not only at all these facets but also at their interactions. As total quality management expert W. Edwards Deming famously said, changes to management systems "require knowledge of the interrelationship between all components of the system, and everybody who works in it."[4] On the final day, the executives decide on organizational changes and other priority actions.

At SGDU, Camp and her team wrestled with the fundamental but politically sensitive question of whether the functional departments, geographic entities, or businesses were going to drive the company. The team collectively agreed to move to a product-based rather than a geography-based business-unit structure. In this structure, the geographic teams and functional departments would now play a supporting role rather than a driving one. The businesses themselves would be responsible for R&D, product planning, marketing, and delivery. According to Camp, "We agreed to have the whole organization in place in six weeks."

There was a real passion to demonstrate results because of "the candid feedback and because we hadn't historically done that." Although Camp had favored a strong matrix organization in which product leaders and functional leaders had equal power, her team's factual discussion of the task force's report persuaded her otherwise. An organization built around several accountable product-based business units would be the best approach. The senior team had converged quickly on the new organizational design even though many of its members were functional managers who would lose power in the new structure. SGDU's rapid transformation may sound too good to be true, but my colleagues and I have seen it happen many times. When the right conditions are created for people to put the greater good ahead of their own, they are very likely to do so. It's an uplifting experience to play a part in that.

Stress-test the plan

Once the senior team has developed its plan, it meets again with the task force to present what it has heard ("This is what you said to us, and yes, we really heard you"), its diagnosis, and its action plan. This critical step reinforces the senior team's accountability to the organization.

To ensure honest and thoughtful feedback, the task force takes time to deliberate alone before responding to the proposed plan. Because of this review, the final meeting between the two groups is sometimes more contentious than it otherwise would have been—and it's more productive as well. One task force we observed (not SGDU's) informed the CEO and the senior team that they had not fully addressed the need to streamline an overly layered organizational structure—a structural change that, if implemented, would reduce the authority of a particularly influential member of the senior team. When the task force brought up this issue, the executives changed the plan. The revised plan had much greater credibility within the organization, and the task force then moved beyond its initial role as a group of objective reporters and became a committed partner in the implementation of the plan. At SGDU, the task force was positive about what the senior team had proposed; it also gave the executives useful advice about how to best communicate and implement their action plans.

Implementing the Change Plan

Too often the urgent drives out the important. The best intentions to execute change become waylaid by short-term pressures. Before long, change plans disappear into obscurity. Cynicism and hopelessness take root. Even if change plans are executed, people below the executive suite never learn that their feedback motivated the change. SFP does not end with a plan to change. Honest and collective conversations about the company's progress in implementing the change must continue. Leaders must persistently respond to the unanticipated or unintended outcomes that always occur in organizational change.

Execution of the action plan is itself an iterative process, with people continuously learning. What has been changed? What barriers did the initiatives encounter, and what do these obstacles tell the senior team about what else needs to be done. What does it tell them about the organization and its management of the change process? What else must the top team do to enable the change? Keeping employees actively involved in change initiatives is key to successful and sustained change and motivates people to embrace continuous improvement. A change-ready organization is developed over time.

Camp asked the task force members and, sometimes, others to lead one of several aspects of the change plan. One senior team member became the program manager for ensuring that the action plan was executed. Target dates for completion of initiatives were set. The program manager reviewed the results and reported to the senior team regularly about progress. The leader of the change initiative should be part of the review and report not only on substantive changes made but also on further challenges encountered.

At the Santa Rosa Systems Division of Hewlett-Packard, the senior team took on the development of the organization as a strategic task worthy of time and attention. For the first few months after the SFP, the group met weekly to review progress. It met less frequently later but continued overseeing the organization's effectiveness. To learn how people closer to the front line saw progress, the executives met quarterly with the fitness task force members, who informed the executives about what their interviewees were telling them. As I discuss in chapter 4, the division repeated SFP every year to continuously improve organizational effectiveness by sustaining and building on the changes made the first year.[5]

These reviews should be seen by senior teams as an important opportunity to learn about their organization and their leadership of change. Why is change progressing too slowly or not at all? Learning about these matters and reflecting about them is like peeling another layer of the organization and leadership onion.

The Bottom Line: Better Business Performance

Senior teams that have engaged in SFP have dramatically changed how their businesses were organized and managed—and their firms' bottom line. You will see examples of this success in chapters 3–6.

Six weeks after Lynne Camp and her team tested their plan with the task force, SGDU was operating as a decentralized, business-focused, accountable organization. The speed of that transformation seems incredible to those who have never experienced an honest, collective, and public conversation, but among the companies that have taken the plunge, such rapid transformation is not uncommon. What makes it possible is that senior management teams are made to *feel* accountable to the organization.

Just as important, the success that begins with honest conversations begets future conversations that further improve performance. The first time is, of course, the hardest. Once everyone has had a chance to see that real change does emerge out of the initially painful truth-telling, the organization gets better at having an honest collective conversation.

The managers whose leadership was questioned the first time, far from emerging discredited, are typically seen as leading more effectively if they embraced the process and responded to the feedback. Camp's cachet rose dramatically because she courageously acknowledged her role in the organization's problems and responded by changing the organization and how she herself managed it. By enabling a complicated organizational truth to emerge, senior managers reduce cynicism, increase trust, and develop selfless commitment. As a result, they create a mandate for change that even the most entrenched and resistant power centers cannot resist.

Thirty years of facilitating, observing, and researching the effectiveness of honest organization-wide conversations in culturally different regions around the world has provided insights into the power of such conversations and into the situations that moderate their effectiveness. My colleagues and I have come to realize that SFP is far more than a method for aligning the organization with strategy and values. It is a powerful means—arguably the most powerful—by which leaders can lead change authentically and develop a shared determination to succeed. Without honest conversations that engage people intellectually and emotionally in what top management is trying to achieve, the barriers that most assuredly stand in the way will prevent you from achieving your objectives.

SFP has been implemented in some nine hundred companies or organizational units in the United States, Latin America, Europe, India, China, and Japan. It has also been applied to a variety of strategic challenges beyond overall organizational corporate or unit effectiveness. Examples include mergers and acquisitions, operating cost and quality, racial tensions in a functional unit, integration of three previously competitive sales and marketing organizations in fifty sales districts, and cross-company strategic initiatives.

Multiple studies using different methods have shown the effectiveness of SFP, though the research also shows that its success depends on leadership and the organizational context. Most important are leadership's determination to close a performance gap and the extent to which leaders' values align with SFP's underlying values, namely, openness to learning and acting on the unembellished truth. Of course, SFP has also changed leaders' readiness to be open to difficult feedback and learning. (Appendix B summarizes the research my colleagues and I have conducted to evaluate SFP.)

Transformation Principles

As discussed, SFP is not the only way to have an honest, collective, and public conversation. But SFP is the approach that I have been studying and for which I have found empirical support. Embedded in SFP are six essential principles for leading such a conversation. Should you want to develop your own version of honest conversation, these six principles will help you succeed:

- **Focus the conversation on issues that matter most.** The senior team should direct the conversation to be about strategic and cultural issues central to the organization's success.

- **Iterate between advocacy and inquiry.** The leaders advocate where they want to take the organization and then launch an inquiry into the organization's strengths and its barriers to success. Later, the leaders would advocate an action plan and then inquire into the strengths and weaknesses of that plan.

- **Make it safe to share the whole truth.** The process must be disciplined and structured to prevent missteps (e.g., to avoid defensiveness: "That's not true") that will shut down the conversation.

- **Reflect, diagnose, and develop a plan.** The leadership team needs to reflect on the truth, diagnose the root causes of problems, and develop a systemic action plan for change that will realign the organization—the whole system—with the team's espoused strategy and cultural values.

- **Make yourself and the rest of the leadership team accountable.**
  Leaders need to show those who provided the feedback that they
  are accountable for having listened carefully to them and for the
  transformation they plan to make.

- **Repeat the process periodically.** Iteration generates continuous
  organizational learning that will steadily improve the quality of
  the organization.

Alternative Modes of Honest Conversation

Leaders have used these six principles to craft alternatives to the strategic fitness method for valuable conversations. Some of these alternatives are described in the following sections. All the methods aim to
enable honest conversations about both the system of organizing, managing, and leading and the barriers to effectiveness, and all accelerate
realignment and change. As with SFP, the most important ingredient
is the leaders' authenticity—that is, *your* authenticity—in leading these
conversations.

Inquiry by the senior team

Kevin McVey, head of Geiger, a business unit of Herman Miller, decided
to lead an honest conversation to improve his unit's effectiveness, trust,
commitment, and performance. He and his senior team developed a
higher-ambition statement of strategic direction. They then developed
a questionnaire to assess which capabilities employees thought were essential to achieve the direction. Using the questionnaire as an interview
guide, senior team members themselves interviewed a cross-section of
employees, as opposed to having a task force do it. The team as a whole
discussed its findings and identified three issues requiring action. The
team members began to change the organization immediately, and
they periodically updated the employees on their progress. Three years
later, the general manager gave employees a comprehensive progress

report, including the unit's financial performance. The team then repeated the process, using the same survey and interview process, to continue improving the organization's performance and to sustain the trust and commitment that the team had generated in the previous three years. "The most amazing thing to see," McVey reported, "has been the continuing trust built throughout most of the organization and the improvements in performance."[6]

Leading the honest conversation yourself

Camp became a believer in the power of honest, collective, and public conversations but found herself running a different business a few years later, when circumstances and the available time and funds required a different approach.[7] She and her senior team defined a strategic direction and then put the "whole system in the room," convening a group of her key people from different parts of the organization for an extended meeting.[8] The senior team presented their statement of direction and engaged the group they had assembled in answering clarifying questions. These key people then met in smaller groups, without the senior team members, to discuss the strategic direction, identify organizational strengths and barriers, and develop recommendations for change. One representative from each group reported back to Camp and the senior team the barriers his or her group had identified, but the representative did not reveal who in the group had raised the issues. The reports were then synthesized and an action plan was built to update the strategic direction and address the issues that had been surfaced. Camp said that "inviting and listening to feedback and incorporating it into your strategy is powerful. It transfers ownership of the strategy from the senior team to all of the leaders in the room. We walked out of the room all aligned on our strategy and action plan."

Pathfinder initiatives

Both Becton Dickinson (BD) and another company, Waste Management, developed yet a different way to learn what capabilities they needed in order to drive improvements in their system of organizing and managing.[9] This learning-by-doing approach started with the identification of a group of unit leaders whose capabilities were essential to execute the corporate strategy. These "pathfinder" unit managers were charged with leading change in their units and becoming primary examples for the corporation. They were asked to do three things:

- Achieve results for their units by leading and managing the development of new strategic capabilities the company had to develop. At BD, this charge meant bringing major business innovations to market, whereas at Waste Management, it meant developing new market segments such as real estate and health care.

- Provide feedback and serve as an ongoing partner to corporate leadership by reporting barriers they experienced and what they learned from speaking with their peers. This information gave senior management an honest diagnosis of the whole corporate system. At BD, for example, the pathfinder unit managers highlighted a critical need to protect or "ring-fence" funds for innovation, so the money didn't just disappear into sustaining engineering.

- Present to the company's senior team which of their changes had made their units more successful. These leaders and their units became shining examples of what is possible and were charged with being corporate change agents by helping their peers transform their own units to the new model.

Structured and required inquiry groups

Structured customer and employee circles were used by Archie Norman, CEO of Asda, a UK grocery chain, to turn around its two hundred stores.[10] Store managers were required to implement these circles quarterly to hear directly from customers and employees about their experience of shopping or working at Asda. The structure of the inquiry was designed by a consultant, but store managers were required to lead these circles quarterly and to act on what they heard needed improvement.

You might think that if a store's culture were one of fear, the whole truth might not come to the surface. But Norman held store managers accountable for results. Improvements in customer and employee satisfaction were certified by a "driving" test, an assessment made by a corporate staff group (through interviews and survey results) of whether significant change had occurred. If there was no improvement, the store manager was given help. If there was still no improvement, he or she was replaced. Of course, improvements in sales and cost were tracked as well. That in itself was an incentive—the most powerful possible—to listen and to act on what was learned.

Summing Up

This chapter aimed to show how senior managers can lead an honest, collective, and public conversation and make dramatic and rapid changes in their organization. Leading such organization-wide conversations is difficult because managers and those below them find it difficult to be completely honest with each other. The strategic fitness process (SFP) is a high-engagement nine-step leadership platform that overcomes these challenges. Lynne Camp's experience at the Systems Generation and Delivery Unit at Agilent Technologies demonstrates how SFP can work.

In light of our decades of experience, my colleagues and I have found that SFP's success rests on six features:

- The fact that the senior team, not a staff group such as HR, commissions and leads the process signals to lower levels that the senior team means to lead change. (Internal HR specialists who have learned the process, however, are sometimes asked by senior management to help move it along.)

- Using a task force of eight or so to interview key employees in all parts of the organization provides the senior team with an honest and systemic view of the organization's effectiveness—the good, the bad, and the ugly. No individual—a consultant, for example—could gather the same trove of rich information as comprehensively and quickly (in just six weeks) or with as much engagement and improved trust and commitment as a task force representing different parts of business can.

- The senior team members' public commitment—before the SFP gets under way—to share with the whole organization what they hear and what they plan to change signals their determination to change the organization and renders them accountable for completing the process.

- The honest conversation is made safe by its structure and rules of engagement. These guidelines have helped people overcome their reluctance to share unwelcome truths.

- The task force and the interviewees are energized by the conversation and can become change agents if management assembles further task forces to dive deeper into some issues, recommend changes, and help implement them.

- When top executives inform the whole organization about what they heard, what they plan to change, and—later—what they have actually done to act on the feedback, they instill trust and commitment to change throughout the company.

Leaders have used these principles to create their own forms of honest conversation—different from SFP—when circumstances warranted. Several examples were given in this chapter. Whatever the variation, the purpose is always to ensure completely honest conversations that will transform an organization systemically and with commitment.

SFP *always* puts the truth on the table. But if the process is to stimulate change, leaders must act on what they hear, as the experiences of Lynne Camp and other leaders will illustrate in later chapters.

Chapter 2

Why Discussing the Undiscussable Is Transformative

Before senior management launched an honest conversation through the fitness process, the morale of our division's employees was at an all-time low. There weren't too many people that thought we had a prayer as a new division. But the reorganization that resulted from SFP really lifted people back up and energized us to start moving to where we needed to go as a division.

—Len Hirschi, Production Manager, Hewlett
    Packard's Santa Rosa System's Division

oth research and daily experience teach us that confronting others' deeply held, emotionally based beliefs directly will lead to defensiveness. Using rational arguments to change minds, as social psychologist Jonathan Haidt has shown, will not work either.[1] People in an organization are compelled to action when they confront realities for the first time—when those below the top team hear sometimes-alarming truths about the competitive demands of the environment from senior people, and executives at the top hear the sometimes-discouraging truths about barriers to change.

My colleagues and I have repeatedly seen that such revelations and subsequent action can be brought about by honest, collective, and public conversation. But why does this kind of conversation work? What facets of SFP make it transformative?

Senior Teams Develop a Direction as a Group

A clear strategic direction for the organization—its strategy and values—owned by the whole senior team is necessary for conducting a valid inquiry into the extent of the organization's alignment with that direction. A genuine strategic direction (not a politically expedient agreement) cannot be created without an honest conversation by the whole top team. As I will show, most employees think the organization's strategic direction is unclear, and this lack of clarity also means the strategy may be flawed. Confusion like this is a barrier to organizational effectiveness. Recent research has shown how important a clear direction is to employees' sense of purpose and engagement.[2]

In many cases, we found that the direction had not been developed by the senior team as a group. Rather, the CEO or business-unit leader and the chief strategy or marketing officer, sometimes with the help of strategy consultants, developed the direction. The rest of the team was not directly involved in the conversation until later.

In a typical change effort, a few top executives develop numerous documents and roll out data-filled presentations to communicate the new direction. It is not condensed into a simple, direct written statement about what the organization needs to do to succeed and the values by which employees (at *all* levels) are expected to live—and why. Priorities are not made clear. Neither is there clarity about what the organization will *not* do—the strategies or behaviors that are out of bounds given the organization's purpose, values, and capabilities. In short, the senior team has not clearly defined a distinctive identity or advocated it clearly. This failure leads, as you will see, to a number of organizational problems.

Not surprisingly, senior team members often lack a fully shared understanding of their company's strategy and values. Different members have very different ideas and prefer to hold onto them. One task force we worked with reported that "the organization was being torn apart by two conflicting strategies." The leadership had not had an honest conversation about its purpose, values, and strategy or the legacy it wanted to leave. Some of the SFP task forces we encountered told us: "We have no human values." This conclusion didn't mean the company was evil. It meant that implicit assumptions and values of top managers about how to lead felt inhuman. Individuals had values, which they applied to their work, but these values were not always consistent or aligned with a strategy.

SFP therefore begins with the senior team meeting to draft a two- or three-page statement of direction. Inevitably, team members discover that they have different understandings of the strategy or how the organization is supposed to enact it. "When it came time to write down our strategy," Lynne Camp said, "we found out there were several areas where we weren't aligned." Camp was describing her leadership team's efforts to write a two-page statement of strategic direction for SGDU (see chapter 1). These differences precipitate misunderstanding about priorities in an organization. A clear, concise statement of direction is an essential first step for any meaningful inquiry into the organization's capabilities. You can't answer the question "Are we capable?" until you have answered the questions "Capable of what?" and "To what end?"

Consider this best-practice example of two honest conversations that CEO Joshua Duncan led shortly after he took charge of American Diner, a national restaurant chain. The first conversation was about purpose and values, and the second was about strategy:

> **Purpose:** "In one of my first meetings with the senior team, we talked about what kind of legacy we wanted to leave. The team had a lot of energy for this. Everyone had something to say about it, and we put all the ideas up on the wall. We then looked for

commonalities around what kind of difference we wanted to make. All of the ideas had to do with people, touching people in a positive way, and giving people a chance to grow. Today, we don't talk about vision, but about the legacy we are trying to build."

Strategy: "Each team member brought important insights and perspectives. We had two seasoned field leaders with almost fifty years of experience between them. We had a financial leader on the team who knew the numbers and had a great sense of the pulse of the organization. The head of franchising had led those businesses to a string of successful years. Our marketing leader had created some of the most effective advertising I have ever seen. Our head of real estate brought strategic financial and real estate skills to the party. The challenge was to achieve more from the whole than just the sum of the parts."

Valid and Compelling Data

Top executives can tell when the company isn't accomplishing its strategy. But they have a hard time gathering valid data to diagnose the root causes. By valid data, I mean the *whole truth*, with nothing left out about what's working and what isn't.[3] Honest, collective, public conversation delivers this truth because the inquiry is open-ended. An employee survey, in contrast, is based on presumptions about what the specific issues are and may therefore miss hidden, complex truths. In other words, those who construct surveys do not know—or may not be ready to know—what they don't know. SFP, however, is based on broad questions—what we have called firehose questions—about the organization's capacity to execute a strategic statement of direction. People are asked "What do you see as the organization's strengths that will help it move in this strategic direction? What barriers within the company will stand in the way?"

The responses—whatever they turn out to be—are then integrated into themes. The important themes are not figured out in advance and investigated. They are derived from participants' unguided answers. That's what makes them the important themes: they reflect what is really going on, what is not known, or what is known but difficult to say openly. This information is the gold that usually slips through the pan in an employee survey. Leaving out essential truths, such as the leader's or the senior team's own contributions to the problem, reduces the credibility of the change effort, which reduces trust and creates cynicism. People readily grasp that a strategy or change effort won't work if it doesn't explicitly address what they know to be the real sticking points. Isn't this what often happens?

Camp explained why the anecdotal feedback she had heard—before hearing from the task force—failed to show her the division's system for what it was and then how to act on it:

> I didn't know how pervasive or right the anecdotal feedback I had received was. I'd be in Taiwan and I'd hear one issue. Then three months later, I'd be in Germany and hear a different issue. Then four months later, I'd hear another issue. If you're a data-driven person like I am, you don't know what to make of these diverse and sometimes contradictory pieces of information. People always complain. There are always issues in an organization, always. The question is, what are the ones that really require action?

SFP translates the anecdotal information that leaders like Camp experience as a kind of indecipherable buzz into an actionable change plan. Ed Ludwig, former CEO of Becton Dickinson, observed that SFP transformed "the anecdotal into an actionable [plan]. It reconfirmed my concerns." In every SFP-guided conversation, truth is delivered in a way that provides a compelling and holistic picture of the organization. Sometimes left out of the feedback is the emotional intensity with which interviewees talked about problems and—deliberately and necessarily—the names of people embedded in the problem.

SFP hinges on keeping the data about people anonymous. Of course, interviewees do sometimes have complaints about specific people. But if employees believe that giving their honest feedback can cost someone his or her job, most will consider honest conversation too dangerous or punitive rather than developmental (even if they were temporarily satisfied by a person's being fired). SFP would collapse if individual managers were being fingered publicly in the feedback presentation. Consequently, an important guideline is to prohibit senior leaders from replacing any managers below them immediately after the feedback, no matter what it revealed. Otherwise, this dangerous possibility would shut down future honest conversations and undermine trust.

By the same token, if a manager doesn't eventually improve a department's effectiveness in terms of organizational direction and the subsequent action plan, he or she can certainly be replaced. But then it will have been for failing to carry out stated goals, not for getting a bad review during the task force interviews. Archie Norman replaced store managers at grocery chain Asda when they did not improve their stores after the honest conversations they were required to hold with their employees and customers (see chapter 1).

In some of the organizations we studied, a consultant had previously collected the very same data that the SFP task force collected and had made excellent recommendations, but these had been implemented ineffectively or not at all. The senior team and other key managers were not fully committed to leading such fundamental change either in their part of the organization or in their own behavior. This problem is averted when the feedback comes from a task force selected by the senior team. The task force members know the organization and are well known within it. They have been chosen for their objectivity and high potential. Furthermore, you can't just say, "Well, they got their fee. We don't have to do what they say." It's a lot harder to ignore what your own chosen task force comes up with.

A manager at Hewlett Packard's Santa Rosa Systems Division explained why the task force's feedback was compelling to the team *and* to employees:

Not only did it function as a powerful tool to communicate difficult issues, but it also showed that the top team cared about what employees thought and that we would not institute a change process without asking for their input. Also, I believe that by [senior management] asking for their "unvarnished" opinions, the employees realized just how serious we were about improving effectiveness. To [the division manager's] credit, he probably took the most amount of risk initiating a process like this. He acted as the linchpin, and without his involvement, a process like this would have been spinning its wheels.[4]

Once they heard from their task force what was not working and how emotional people were in delivering the truth, senior leaders knew instantly they could not ignore the feedback. If they did, it would undermine the legitimacy of their transformation and inoculate the organization against the truth.

Respectful Conversation

Executives don't always like the data that is fed back to them, particularly when it is explicitly or implicitly critical of their own leadership, yet they almost always perceive the process as respectful. It never erupts into accusations or hostility. Consider this task force member's description of her group:

When we met to prepare [for the feedback session], we decided we would not hold anything back in our presentation to the executives, but also that it would not be a public appraisal of individuals. We would not feedback juicy quotes about people or issues unless it really added to the discussion. We did not, however, hold back the personal stuff [about the CEO]. People really like him. He is balanced and an easy person to like, but if you say [the company] does not have a clear vision, that is personal to him.[5]

All the civilized conversations my colleagues and I have observed in SFP are shaped by several forces. The task force members are anxious about how their senior team will respond to the feedback, so they are careful about how it's couched. Their attitude is partly shaped by the structure of the process and partly by their natural inclination not to be mean. So they edit out the more emotional or angry things they hear in their interviews. The structure of the fishbowl and the ground rules for engagement that participants are given prevent uncontrolled anger from breaking out. If you make the people in power too angry, you don't get anywhere. SFP is designed to get somewhere. In the rare cases in which anger creeps in, the conversation rights itself with the help of a facilitator if one is present but just as often through the intervention of another senior team member who reminds everyone about the rules of engagement. Importantly, those involved understand the opportunity they have been given to improve the organization, and they see the need to right themselves.

Systemic Change

As Camp's story and others in this book illustrate, honest conversations make systemic change possible. Multiple facets of the organization, illustrated in figure 2-1, did not fit together. They were and are typically surfaced directly or indirectly as contributing to the difficulties in executing the organization's strategy.[6] The comprehensive nature of honest, collective, and public conversation stimulates discussion of each facet of the organization and its relationships to other facets. At first, such a comprehensive conversation might seem like taking the whole car apart just to change a flat. In fact, it is what allows senior teams to fit or realign their system of organizing, managing, and leading with their new strategy and values. As explained earlier, the change has to be systemic—not just a new tire—so you need a process that calls all aspects of the organization into question.

FIGURE 2-1

Organization effectiveness requires a high-fit system

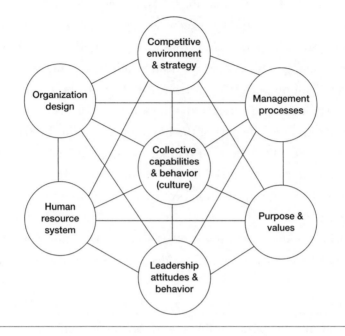

Recall how the bottom-up, honest conversation in Corning's business unit described in the preface led to the unit's rapid (I was awarded the Emotional Oil Can after just one year) and systemic change. Improving the rate of product development required multiple changes. Product development teams that did not exist had to be formed. They had to be led by the appropriate function (in this case, marketing), with people who had the ability to lead a team. The ineffective senior team needed to be effective and able to agree on priorities and a review process. None of these capabilities were in place and had to be developed rapidly, which required the commitment that honest conversation enabled. Top-down, initiative-driven transformations do not accomplish this; the necessary changes happen slowly, incompletely, or not at all. A remarkable 70 percent or so of transformations fail to achieve their intended outcomes.[7]

In virtually all the organizational transformations that honest conversations have facilitated through SFP, changes in various facets of the organization had implications for the roles, responsibilities, and behavior of the senior team and key executives in business units. The systemic discussion gives leaders a chance to evolve their thinking about what corporate changes are necessary. It's unrealistic to think that a plan of that scope can be perfect right from the start, so the process needs a mechanism for course correction. One way to do that is to make honest conversations a regular part of the life of the company, as Becton Dickinson has done. (The effects of regular—as opposed to onetime—honest conversation are discussed more fully in chapter 6.)

As noted in the introduction, systemic change requires changes in both the tangible, or hard, facets of the system and the intangible, or soft, socioemotional facets (figure 2-2). Because the intangible issues on the right of the figure tend to be deep and off-limits for discussion,

FIGURE 2-2

Organizations as socioemotional and technical systems

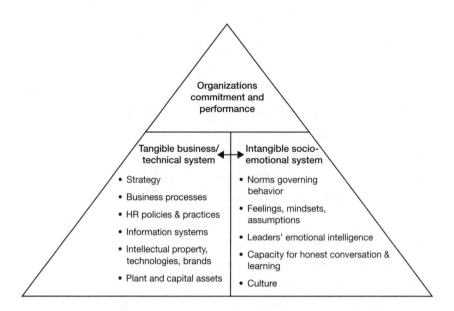

Source: Courtesy of Malcolm Wolf.

they seldom surface in conversations about change. Leadership is more comfortable focusing on the issues on the left—exactly what happened at Nokia (see the introduction).

Our experience with many organizations in various industries has shown us that these intangible issues are made more discussable when people engage in honest, collective, and public conversations. In chapter 4, I will discuss the silent killers, the hidden barriers to fitting the organization to the necessary strategic and cultural criteria. Honest conversations make those barriers discussable at last. At BD, for example, honest conversations allowed stakeholders to discuss constructively how the distribution of power between global businesses, functions, and regions—an arrangement that had worked so well for a strategy of incremental product improvement—now stood in the way of the company's new strategy of providing innovative solutions.

Vince Forlenza led one of several successful transformations at BD. Interviewed for a 2018 study by the Boston Consulting Group about the CEO's role in a transformation, he described the importance of the systemic approach that honest conversation facilitated by SFP had made possible: "We had to make it understandable to our people that the pieces of our transformation fit together and that they weren't just a series of independent initiatives. There was a sequencing—a logic—to what we were doing. You can't try to do too many things. If your efforts to change multiple facets reinforce each other, you will get more momentum."[8]

A Mandate for Change

With good reason, employees are generally pessimistic about their company's capacity to change—except in ways they didn't want. That is why people almost always view the opportunity to serve on a fitness task force as the opportunity of a lifetime and consider their selection an honor. People want to make a difference. Of course, they can make a difference in their own particular jobs, but they seldom feel they can make a companywide difference, despite finding plenty that would be worth changing.

The tragedy is that companies that need to make big strategic changes need their employees to make a difference. But these companies generally don't realize this need, are afraid of it, or don't know how to fully engage their employees. A strategic initiative requires collaboration between the various activities in the value-creation chain. The ability to carry out such a collaboration is largely determined not by any specific decision or directive but by the company's whole system of organizing, managing, and leading. Unfortunately, those below the top have no power to reshape this system. (It's not so easy for those at the top, either.) Fear of getting in trouble makes it hard for even the best people to speak up. In fact, as I will show later in this book, those at the top rarely have honest conversations even among themselves. Even when employees do share their concerns with the senior team, they seldom find that anything has changed. The result throughout the organization is increasing frustration and, ultimately, cynicism. People feel the organization is stuck, and those with the most to offer feel it most keenly and often leave.

For all these reasons, the opportunity to speak the truth to senior leaders about why the organization is stuck is very energizing, particularly for task force members. Here's how one member explained it to me:

> The whole process was very cathartic and quite energizing. Most task force members knew at least a few of the other members, and we came together and clicked into a sense of openness and trust. There was nothing held back when we were together as a group. We felt we had been handed an important responsibility, and we wanted to do it justice. The process and the group seemed to be very good at encapsulating the essence of what we learned rather than getting caught up in any individual's hobbyhorse.

This sense of excitement extends to the people interviewed by task force members and even to those who are not interviewed, but who know that an honest conversation is in progress. Here's what another task force member told me:

> No one refused to be interviewed, and I really had to struggle to keep people to two hours per interview. Everyone was very passionate about the company [and its problems]; there was a lot of emotional engagement. The word that struck me at the end of the interviews was disappointment. It felt like something that you loved was not working well as opposed to something that you did not like. There was negative feedback, but . . . [there] was passion . . . to really make this work. I came away thinking that if we can get this thing right, there is a lot of energy that we can release.

Honest conversations energize senior teams, too, as they come to understand how people below them see their effectiveness as leaders. Consider this recollection from a senior team member of a regional organization of a cable company employing SFP: "At the time, I do not recall thinking any of this was earth-shattering, but what I did think it said was there was a great need to get on with the things we have to do. We were seen as a soft, slow-moving organization, and the task force wanted us to get on with some pace. They would like strong leadership and for us to be a bit bolder."

The collective and iterative advocacy and inquiry that make up honest dialogue, involving all parts and multiple levels of the organization, bring some one hundred key people into the conversation. Its public nature energizes those who do not participate directly; people below the senior team know that the dialogue is going on and then hear the results. I have learned to enhance a sense of participation in the dialogue by asking task force members to call the people they interviewed right after meeting with the top executives. By doing so, the task force lets the interviewees know that they delivered their message to top management. The task force need not detail the substance of the meeting—everyone will hear that later—but can tell the interviewees that management has listened nondefensively and that they are still "alive."

Conversion of Self-Interest into Commitment to the Larger Good

Reorganizations inevitably result in felt losses because some people or groups really do lose some power, resources, and decision rights.[9] Thus, people often make self-interested political efforts to prevent those losses. This political struggle is a by-product of the competition for promotion, resources, and recognition that hierarchical organizations naturally create. Such maneuvering is not necessarily a deliberate effort to undermine change. Individuals and groups are often unaware of how their assumptions and feelings are undermining organizational effectiveness; therefore, they don't see why *they* have to lose something they value.

Organizational change cannot work unless managers become aware of the deeper intangible issues and are ready to sacrifice for the common good. Honest conversations transform a psychology of *me* to one of *we*. In effect, they are instruments for developing teamwork, for creating the collaborative community and shared purpose essential to any company wanting to innovate and compete in any rapidly changing market.

How does honest, collective, and public conversation enable individuals and groups to sacrifice for the larger good? It is the sense that we are all in this together. I have observed the sobering effect that straightforward feedback has on senior teams. The nature of the feedback—coming from outstanding managers selected for their competence and integrity and reporting on what the front line has told them—has powerful consequences. Leaders are put in touch with the reality of organizational behavior that is otherwise hard for them to see and—importantly—hard to feel from their perches in the hierarchy.

Senior teams seldom realize that employees often know what upper management thought was hidden. Finding out that others know what you thought they didn't know arouses emotions that turn self-interest into commitment to the community. Although the senior team is always told how SFP works and how it tends to work out, more than one leader has told me, "I didn't know what I was getting into." Honest conversations are an emotional experience that causes the senior team to come together to discuss and change the organizational reality that they now fully understand at both a cognitive and an emotional level. The same transformation also occurs in the task force and at lower levels, particularly if the people on the senior team communicate truthfully what they have heard and how that is reflected in their agenda for change. For example, when the CEO of a large company informed a group of two hundred key managers, with the aid of the task force, about what he had heard and planned to change, the managers told my colleagues and me that they were impressed by the CEO's courage. They were now more committed to helping him change the company that they now loved even more. (The meeting replicated the fishbowl arrangement the task force had used a few weeks earlier to gather feedback, but this time it was with the large group.)

The honest conversation transforms the distance created by hierarchy into a sense of community in which many people are willing to sacrifice their parochial interests to serve the larger purpose of the organization. In one company, senior team members wrote letters of resignation to the CEO and asked that he accept the resignations if changes had not occurred by the following year. At Hewlett-Packard's Santa Rosa Systems Division, honest feedback from the task force about low morale and a "cold war" between two departments about strategic priorities caused one of the department heads to take responsibility (see chapter 4). His well-intentioned zeal to increase badly needed revenue, he told the team, had undermined organizational effectiveness. When the reorganization that resulted from the honest conversation eliminated his department and changed his role and responsibilities, he not only accepted the change but also remained committed to making it work.

Transparency, Learning, and Accountability

Honest conversations create transparency that the leaders we have worked with have come to value. Leaders learn for the first time how people really feel, something that the natural culture of a hierarchy has kept hidden from them. Not only do they find out more than they ever knew about what's wrong, but they also find out more than they ever knew about what's right and worth preserving. Too often, organizational changes are made with little regard to the assets they may undermine. Lower levels should therefore be asked about strengths to be preserved, not just about barriers to be removed. Task forces have come back with positive feedback such as "We have great people" and "People love our high purpose, performance, integrity, and ethics." Acknowledgment like this gives the senior team pride in their company and its people. And it increases the care with which they approach the transformation to avoid undermining their culture.

When senior teams hear the truth through this process, they become more accountable to lower levels for creating change. It turns out that they often know about many of the issues raised by the honest conversation, but at a rational level, not at an emotional level. The emotions aroused by honest feedback make leaders take more responsibility for leading change. That sense of accountability often deepens when task forces ask to speak for themselves, not as reporters, about the urgency for change. Senior teams are told that if they do not lead change quickly, frustration could drive some people out of the organization. Consider what one executive at a Hewlett-Packard unit reported:

> I was taking a lot of notes, but all I could think of the whole time was, how did it get this bad? The discussion the top team had about how we worked was even more painful. The whole thing was easily the worst day of my HP career. In my room that night, I was considering writing a resignation letter, until I realized that [the general manager] probably wouldn't accept it. It hit me that we were in it up to our necks now and there was no turning back.

In his groundbreaking book *The Righteous Mind*, Jonathan Haidt asserts that we *Homo sapiens* base our decisions on our deeply held assumptions—our beliefs—and then rationalize our actions according to those assumptions.[10] A system of organizing, managing, and leading is based on assumptions, often unexamined, of the senior team. The executive in the quote above and his senior team did examine their assumptions about how to lead, manage, and organize their business after they received feedback from their SFP task force. They learned that the business unit they were running was failing badly because they had failed to recognize how different their business was from the traditional HP business units in which they had all "grown up" (see chapter 4). In accepting the honest feedback, they had become open to changing their assumptions.

Haidt cites research findings that tell us what conditions decision makers like the HP unit's senior team need for critical examination of their preexisting assumptions about how to manage their business. These conditions are remarkably similar to those created by SFP and explain the power of honest conversation to help people change their assumptions.

The central principle is accountability. If we know in advance that we will have to explain a decision to others, we base our decisions on data rather than on our beliefs. And we will especially apply this data-driven approach when we are unsure that the audience will accept our decision and when we also believe that the audience knows something about the problem and desires accuracy in its solution.[11]

When conducting an SFP, the senior leaders must make themselves accountable in advance for confirming *to* the task force what they heard *from* the task force (the data) and what changes they plan to make in response. They also commit beforehand to ask for the task force's critique of their action plan and later to communicate to the entire organization what they have heard and their resulting action plan. Consistent with the conditions identified by Haidt above, leaders are never sure how their action plans will be received by the task force (SFP requires the task force to meet alone to develop its critique) or by the potentially skeptical people in the larger organization. They also recognize that the task force and the people interviewed know what the problems are and have their own ideas about how to fix them. While we were not aware of the research by Haidt and others when we designed SFP, we also understood these principles intuitively. They were our own assumptions and beliefs, and the evidence suggests that they were right.

While you might think that learning the truth about difficulties in executing strategies would make leaders less certain about what to do, the opposite is true. Becton Dickinson CEO Ed Ludwig described how feedback about barriers—revealed in an honest conversation he led as the new leader of a BD business unit—gave him conviction: "It began a solution process. So rather than creating anxiety, it created a sense of, 'Okay, I know what's wrong. It's a big issue, but we have ways forward.' And it gave me the strength of . . . conviction that I would not have had on my own, as a new leader. I just wouldn't have it on my own."[12]

At the lower levels, too, honest conversations increase people's courage, conviction, and commitment to change. People want to make a difference, to move beyond just being resigned to the belief that things can't change. Being part of a two-way, authentic conversation with senior management increases a person's commitment. The American Diner restaurant CEO discussed later in the book reported that SFP was "powerful because it gave people an opportunity to make a difference." That's also why many task forces we worked with reported that people loved the process.

Hope for Fundamental Change

In recounting his experience as a survivor of concentration camps during World War II, Viktor Frankl, a therapist and keen observer of human behavior, attributes his and others' survival to "hope in the future." He elaborates: "With the loss of belief in the future, [the prisoner] lost hope; he let himself decline and became subject to mental and physical decay."[13] In many organizations I visited, I observed a similar phenomenon. Previous top-down initiatives and employee surveys had brought about little change, leaving employees with cynicism, passivity, and no belief in the future.[14] People who are this discouraged stop bothering to collaborate with others to improve the organization. Of course, their loss of hope didn't lead to the drastic physical decay Frankl described in the concentration camps, though research has shown that human health is affected by loss of control and meaning.

In all the honest, collective, and public conversations my colleagues and I have facilitated, we have noted an increase in people's optimism that the organization can change. The hope is palpable in the excitement we see in the fitness task forces and in the interviewees, who sometimes make their cases very emotionally and want to talk well beyond the scheduled time. "There was negative feedback," reported one task force member, "but . . . [there] was passion . . . to really make this work." Witnessing the senior team's readiness to hear the truth does much to increase people's optimism. Ludwig recalled that when, as a division manager, he asked his fitness task force for feedback, they were "relieved" to know that "these guys [the senior team] get it." He added that "this ripped through the organization."

Thus, the act of inquiry reduces cynicism—but not indefinitely. We found that to sustain hope after that initial burst of optimism, leaders must *close the loop* by communicating to lower levels the complete truth they have heard, their diagnosis of root causes, and the resulting changes they plan to make. If this act of accountability does not occur, lower levels will not know that they have been heard and that they have made a difference. Recalling the first SFP he ever led, Ludwig explained: "We never reconnected [the employees] to the process. We never told them 'You gave us feedback . . . Here is what we learned from the feedback. Here is what we are doing about it . . . ' There were times . . . in the next year or two when people were saying, 'Whatever happened to that process when we gave you feedback?'"

Telling the complete truth to the extended senior team—that is, the hundred interviewees plus other key people—is an important step in convincing people that senior management is leading a fundamental systemic transformation. This sort of openness, one of many ingredients of honest, collective, and public conversations about organizational effectiveness, unleashes commitment to change. Moreover, it leads to perceptions that senior leaders are authentic, which in turn enables leaders to hold those below them accountable for implementing change.

Not only does the honest conversation need to be followed up, but it also needs to be repeated from time to time. The hope, engagement, and commitment engendered by one instance of SFP can quickly decay if good conversations about the organization's effectiveness are not repeated periodically. Moreover, the opportunity to develop a company of innovators and change agents will have been missed.

Martin Seligman, the leading researcher in the psychology of optimism, has found that people's sense of hope—their optimism—depends on the degree to which they attribute positive changes in their lives to their own efforts.[15] Extrapolating this research to the sphere of organizations helps explain why honest, collective, and public conversations about the organization's effectiveness rekindle collective hope and optimism, as we have consistently observed. People *take part* in the improvement of their own working lives. Employees provide the feedback, and the task force assesses the action plan, not to speak of the many opportunities to involve task force members and others in helping to implement change. Seligman's findings also explain why we found that organizations that institutionalized honest conversations, making them a tool for continuous improvement, were able to sustain collective optimism and repeatedly adapt, as I will discuss later in the book.

A Developmental Process

Successful conversations about the state of the enterprise must be developmental, not remedial, although they can and should lead to replacement of leaders who do not demonstrate learning, change, and improved performance over a reasonable period. Never should the negative feedback from SFP be a cause for immediate dismissal or removal of individuals. If this happens, the process will become tainted as punitive and will be avoided, its purpose and value defeated. Such a problem arose briefly in one company before management fully understood SFP's developmental purpose. Senior management had asked unit leaders already under scrutiny for their management and results to carry out SFP. When the honest feedback amplified management's existing doubts, the managers fired the unit leaders. For several years after this unfortunate episode, SFP was seen as a booby trap and did not take hold institutionally.

As I will describe in chapter 7, Grey Warner, senior vice president Latin America at Merck, wisely framed SFP as an opportunity for leadership and organizational development when he asked his ten country managing directors to use the process in his successful turnaround of Merck's Latin American region in the 1990s. He did remove some leaders, but only after they consistently failed to show progress, so he avoided poisoning the way people felt about SFP.

Discipline for the Necessary Conversation

Anyone who has tried to discuss something difficult with another person will know how hard it is to make such conversations productive. Defensiveness can easily send such conversations off the rails, while reluctance to come down too hard on another person can make the conversation vague and disturbing without being constructive. Little things like body language or quick, thoughtless responses can easily destroy trust and make whatever is already wrong even worse. For these reasons, the sequence of steps in the conversation matters: how it progresses from the laying out of the issues to the development of a plan for improvement. The structure that SFP provides to the conversation, the fishbowl, and the ground rules for engagement are also very important. Honest, collective, and public conversations are even more complicated than difficult private conversations because of the number of people involved and because of the power some people have over others.

For these reasons, SFP could be considered a container for the conversation—something that both gives it shape and keeps it from spilling out. This SFP that my colleagues and I carefully designed, along with the rules of engagement, has proven very helpful, particularly if organizational problems are complex and the level of trust within the organization is low. Furthermore, we have kept improving it as years of experience have taught us more.

SFP is not the only container that works, of course. My aim in this chapter and the rest of the book is to show the transformational power of any structured, honest conversation. That's what matters, and SFP is one well-tested way to get there. Courageous leaders with the values and skills embedded in SFP should be able to enact the six principles defined in chapter 1 even without the structure of SFP or some similar process. Chapter 8 will discuss in detail what experience has taught us about the leadership qualities required. Unfortunately, experience has also taught us that these qualities are hard to come by and constitute a major talent gap in most companies.

Better Implementation

As explained in this chapter, the honest conversations enabled by SFP are not the same as an employee survey. They demand that senior teams take visible action based on what they have learned. There is no formula for this requirement. It depends on what the participants learned about the barriers to execution. In my colleagues' and my own experience, changes in organizational design—structure, processes, and, very importantly, roles, responsibilities, decision rights, and relationships—are an outcome. Indeed, serious conversations about what needs to change empower senior management to make these bold changes rapidly without the resistance and loss of commitment that often accompanies such fundamental changes. As leader after leader has told us, SFP accelerated their companies' transformations.

If fundamental change has already been made, honest conversation can help you evaluate how well the change is being enacted and, if not very well, why not. Leaders can then initiate other interventions to support the necessary changes in behavior. My research has shown that organizational changes founder because of underinvestment in helping individuals and newly created teams learn the requisite skills and behaviors in vivo—that is, while they are actually performing their newly changed roles. This is a much more motivating, relevant, and powerful way to learn than classroom training programs, though these can be a helpful supplement.[16]

Not a Magic Bullet

Honest conversations almost always change the harder, tangible facets of the organization—for example, organizational design changes in structures or processes like business planning and reviews. The conversations are not always equally successful in *sustainably* transforming the less tangible barriers, or silent killers.

An in-depth study of twelve organizations whose leaders implemented SFP showed that the degree of success depended on leadership and the organizational environment. Most important was the leaders' determination to close a performance gap, to transform the organization, and how well their values aligned with SFP's underlying values, namely, openness to learning and acting on the straight truth. Of course, the reverse also applies. While the success of SFP depends on the environment, successful SFPs can and have changed organizational behavior and culture and the leaders themselves. That is the nature of systems: everything depends on everything else. Table 2-1 shows the variability in results. Success depended on the leader following SFP guidelines in practice *and* in spirit. (See appendix B for my and my colleagues' research on the effectiveness of SFP.)

In practice, leaders who did not complete all the steps of SFP, including sustained implementation of solutions developed through the collective conversation, did not achieve the promise offered by such a conversation. Leaders who did not lead the honest conversation with sincerity or in the spirit of SFP were also less successful.

TABLE 2-1

Extent of change in twelve organizations after SFP

Industry and type of organization	Extent of change*
Technology company A, business unit	7.00
Toy company	6.00
Pharmaceutical company, Mexico unit	5.90
Technology company B, business unit	5.50
Technology company C, business unit	5.20
Pharmaceutical company, Brazil unit	5.00
Hotel company	5.00
Technology company D, business unit	4.36
Banking business unit	3.50
Pharmaceutical company, Argentina unit	3.33
Medical technology company	3.09
Privatized government agency, Canada	2.55

* *Extent of change*: The mean difference between pre- and post-SFP assessments of twelve organizations. The researchers rated questionnaire items describing organizational qualities such as effectiveness, commitment, and trust on a seven-point scale (where 1 = "strongly agree" and 7 = "strongly disagree"). Pre-scores were subtracted from post-scores so the higher the difference, the greater the change in overall quality of the organization. See appendix B for details.

Success in our sample—and in our overall experience—depended on the leader's assumptions about people and how to manage them. Over fifty years ago, Douglas McGregor, in his classic *The Human Side of Enterprise*, argued that managers' deeply held but *unconscious* assumptions about human motivation underlie their choices about how to lead.[17] He described two fundamental types of leadership—theory X and theory Y—both of them based on deep, unconscious assumptions about people. Theory X managers exercise directive, top-down management (command and control) because they assume that people eschew hard work, learning, and taking initiative and responsibility. Theory Y managers believe in high-involvement, participative leadership because they expect that people want to make a positive difference, can learn, and can become motivated and committed to do their best.

SFP is clearly based on theory Y. A theory Y manager is more likely to unleash its full power. By and large, the courageous leaders in this book were theory Y managers or were influenced by their experience with SFP to embrace theory Y assumptions that they had not previously held.

The leaders' assumptions were formed by factors that we did not study in depth. Sometimes the assumptions were rooted in family values or their religion. Other assumptions were shaped by a boss they admired or were a reaction to a boss they disliked. And still other assumptions were shaped by a company culture that valued human-centric, theory Y management. Of course, honest conversations, when led with sincerity, also helped organizations develop theory Y cultures. Those leaders modeled theory Y leadership by choosing to employ SFP and how they guided it and then evaluated and promoted leaders below them. In effect, organizational culture changed through a sorting process—moving theory X managers out and hiring and promoting theory Y managers.

Interestingly, the national culture in which the organization was embedded did not determine success or failure per se. We have seen honest conversations succeed in Asia—China, India, and Japan—as well as in Latin American countries and, less surprisingly, in Europe, particularly in Scandinavian countries such as Sweden. Most successful SFPs outside the United States either were led by expatriates or had adopted assumptions about leadership through education or experience outside their native country. In some countries the structure of the honest conversation had to be modified slightly to relieve the anxiety of task force members about speaking truth to power.

The organizations that used honest conversations the most successfully adopted SFP and its underlying principles to continue to learn about the progress of the transformation as new barriers and unanticipated consequences arose. SFP enabled business leaders to build a partnership—a high-commitment, high-performance collaborative community. That happened in the most changed organization in table 2-1 (rated as 7 in amount of change), a case I will discuss in chapter 4. In short, honest conversation through SFP can produce powerful change but does not guarantee it.

Summing Up

Honest, collective, and public conversations through SFP are effective because they surface valid and compelling data and enable nondefensive, respectful dialogue and learning about the system of organizing, managing, and leading. The open, dynamic conversation gives senior leaders a mandate to make the bold and systemic changes required to accelerate change. SFP was most successful when leaders followed SFP in both practice and spirit.

The leader's readiness to engage in honest conversations and the relative success of those conversations are moderated by four leadership characteristics: (1) commitment to take the organization to the next level of effectiveness and performance, (2) a human-centric philosophy of management, (3) eagerness to learn rather than tell, and (4) immersion in an organizational culture that supports that philosophy. SFP led with sincerity always helps start the process of changing the organizational culture.

In part 2, I will show that honest conversation helped leaders achieve important outcomes. All the organizations described in this part of the book achieved all three essential outcomes for sustained performance. They became fit to perform, fit to trust, and developed fitness to adapt. In chapter 3, I describe the transformation of Becton Dickinson to show the power of these conversations to transform a large, complex, global company. Chapters 4, 5, and 6 each focus in more depth on one of the three organizational outcomes, with each chapter examining one outcome, though in each case, all three outcomes were achieved. Each chapter also explains exactly why and how these outcomes are achieved through honest conversations enabled by SFP—the underlying theory, if you will. Let's now look at the theory in action.

Honest Conversations in Action

PART TWO

Chapter 3

Fit to Compete: Becoming a Corporate Olympian

We have to become an Olympic athlete even though we are a pretty darn good runner.

—Gary Cohen, executive vice president, Becton Dickinson

SFP really energized the transformation in multiple dimensions . . . The changes we made happened because of SFP . . . I had a lot of these ideas, but . . . SFP gave key people in the organization a voice. They could have a dialogue with me . . . and with others. I didn't have the whole thing scoped out in my head. It was information from SFP that enabled me to refine my thinking.

—Vince Forlenza, CEO, Becton Dickinson

As described earlier, Vince Forlenza is CEO of Becton Dickinson (BD), a $16 billion global medical technology company. Between 2011 and 2019, he not only led the company, as any CEO might have done, but also led its successful transformation—something far more often attempted than achieved.[1]

Forlenza had a reputation as a smart, can-do manager who valued constructive debate but who expected those who saw a problem to come ready with thoughts for a path forward, not just complaints. On his desk was a small rock embossed with the words "No whining." He had come to Becton Dickinson thirty-eight years earlier as a young MBA with an undergraduate degree in chemical engineering and an extraordinary capacity for thinking systemically. He had applied this capability to succeed in every job—line and staff—he had held on his rise to CEO and then had applied it to the transformation of BD he led.

The purpose of that transformation was to realign BD's corporate organization from an excellent operating company—highly effective at incremental improvements to a relatively stable product line—into a company capable of delivering innovative solutions and of growing more rapidly than it had been. In the end, the transformation was successful by almost every measure. Between 2011 and 2016, the period of the transformation I describe here, BD's portion of sales attributable to new products grew from 8 to 16 percent, revenues rose by 26 percent, and stock price by 39 percent, and BD consistently outperformed the S&P 500 by a large margin. Commitment to executing the new strategy had accelerated the transformation. The company had also successfully acquired and integrated CareFusion, a company half its size, an accomplishment that is particularly notable given that, during an SFP held in 2011, BD's own key people identified partnering and acquiring as company weaknesses.

The company was now more *fit* to compete—better aligned with its current competitive realities. It had also improved its *fitness*—its capacity to adapt through periodic honest conversations about its own weaknesses and the resulting plans for improvement. Of course, much more had to be done. Nevertheless, in a relatively short period as transformations go, many changes had occurred and the whole company [or the leadership] was ready for further change.[2]

The transformation actually began in 2010, when CEO Ed Ludwig was planning to retire in a year and wanted to leave Forlenza, his chief operating officer (COO) and designated successor, a company capable of innovating and growing more quickly. Ludwig suggested that the two collaborate in leading an honest, collective, and public conversation about BD's capabilities to do just that, and he proposed using SFP as their leadership platform. Forlenza was a more-than-willing partner, and that conversation launched the transformation.

Although SFP is an unorthodox *leadership platform for corporate transformation*, the process already had a long history at BD. Ludwig recalled the senior team meeting at which he and Forlenza kicked it off:

> We were genuinely concerned about growth. We sat down with the leadership team, and I explicitly remember that we said: "You guys [the senior team] may not want to think about doing an SFP. We've done it in the past. We believe that a fitness process would really help us learn what is holding back growth and innovation and to change." And I think it was during that discussion that someone said, "Let's really go looking for insights, criticisms, ideas regarding our growth agenda, because we're spending more and more money and we're not seeing [good results]." We had been through a couple of acquisitions that weren't quite right and a couple of products that sort of died upon launch. There wasn't the burning platform we clearly had in 2000 when I became CEO: [poor] performance, problems with Genesis [a new information technology enterprise system], dating of orders, hostile shareholders. We didn't have any of that in 2010. This time we could really stimulate excitement to go for something as opposed to scaring them to death and running away from something.[3]

Like Forlenza, Ludwig—an accountant by training—had spent his whole career at BD. In several instances, Forlenza had worked for Ludwig on his way up through the company. Both men were deeply committed to the company and saw themselves as stewards of its future. In the hallway leading to Ludwig's office hang pictures of the founders and the three CEOs who had preceded Ludwig. He told me that when he passed those pictures, it reminded him "not to screw up." Though

Forlenza was less emotionally expressive than Ludwig, he felt every bit as committed to BD and determined to ensure its future success.

BD was already familiar with SFP. Over the previous twenty years, many senior executives—including two of Ludwig's predecessors—had used it to take charge of the company and implement their strategic vision of what the company had to do to compete. Many key senior managers had also implemented SFP during that time period in their business, functional, or regional organizations.

Ludwig himself was naturally attuned to the idea of honest conversations. In meetings, he was generally the last to speak, waiting for others to express their views and then summarizing what he had heard, adding his own view, and offering a direction that integrated it all. He was also a serial user of SFP. In 1990, he was one of the first business-unit general managers to use SFP to launch the successful transformation of a business unit when he took charge. He recalled that as an inexperienced and young-looking thirty-eight-year-old in his first general-management job, he found that honest conversation helped him gain commitment to his change effort from a group of older and more-experienced managers. In effect, it had legitimized him as a change leader. When Ludwig took charge as BD's new CEO in 2000, the company was facing a serious crisis in performance and a plummeting stock price. He used SFP to transform the company. Forlenza, who had been a member of Ludwig's senior team at the time, recalled: "We all lived through the 2000 SFP, and we knew it worked and it had been a major success. The outcome of the programs that we had put together really put the company back on track."

In 2010, when Ludwig and Forlenza decided to launch an SFP, it was a different story. Becton Dickinson wasn't in any immediate trouble. It had been outperforming its industry because its management had fostered excellent operational capabilities. On hearing about Ludwig's planned retirement, a Wall Street industry analyst wrote a note to him praising his leadership of the company between 2000 and 2011. BD had a stable of good products that, year by year, it kept making a little better. For example, the company led the industry in making its syringes safer in response to the HIV crisis and had kept improving over nearly twenty years. BD's corporate conduct was ethical, its associates (BD's name for all employees) were committed, and its customers were happy. In the last two years of the decade, however, BD's stock price had stagnated, growth rates were declining, and the company was achieving its earnings-per-share goals through stock buybacks rather than through organic growth. These problems were in part due to the Great Recession of 2007—but only in part.

Ludwig's senior team determined that the formula that had made the company successful for many years would not work as well in the future. BD's focus on improving existing products left it vulnerable to increased competition, lower margins, and commoditization. Customers were looking for high-quality solutions—not just products—and at lower prices. BD had to find ways to redefine itself as a solution provider capable of integrating its own products with new information technology and with other products—both existing products and new products it could obtain through acquisitions.

But Ludwig, Forlenza, and the senior team could also see that this necessary shift would take the company well outside its comfort zone. Innovation and incremental improvement require different kinds of organizational arrangement, different management processes, different kinds of judgment, and very different cultures. BD had already been trying for several years to be more innovative, but the effort hadn't been working. The company had developed a process that improved the efficiency of new-product development, but the improvement had not yet yielded major innovations. Several acquisitions had also proved to be disappointments.

Ludwig and Forlenza were also aware of organizational conflicts that reflected the corporation's inability to innovate and grow. BD sales and marketing regions around the world, particularly in Asia, complained about their lack of influence in a strategic planning process controlled by powerful global business-unit leaders who were not knowledgeable about regional markets. The tensions arose partly because these leaders were accountable for sales in the United States and consequently prioritized the US region for resource allocation. Regional managers were also frustrated with the power of corporate staff functions to say no to investments in new products and opportunities, applying rules and regulations that were not always applicable in far-flung regions. One marketing manager—who became an SFP task force member—decried the bureaucratic hurdles to her efforts to introduce a new, lower-cost catheter in China. There was also dissatisfaction about a cumbersome planning process and—from managers responsible for innovation initiatives—objections to the allocation of investments. Short-term engineering extensions of existing products were enjoying greater investment than were the breakthrough innovations for which the managers were responsible and which they desperately wanted to succeed.

So, if innovation was where BD wanted to go—or *had* to go—Ludwig and Forlenza understood that the company had to be transformed, though they had no clear vision of what precisely to transform or how to do it. They did know, however, that an honest, collective, and public conversation using SFP would answer those questions, enabling a holistic transformation and giving them a much greater chance of success. Forlenza recalled:

> When I came into the role, I knew what I had to do was transform this company . . . to become more innovative . . . SFP began to give me a very coherent way to go about that . . . It involved the organization from the start, and it enabled me to go back to the organization and say, "We are working on this." SFP gave me the starting point and a way to structure the inquiry with input from the organization. It broadened my thinking . . . It didn't give me the answer.
>
> SFP really energized the transformation in multiple dimensions . . . The changes we made happened because of SFP. I had a lot of these ideas, but . . . SFP gave key people in the organization a voice. They could have a dialogue with me . . . and with others. I didn't

have the whole thing scoped out in my head. It was information from SFP that enabled me to refine my thinking.

That is very different from starting with, "Hey, here's what I'm thinking." And so, you had people who were involved in the solution and the formulation of the solution who felt that they were being heard.[4]

With the honest conversation made possible by SFP, BD's leadership team could see in great detail how its system of organizing, managing, and leading was really working. Armed with this comprehensive knowledge, the team could form an agenda for change, which was then carried out over a six-year period. In my travels around BD in the years after that SFP, people referred to this conversation quite often when speaking about the transformation the company was undergoing. I observed how powerfully the conversation had enabled collective understanding and commitment. It was a defining moment, not only for Forlenza but also for many others.

Advocacy of the New Direction

BD's management committee—the company's senior team—began the SFP with a conversation that created, over several meetings, a statement of direction. In reaching this agreement, the team developed both an understanding of the new direction and a commitment to it. Here is a summary of, and some excerpts from, the statement (which elaborated on each of these goals):

- **Enduring purpose and values:** "Helping people live healthy lives" and making BD a high-performance company that is also a great place to work.

- **Performance:** "Our goal is to increase BD's sustainable revenue growth rate (normalized for acquisitions and foreign exchange rates (FX) to 8–10% and remain consistently in the top half of our peer group, while continuing to be among the top quartile of companies in the medical technology industry on bottom-line growth, cash flow, and ROIC."

- **Innovation:** Moving from a product company to a solutions company. This goal includes "reinvigorating the core," "expanding into near adjacent spaces," and "deeper geographic penetration."

- **Capability improvement:** Targets include product development, strategic marketing (the capacity to identify strategic opportunities), collaborative capabilities between R&D and marketing, and external innovation partnerships.

- **Efficiency:** Investments required for new innovations will have to be "financed" through improved efficiencies and the resulting cost reductions.

As we will now see, systemic organizational transformations aimed at aligning the organization with a new direction are not linear. Granted, a transformation starts with the senior leadership team's *advocacy* of the new direction—leaders' aspirations for the company's purpose, strategy, and values. But advocacy has to be followed by the leaders' inquiry into what strengths must be preserved to pursue that new direction and what internal barriers will stand in the way. Beyond that, leaders need to iterate between advocacy and inquiry (see figure I-1) to correct for unintended effects and, importantly, to build up a selfless, collaborative community that is committed to change and the larger corporate good.

The Inquiry

BD's top management team, having completed the statement of direction, next commissioned a fitness task force of twelve key managers one to three levels below the team itself and from all parts of the corporation. These individuals—who represented BD's various businesses, functions, and geographic regions—were also considered credible and objective by the leadership team. In short, the task force constituted people whom the senior team would believe when the twelve came back with the complete, unbiased truth.

The task force's job was to talk with people inside and outside the company; outsiders included customers, Wall Street industry analysts, academic partners, and CEOs in the industry. Each interviewee was presented with the statement of direction and asked three broad questions: Does the statement make sense? What company strengths should be preserved and strengthened because they support the new direction? What are BD's barriers to achieving the new direction?

Throughout all parts of BD's global footprint, key people one to three levels below the top were informed that senior management was launching SFP. Specifically, they were told that the purpose of the process was to assess BD's strengths and barriers with respect to becoming an innovative company, that 150 people would be interviewed, and that senior management would hear directly from the task force about what it had learned. SFP was not to be a paper survey or a third-party investigation, but rather—as much as possible for such a large organization—a conversation between senior management and the whole company.

Within a week of their appointment, the task force members met at headquarters in Franklin Lakes, New Jersey. They were briefed by Ludwig and Forlenza about the statement of direction—that is, the senior team's idea of BD's growth and innovation goals—so that the members could understand it and communicate it clearly to their interviewees. Ludwig and Forlenza urged the task force to bring back their unbiased observations—that is, the whole truth as perceived by lower levels, which would not be the same as top management's whole truth. But as has been proven with many organizations, it wasn't the senior team's urging alone that would uncover this truth. It was the structure and sequence of SFP steps designed to promote honest conversation while avoiding the many missteps that often creep in (see chapters 1 and 2). These missteps include, in one direction, disrespectful, aggressive feedback from uninhibited individuals and, in the other direction, top management's defensiveness, whether expressed in words or through body language.

When my colleague and I, who were acting as facilitators, asked the BD task force members how they felt about their assignment, their responses reflected anticipation. They saw it as an opportunity to make a difference but were also somewhat anxious and uncertain about its outcome. They also briefly discussed their own views of the barriers to innovation. For example, the marketing manager from China described the delays she had experienced as she tried to navigate the bureaucracy at headquarters to get approval to launch a new product developed for the Chinese market. Others chimed in with their stories and perceptions of what stood in the way.

Training in how to conduct an interview followed. Then task force members interviewed each other. These interviews gave them some practice, but also helped put their own perceptions—the ones they had alluded to in the earlier conversation—into the findings. Their views mattered as much as anyone else's, but a key to SFP's success is that, from then on, they would be reporters and would not be speaking for themselves.

It didn't take long for this group—most of whom knew each other but had not worked together—to feel a sense of unity. Despite being handed a big job to do on top of the big jobs they were already doing, everyone was excited about the opportunity to make a difference in BD's effectiveness and regarded the assignment as an honor.

To ensure anonymity with senior management, the task force members themselves selected the sample of key managers and external stakeholders to be interviewed, though the senior team did provide overall guidance about the constituencies it wanted interviewed. The task force was also given guidelines on how to analyze the set of up to twelve interviews (a manageable number for busy key managers) that each manager would conduct. The guidelines included how to identify themes that would be consolidated for the subsequent feedback presentation to the senior team.

The task force spent approximately four weeks interviewing people around the world—always people *not* in their own organizations—function, region, or business unit. The interviewees were told that senior management would share what it had heard and would describe the changes the company planned to make because of the feedback. The day before the task force members were to provide feedback, they met with my colleague and me to analyze their data and agree on the key strengths and barriers their interviews had revealed. (Below, I will describe the feedback process and the issues presented by the task force.)

The next day, the task force provided its feedback to the senior team. There was anticipation and some nervousness in the air. As described earlier, a fishbowl seating arrangement enables a task force to speak truth to power safely and prevents senior management defensiveness that would shut down honesty (see figure 1-2), We find that this arrangement gives the task force members *psychological and career safety* because it allows them to speak as a group.[5] In this case, however, because of BD's long experience with the process and people's trust in Ludwig and Forlenza, the task force members said they wanted to sit in a semicircle facing the senior team.

The task force's courage to report the truth was bolstered by reminding the senior team that the task force was acting as reporters and not speaking for themselves. To prevent defensiveness by the senior team, time-tested rules—such as "perceptions are facts and cannot be challenged" and "senior management can only ask questions for clarification at the end of each theme"—were listed on a flip chart. These rules had been developed in 1990, when a business-unit leader at BD had responded emotionally to the task force's feedback about a problem he did not see by saying, "That's not true." Ludwig opened the feedback meeting by underscoring top management's willingness to listen and the importance of the task at hand: "This is a very important time for this company, thanks to the task force members. This is not about just being better. We need to do something different. This is not a nice-to-know, cherry-on-the-cake exercise. This is fundamental to the company."

Facing the senior team were flip charts. One chart outlined the themes the task force had developed, and another listed the ground rules for the conversation. Other charts were dedicated to each major feedback theme (see figures 3-1, 3-2, and 3-3, discussed below), and one chart depicted the relative power of different parts of BD. The interviewees considered the power arrangement an obstacle to BD's becoming a more innovative company. Addressing each other, the task force members reported what they had heard in their interviews (often providing quotes and specific examples), devoting a designated period to each barrier, while the senior team members *listened*. In accordance with the ground rules, the senior team was not permitted to interrupt the task members' discussion, though they could ask questions for clarification afterward.

Conforming to the SFP rules of engagement, task force members reasserted several times that they were not speaking for themselves but were reporting what they had learned from the data they had collected and analyzed. Members of the senior team sat in a circle facing the task force, listening and taking notes.

The first topic was what interviewees had said were strengths that BD needed to preserve to achieve the transformation set out in the statement of direction. The point was to make sure BD didn't throw out the baby with the bathwater, as is easily done in attempted transformations.

Associates, the interviewees said, were highly motivated and committed, the task force reported. They loved BD, which they saw as an ethical company with high integrity and an excellent reputation. They felt the company tried hard to make excellent products that would do good and not do harm. They were energized by the goal of "helping all people live healthy lives"—something that transcended just working and getting paid—but they were also energized by senior management's aspiration to make BD a high-performance company and a great place to work (figure 3-1).

BD was seen—both from the inside and the outside—as strong in manufacturing and continuous improvement, though not in innovation. The task force reported on the opinion of one respected CEO in the industry: "[The executive] views us as terrific at what we do, but not

FIGURE 3-1

Task force's flip chart on BD's strengths

STRENGTHS

BD is a great company to work for
- Ethics
- Manufacturing
- Quality
- Worldwide

"BD is a company that it is different from the others by its genuine concern about improving health care — business is a consequence. We can notice a strong ethical culture that brings credibility and trust. The BD associates always add value to the health care system."

innovative." The twelve ended their discussion of strengths by reporting that people loved the opportunity to have their voices heard through SFP and were impressed and appreciative that the leadership team was willing to challenge itself with the complete truth.

They weren't kidding about the senior team being in for a challenge. After about a half-hour of discussion of BD's strengths, the next three hours were devoted to a discussion of the following barriers to change (and this was a company whose associates were generally positive about their top management; in another company with which we worked, the discussion took six hours):

- **Short-term financial focus:** BD focused too much on short-term financial performance and on meeting budgets. This focus left insufficient slack in the system for the company to fully pursue innovation, and it undercut long-term investments in products and business development. Said one interviewee, "Fifty percent of my time is spent on the budget."

- **Talent management:** Talent management, attracting and retaining the right people, addressing skills gaps, and the willingness to cut mediocre or underperforming personnel all remained challenges.

- **US-centricity:** Although over 50 percent of its sales came from outside the United States, BD was dominated by a US perspective and had US people in the key positions of power. Emerging markets were often seen as a way to sell more of BD's existing products—true enough—but not to discover unmet needs around the world. This US-centric perspective was particularly reflected in a planning process that gave control to US-based global business-unit managers and insufficient power to regions. The United States was not considered its own region; rather, the global business-unit heads resided in the United States and headed the US sales and marketing organizations. This meant that the US region and regions around the world were not at all on equal footing (figure 3-2).

- **Organization structure and control:** BD's matrix structure gave individual business units too much power in setting direction

FIGURE 3-2

Task force's flip chart on US-centricity

US-CENTRICITY

- "We have WW teams but they do not listen to the world"
- "The US is not treated as a region"—Geo leader emerging markets
- CEO GE China—"need greater autonomy"
- "US-driven processes are too complex for rest of world"
- "Emerging markets are seen as markets to accelerate growth with current products vs understanding unmet customer needs to develop innovation"

and budgets. Furthermore, regions outside the United States had too little power to obtain resources to exploit local opportunities. Interviewees thought the matrix was difficult to work in and slowed decision making. BD also had a silo mentality, which limited cross-business opportunities and made it difficult for new ideas to emerge. "The structure kills new ideas," a task force member reported that his interviewees had said. "Many are empowered to say no. Few can say yes."

- **Customer focus and strategic marketing:** BD tended not to listen carefully to its customers, and its strengths in internal operations and systems overshadowed customer input. The company's strategic marketing (inbound marketing) was weak and limited BD's ability to understand its customers. This limitation was particularly true outside the United States.

- **Partnership and collaboration:** BD had failed to manage its partnerships effectively. It had underfunded them, often terminating them when internal financial pressures arose.

- **Acquisitions:** The company had made a few small acquisitions, but had not aimed high enough, moved quickly enough, or used acquisitions to pursue breakthrough innovations. Acquisitions were typically driven by individual business units. Bill Kozy, then BD's executive vice president and later COO, recalled, "Bankers told us, 'Don't try any transformational acquisitions. You don't have a clue what you are doing.'"

- **Innovation:** BD lacked an effective means to vet new ideas, and when ideas arose, there was often little freedom or budget to pursue them. Investment favored product-line extensions at the expense of riskier, more innovative products. Processes were too slow, and BD had not done enough to "reward success or celebrate failure" (figure 3-3).

FIGURE 3-3

Task force's flip chart on innovation

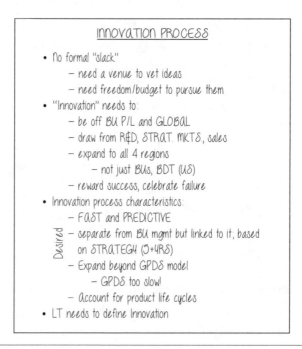

Innovation PROCESS

- No formal "slack"
  - need a venue to vet ideas
  - need freedom/budget to pursue them
- "Innovation" needs to:
  - be off BU P/L and GLOBAL
  - draw from R&D, STRAT. MKTS, sales
  - expand to all 4 regions
    - not just BUs, BDT (US)
  - reward success, celebrate failure
- Innovation process characteristics:
  - FAST and PREDICTIVE
  - Desired — separate from BU mgmt but linked to it; based on STRATEGY (3+4RS)
  - Expand beyond GPDS model
    - GPDS too slow!
  - Account for product life cycles
- LT needs to define Innovation

- **Culture:** BD's culture—including its tendency toward process-oriented, risk-averse consensus making—at times held the company back from bolder, innovative pursuits and from constructive conflict that might improve ideas or processes or eliminate projects unlikely to meet performance expectations. As one interviewee put it, "Failure impacts career and status."

The feedback ended with one final powerful flip chart that captured the underlying cause of many barriers: differences in the power and decision rights of key activities in the business value chain (figure 3-4). BD's system of organizing and managing had a strong arm—including finance, operations, regulatory, quality, and US marketing—and a weak arm of marketing, sales, R&D, and non-US regions with rapidly growing opportunities for innovation and growth. Yet, to grow faster

FIGURE 3-4

The task force's flip chart showing the associates' perception of power and influence

through innovation—BD's new strategic direction—those weaker functions are precisely the ones the company needs to be strong.

That's quite a list of barriers. In fact, the top executives were aware of some—perhaps even most—of these issues. But they had never heard them reported together and had certainly never from a task force that the leaders themselves had appointed to bring them the unembellished truth. This wasn't "I heard it through the grapevine"; this was data that had been systematically collected and rigorously analyzed. Trusting the rigor of the data gave the senior team confidence that these were real and valid issues that had to be dealt with if they were to do what they were already convinced they needed to do—grow through innovation.

Ludwig contrasted how this feedback differed from the feedback he heard when he took charge as CEO in 2000:

> The feedback in this SFP was less emotional than in 2000, when BD was underperforming. There was no confrontational emotional feedback associated with underperformance. People were very happy that we were talking about growth . . . but there was a deeply embedded dissatisfaction with . . . the culture. We thought the culture needed to be edgier, without being unfriendly. We needed,

as Gary [an executive vice president] put it, to become an Olympic athlete even though we were a pretty darn good runner. These were more sophisticated problems.

Now, on the second day of SFP, the senior team met alone to develop a consensus about the barriers and to examine their root causes. The discussion continued in several subsequent meetings. (This extension departed from the three days we recommend for the fitness meeting but was appropriate given the complexity of the corporate change being contemplated.) The result was a transformational agenda: a plan to carry out the goals in the statement of direction and to change how BD would be organized and managed differently in light of the factual observations brought back by the fitness task force.

The senior team developed eight initiatives. A transformation agenda does not necessarily address everything revealed in an SFP. Not all problems, even if they are publicly acknowledged, can be targeted for change or will be considered urgent by senior management. The leaders need to decide which changes are most needed and which they are most willing to undertake immediately. Others can wait until later. They must also explain these choices to the task force and later to the entire organization.

The task force was then asked to meet and evaluate the action plan. Because the task force members were now scattered around the globe, the critique took place by teleconference. The members agreed that senior management had understood the feedback and that its initial plans for change made sense. Naturally, this level of accord does not always happen. When a task force is not collectively satisfied with the senior team's response, the two groups collaborate to reshape the action plan. This conversation can, of course, be tense, but it is also an important step—practically, emotionally, and symbolically—in reinforcing the partnership between senior management, the task force, and—by extension—the whole organization. To solidify the partnership further at BD, task force members were also invited to lead or participate in the change initiatives. Several new task forces were created to dig deeper into problems and solutions, each including a representative of the senior team. Ludwig recalled that all of BD's task force members welcomed this involvement.

With commitment from the task force to the agenda for change, members of the senior team hit the road, making in-person presentations to BD staff around the world to communicate the outcomes of the organization-wide honest conversation that had taken place. People in the organization already knew this conversation had been taking place. Not everyone had taken part in it, and a few may not have had much faith in it, but no one was taken by surprise. (No one would be silently saying, "So, they've been plotting something behind our backs, and now we find out what it is.")

At these presentations, associates heard from senior team members exactly what the senior team itself had heard from the task force: the feedback from some 150 interviewees. The associates heard what the interviewees considered BD's strengths and weaknesses. They also learned about the eight change initiatives that senior management planned to take.

Small groups were convened at the site of each presentation to discuss the change plans, specifically, what they would mean for the local organization and how it could transform itself to support the overall corporate change. This process took a couple of months, but it was tracked, and the resulting observations were discussed by the senior team. Of course, the plans for change evolved as everyone in the company learned more about the barriers and the effectiveness of actions already taken.

Once the far-flung presentations had been concluded, Ludwig and Forlenza did something that is counterintuitive to most CEOs. They gathered both the task force's feedback on the strengths and weaknesses of BD and the senior team's suggested changes and presented all this to the board of directors. If their planned transformation failed, the board would know it and would know whom to hold responsible. Ludwig began this courageous practice back in 2000, when he was a new CEO taking over in a crisis of performance. Back then, he had needed to tell the board that a new IT enterprise system for which he had been responsible as chief financial officer was, according to the task force's report, off track and that he would delay its introduction at a cost of millions.

Ludwig and Forlenza both understood that they were not only making themselves accountable to the board for specific results but were also drawing the board into an active partnership, one that continues to this day. And making themselves accountable to the board for the results, they were also making the board accountable for those results. As T. S. Eliot once wrote, "After such knowledge, what forgiveness?"

The Transformation

It is impossible to fully convey the rich and complex transformation that Vince Forlenza led over the next six years, with important contributions from his newly designated COO Bill Kozy and others on the senior team. Between 2010 and 2016, BD made fundamental changes in how the company was organized, managed, and led—changes that rarely occur in most companies without a near-death experience or without a new CEO.

I will tell the story of how the transformation unfolded, with the help of SFP, largely using Forlenza's and Ludwig's own words. First from Forlenza:

> Ed Ludwig started down the path when he suggested we employ SFP. It was not imposed by the board . . . Ed thought of SFP as a strategic tool to validate (or modify) the strategy and identify areas we had to change. It would give a voice to people in the company as well as outside stakeholders . . . The task force didn't just interview people inside the company. They interviewed other stakeholders . . . the FDA [US Food and Drug Administration], stock analysts, and others in the industry. That gave us a very broad view and perspective. And we received very rich feedback about what was working

and not working in the innovation system. It identified a number of key issues. One important issue I already had in mind that needed change was our weakness in *strategic marketing.*

The outcome—I am simplifying here, of course—was that we strengthened the strategic marketing function around the world. We first validated feedback by the task force with a marketing skills assessment across the company. For the first time in BD's history, we hired a chief marketing officer. This was a transformational event, . . . a radical change in the thinking of the company. It was also the first function we strengthened and began a process that ultimately led us to a strong, strong, strong corporate matrix organization.

The three sides of the matrix that Forlenza was referring to in "strong, strong, strong" were functions, global businesses, and geographical regions. Ludwig recalled just how emotionally difficult a change this was: "Creating a new chief marketing officer was a very controversial move in a company that had some pockets of excellence in marketing. Some in senior management thought of themselves as the chief marketing officer. So, the collective voice of the organization gave Vince the assurance and the conviction to make this move."

Forlenza described the effects of the chief marketing officer position: "The appointment of a new CMO led to the launch of a major customer study that provided new insights. It really energized the transformation of BD on multiple levels. It enabled us to move towards a solutions strategy through a set of tools we used to understand the marketplace. It gave us insights into the customer and changed the way we thought about the company strategy."

The new chief marketing officer launched a marketing study that, Forlenza observed, "supported the need for change and which would be built on." It also began the process of *strengthening functions.* Other outsiders were hired to strengthen functions such as quality and R&D. This accomplished a goal Forlenza had envisioned from the start: the creation of strong world-class functions that would allow BD to pursue the best practices needed for the innovation to which it aspired. "It started to change the way we thought about the organization," Forlenza said. "We looked at multiple different ways to create an effective matrix that would allow functions to make a contribution. The first thing people wanted to do was launch a bunch of programs—the typical approach to change. Bill Kozy and I decided on a *learning-based approach*."

That learning process began with education for the top two hundred leaders about why innovating more radically outside the core business was necessary. They also learned about the innovation system that would be required to execute that strategy. Forlenza continued:

Bill Kozy and I held a town hall meeting about this. There had been a lot of noise about the *innovation system* or lack thereof that came out of the SFP process. We invited some high-potentials working on innovation initiatives to a small session to discuss the innovation system. Innovation leaders were empowered to speak truth to power. That conversation accelerated the change that Bill and I wanted to make in the whole innovation system. This learning approach is different from our leadership development program, where somebody is presenting. We wanted a two-way dialogue with the innovation leaders that was very complementary with the SFP we had undertaken at the corporate level. The concept of SFP is one of a continuous feedback loop. As we built the innovation system over time, we built in feedback loops. That idea came out of SFP; the feedback from SFP was telling us that BD was too bureaucratic, that this slowed us down. It also told us that we didn't know what the hell we were doing. The innovation problem required a learning approach.

I came up with the idea of the innovation councils, one at the corporate level and one for each global business. These councils would put the right senior people—corporate and global business-people—in the room to discuss and review innovation programs in the right way. This was triggered by the corporate SFP. What we learned from SFP was that the money for innovation initiatives we at corporate had funded for each global business was being cut by business-unit presidents when they thought they would not achieve the budgeted profit to which they had committed. The innovation councils enabled us to ring-fence these innovation resources . . . Ultimately, it solved that problem. The innovation councils allowed us to have the [right] dialogue . . . So all those things happened because of SFP . . . It gave us the initial energy.

Forlenza spoke about the redistribution of power and decision rights to the regions—a redistribution that he had implemented:

SFP put on the table that corporate regional organizations were not empowered. It told us that there were some organizations that had all the power and others that needed more if we wanted to accelerate innovation. That was the meaning of the task force's chart that displayed a strong and weak arm of the company [see figure 3-4]. SFP gave us a way to begin talking about that. It really wasn't discussable before feedback by the SFP task force told us that the regions found it difficult to invest in opportunities they saw in their markets. They explained why we were not getting the innovation we needed in fast-growing markets in Asia. Again, SFP enabled us to understand the problem and start to talk about it in a way that enabled us to think more deeply about it. It certainly had a big impact on me.

This feedback led to major organizational changes to rebalance power in BD's three-dimensional global matrix. Historically, planning and budgeting had started with the powerful global business units, making it difficult for regions to propose innovation initiatives that would require resources. Now, the regions would develop their own plans and budgets *first*, allowing for a conversation with global business units about the value of local opportunities. Moreover, to reinforce this change, Forlenza reorganized several regional organizations into two regions, each under a senior vice president who became a member of his senior team, thus giving the regions a voice at the top. "The SFP didn't tell me to do that," Forlenza observed. "It put the issues on the table and made all this discussable . . . Strengthening regional power was a second very positive outcome of SFP. There was, of course, enormous resistance [from business-unit leaders] to strengthening the [regions and functions]. Have we solved it all? No, it will have to be a continuous process, one that will go on forever." The rebalancing of power between businesses, functions, and regions created the "strong, strong, strong" matrix organization Forlenza referred to above, something most companies find difficult to do, precisely because losses of power are so strongly resisted.

There was also significant change in the management process at the top. As Forlenza recalled:

> Everything went to us at the top . . . and it was very consensus-driven. I was frustrated . . . We couldn't have the right conversation with the right people, because the group was too large and half were not directly involved or interested in every issue on the agenda, but everyone wanted to be there [for political reasons]. Reviews of projects became dog-and-pony shows with a lot of slides but little substantive discussion . . . So we changed the management system.
>
> With regard to transformation initiatives, a number of committees were formed, each focused on one of the barriers that SFP put on the table, for example, one on mergers and acquisitions, which the fitness task force had identified as a barrier. This began to create shared responsibility by those involved. That was much better than having a larger group sitting around listening to projects they were not involved in and then a few of us at the top making all the decisions anyway . . . This began to empower my staff.

Top-team ineffectiveness is almost always identified by SFP task forces as a barrier and is, in fact, one of the six silent killers that I will discuss in the next chapter. "SFP put all these issues squarely on the table," Forlenza said. "The data came from key people in the organization. This then allowed us to go back to them and tell them, 'This is what you told us, and here is what we are going to do about it.'"

Feedback about BD's culture of aversion to constructive conflict, one of the barriers reported by the fitness task force, led senior management to create a culture committee. Forlenza described this change initiative and why, as a can-do manager, it frustrated him:

> The barrier that was most difficult to change was our *culture*—our lack of constructive conflict and engagement. I was very frustrated with the culture committee . . . I thought it was a waste of time . . . We ultimately did away with that committee . . . Culture gets changed by doing real work in line with the new strategy—a new governance model, business processes, or performance management systems. Not much happens from pure culture conversations, because they don't result in a clear idea of what needs to change and how it will be changed to reinforce key strategic priorities.

Forlenza made it clear that he was not opposed to culture committees per se. In fact, he created several in 2019. These agility task forces, as they are called, are charged with examining real work processes and recommending changes in them that will enable faster decision making at lower levels, however. This approach to culture change is exactly what I have seen over and over again. Culture emerges, as Forlenza noted, from changing an organization's system of organizing, managing, and leading and from the ensuing roles, responsibilities, and work relationships.

Forlenza did however, find some benefit from the culture committee: "I'll give that committee a little bit of credit for starting a dialogue. That dialogue led us to develop new leadership standards." Those standards incorporated constructive conflict, on which managers were to be evaluated, and were reinforced by a leadership development program for the top two hundred leaders to promote deeper learning about what the standards meant behaviorally. Forlenza also created a structured

TABLE 3-1

Becton Dickinson's future culture as envisioned by its senior team

From	To
• Internally focused managers	• Customer-centric and entrepreneurial growers
• Focus on outbound marketing	• Commitment to strategic marketing pushing growth
• Focus on internal solutions	• Pursuing best solutions through partnerships
• Sustaining engineering focus and iterative innovation	• Nimble product development and breakthrough innovation
• Consensus-driven	• Engaged in debate; decisive
• Risk-averse	• Risk-tolerant managers; balancing stretch and reliability
• Process-managed and bureaucratic	• Learning and effective process enabled
• Disciplinarian; control-oriented	• Disciplined, accountable, and empowering
• People and careers managed through relationships	• People and careers managed through competency and skills-driven performance
• Difficult discussions about people and strategies indirect or avoided	• Difficult discussions about people and strategies embraced directly
• US-focused	• Globally connected to customers, partners, and technology

process he called constructive challenge, which would be applied to all major R&D and business-development initiatives. To force constructive debate about the viability of an innovation, a green team was designated to argue for moving forward and a red team designated to challenge that decision. To make BD's cultural transformation discussable and palpable, the senior team created a document listing the cultural characteristics BD was moving *from* and the new ones the senior team intended to move *toward* (table 3-1).

I asked Forlenza to assess the impact of honest, collective, and public conversations on BD's culture over the thirty years that the company had conducted them in the particular form of SFP. What had been the effect of the process itself, independent of the many tangible changes that it had set in motion? He said:

I think SFP certainly builds openness because people are asked for their opinion and what is going on. Secondly, it leads to the formation of teams that involve people in fixing the issues they are involved in and in which they have a stake. Thirdly, it involves high-potential talent in identifying and solving problems and develops them at the same time . . . Task force members working in a given function or business are asked to interview people in functions and businesses they are not working in and to be involved with people from other activities to solve them. So they develop a [general-management] perspective about how to think about and solve problems. It's very positive from a cultural standpoint."

The Results

By implementing many changes in how the company was organized and managed, Becton Dickinson improved its performance on several fronts—new products as a percent of sales, a large increase in revenue, and outperformance of the S&P 500 by a large margin—as described at the beginning of this chapter.

In 2015, BD extended its capacity to develop innovative solutions by acquiring CareFusion, a company half its size. Forlenza and his team created a new company culture that combined the two companies' strengths. The process they employed departed materially from BD's past acquisition integration practices, which the 2010 SFP had identified as barriers to innovation and faster growth. The result was improved innovation, more risk taking, and faster decision making.

Of course, much more needs to be done. As Tom Polen, BD's new COO, told me in a 2017 interview, BD has still not achieved the rate of innovation he believes is necessary to sustain competitive advantage. Indeed, in 2019, after BD had acquired Bard, another large innovative medical solution provider, Polen and Forlenza launched an honest and collective conversation that employed a variation of SFP—three task forces instead of one gathered data through interviews with key people—about how BD could up its game again, given its increasing complexity, scale, and scope. Constructive challenge and faster decision making were again brought up for discussion.

Transformations are never finished, because companies will always face new challenges. That is why BD's overall capacity to have honest conversations—to learn and adapt quickly and effectively—is itself a long-term competitive advantage. It's the business world's equivalent to a starfish's ability to grow a new arm.

SFP makes a certain kind of leadership possible, but it takes a certain kind of leader to make SFP possible. In Becton Dickinson, SFP guided a collective learning process, but without the determined and courageous leadership of Forlenza and his senior team, the effort would not have succeeded. On the other hand, without the partnership enabled by the unique conversations enabled by SFP, Forlenza and his senior team would not have garnered the necessary commitment to the transformation from key leaders, whose roles and responsibilities changed as BD's organization evolved into a strong matrix. As I noted earlier, fundamental transformations lead to unavoidable changes in some people's power. SFP enabled key people throughout the company to participate in the transformation. The 12 on the task force, the 150 who were interviewed, and the many in all parts of the world heard from the senior team about the honest feedback it had received and the resulting plan for change. All these people, from C-suite to front line managers, metaphorically held hands and moved into the future. Ludwig put it this way:

> I don't think it would've happened as rapidly [without SFP]. I'm absolutely convinced that this is an energy concentrator, an action accelerator, simply because everyone is [engaged]. It's not so much [about] eliminating resistance as it's [about] getting everyone to go in the same direction . . . If you're going to make a major investment to train your top leaders in managing innovation and reorganize to execute an innovation strategy, you need conviction.

These are big things . . . I think SFP took our vague concern about innovation—a notion that something is not quite right, that was un-actionable—to a compelling action plan for change. It accelerated [the transformation].

To extend BD's strategic and cultural change deeper into the organization, Forlenza encouraged the heads of thirty-two major units—businesses, geographic regions, and functions—to use SFP to learn how well their organizations are aligned with their own growth and innovation strategies and with BD's recently formulated cultural objectives and values. For example, James Lim, the head of BD's Asia Pacific region, implemented SFP to improve his vast regional organization's effectiveness and its alignment with BD's corporate innovation strategy and new cultural standards. Also implementing SFP were a business-unit leader in Europe, two functional leaders, and the new US sales and marketing region director—a position created in response to feedback provided in 2010—and still others. Each leader reported to the senior team on what they had learned about their organization and what they planned to change.

Reflecting on BD's remarkable turnaround, Jerry Hurwitz, senior vice president for HR, saw SFP as a catalyst for the transformation of the company from one relying on operational excellence to one excelling in innovation and growth: "I think we took the SFP work in 2010 very seriously. It formed the basis of Vince's agenda for several years and became the focus of key [senior team] members. Perhaps it was not completely obvious at the time, but the SFP was instrumental to many of the changes at BD."

One fortunate by-product of Ludwig and Forlenza's joint leadership of an honest conversation was their own smooth CEO transition. SFP motivated many conversations between them—some of the conversations included my colleagues and me as consultants—about BD's future direction under Forlenza. The agenda for change put forth by Forlenza as the new CEO was driven by a process that had given associates a voice and had been led by both Ludwig, the well-loved CEO about to leave, and Forlenza, the incoming CEO. Thus, the changes, big as they were, were not seen as a break with the past, as is so often the case and so often a source of resistance.

Summing Up

The story of BD's use of SFP—the application of the process, the straight truth it brought into the open, and the organizational and performance outcomes—illustrates the power of honest, collective, and public conversation to accelerate corporate transformations. By engaging key people around the world in this conversation, SFP led to individual and collective organizational learning at BD. Through this acquired knowledge, everyone in the company developed trust in the senior team and commitment to its new strategy and purpose. The conversation was a touchstone often referred to in the early years of the transformation. Not only were people experiencing significant changes but they were also feeling a part of those changes.

My goal in this chapter was to show how the leadership platform of SFP can help transform a complex global company's system of organizing, managing, and leading. I outlined the process and how it unfolds, first at the corporate level and then in major businesses, functions, and regions. You saw how honest conversations enabled an assessment of the strengths and barriers that many key people below the top and even those at the top knew about but which had never been discussed and acted on collectively. As Forlenza and Ludwig observed, this conversation changed mindsets, assumptions, and emotional attachments to a successful past and accelerated a fundamental transformation. This rare change process goes well beyond superficial modifications. And repeated cycles of honest conversation enable continuous partnership in learning and change.

For companies to obtain the benefits of honest conversation, they will have to select and develop leaders with courage. As my colleague Nancy Koehn concluded from her study of great historical figures, such leaders are not born; they are made by the challenges they encounter.[6] Honest conversations are challenging and sometimes painful, but that is why they accelerate systemic change. Ludwig and Forlenza had the determination to transform BD. They knew about some of the conflicts in the organization in advance of the honest conversation. But SFP enabled them and their senior executives to hear the emotions and urgency ascribed to these tensions and allowed the senior team to develop a holistic plan, one that addressed multiple facets of the organization, including structure, planning, senior team size, resource allocation, and culture. With its systemic agenda for change, BD could execute its new strategy. In the process, Forlenza and many of his leaders evolved their own leadership and their roles and responsibilities in a changed organization.

In the next three chapters, I will dive deeper into three desired organizational outcomes mentioned earlier: fitness to perform, to trust, and to learn and adapt. According to my research, leaders can achieve these outcomes through honest, collective, and public conversations guided by SFP. BD achieved all three outcomes through the honest conversation led by Ludwig and Forlenza. I will discuss exactly why and how each type of fitness is developed—the organizational and behavioral dynamics that honest conversations enable. All three outcomes are essential for sustained success; none of them can be achieved without the others. Arguably, honest conversation is the best and most rapid method that makes such a triple play possible.

In the next chapter, we will see how honest conversation guided by SFP can both diagnose and overcome six silent killers—that is, barriers to effectiveness—and thereby create an organization fit to perform.

Chapter 4

Fit to Perform: Overcoming the Silent Killers

It is the work [that Hewlett-Packard's Santa Rosa Systems Division, using SFP] did on alignment that got them to come to grips with what business they wanted to go after and what the business model was that was needed . . . Today I see them as one of our star divisions . . . Compared to other divisions, it probably is the most dramatic turnaround.

—Ned Barnholt, executive vice president,
HP Test and Measurement Sector

I had known that there were some serious issues in the division that needed to be addressed. But when these problems were spelled out in detail to me and the staff by a group of employees, the situation took on a whole new light.

—Scott Wright, general manager, Santa Rosa Systems Division

s Leo Tolstoy observed, "each unhappy family is unhappy in its own way." But hundreds of experiences with the strategic fitness process have taught us that the unhappy companies that find it hard to carry out what should be workable strategies do have several malfunctions in common. These are not specific wrong decisions or bad behaviors. Rather, they are leadership and management failures that render the organization unfit to implement the senior team's strategic intent and performance goals.

As explained earlier, we call these failings silent killers because, as is the case with medical silent killers such as high cholesterol and hypertension, you don't recognize you have them without a proper diagnosis and they need significant changes in behavior. The silent killers were identified by virtually every SFP task force we worked with, and they constituted a syndrome; that is, the weaknesses were usually reported together. The good news is that SFP allows you both to discover all the killers at once and to make an action plan to solve them all at once. It sounds like a lot. It *is* a lot. But it works.

To demonstrate the silent killers in action, I will use the story of Hewlett-Packard's Santa Rosa Systems Division (SRSD). Its leaders wanted to shift to developing and selling solutions rather than single-purpose instrument products to the fast-growing telecommunications industry. Reasonable as this strategy was, it wasn't working. In our terms, SRSD wasn't fit to perform. But why not?

There was plenty of frustration all around the division—and fear, too. But it took an honest, collective, and public conversation to bring SRSD's six silent killers to light and for people to do something about them.

I had just given a presentation to a group of HR executives at HP on why the strategic fitness process was uniquely suited to align an organization's system of organizing, managing, and leading with its desired strategy. One executive in the audience, Jody Edwards, ran up to me and breathlessly said, "Our division is totally ineffective, and we are not meeting our profit and growth goals. We desperately need the strategic fitness process you just described." Among the things she told me that day were problems later articulated by SRSD's fitness task force in the following way:

- We have two competing strategies that are battling each other for the same resources. The resultant factions around these two strategies are tearing this organization apart.

- The members of the top team operate within their own silos. They are like a group of fiefdoms that refuse to cooperate for fear that they will lose power.

- There is a cold war going on between R&D and the Custom Systems Group located within manufacturing.

- SRSD is still not sure what kind of business it wants to be.

As we will see, Edwards was describing the silent killers. But at SRSD, they were not silent; they were screaming to be heard.

Hewlett-Packard Santa Rosa Systems Division: The Business and Its Ailments

SRSD was formed as a new business unit in HP's test and measurement sector in the early 1990s to establish a new solution (or "systems") business to serve the emerging and rapidly growing telecommunications market. HP had already established itself as a leading inventor and manufacturer of single-purpose frequency-measurement instruments (known at HP as "boxes") for engineers working in R&D labs in defense and other industries. Revenues were approximately $8 billion. One key to the company's success was that HP engineers understood intimately what test and measurement equipment other R&D engineers needed, because HP's people had originally developed such equipment for their own use. But there was one weakness in that strategy. Strategic marketing—the process of first identifying market opportunities and then specifying product requirements for R&D—had never been developed at HP where marketing was mostly a matter of promoting sales. This history made R&D the most powerful function at HP, even when it came to marketing decisions.

This power arrangement worked very well indeed until the 1990s, when the test and measurement market changed. The defense business slowed, causing concerns about growth in HP's top management. The internet revolution was just beginning, and manufacturers of telecommunication equipment were growing rapidly. But what they needed for test and measurement wasn't single-purpose instruments like HP's tried-and-true boxes. They needed *systems*—technology platforms that were more complex and durable—to measure the various frequencies emitted by the commercial products they were manufacturing, such as cell phones.

HP created SRSD to meet this challenge. When it was formed, it inherited fourteen customized systems that the box divisions had already begun developing in response to their customers' sudden mission-critical needs. Scott Wright was appointed SRSD's general manager, with a senior team selected from the box divisions. All the team members had substantial experience in their own functional areas. They knew and trusted each other because they had grown up in HP's strong, widely admired, and highly collaborative team culture, known as "the HP way."

Hugely complicating Wright's task was the reality that the new solutions were still in development and early-stage introduction. Their development costs had to be offset by profits from the fourteen custom products that SRSD had inherited. The Custom Systems Group was established within SRSD to manage those fourteen legacy products.

Launching SFP

Edwards was convinced that the process of honest, collective, and public conversation I had described was what SRSD needed. Wright, on the other hand, was not so sure but was willing to have me conduct a one-day seminar for his top thirty people, who included the senior team. As it happened, I led a discussion of a case about a business unit in which low trust and cross-functional conflicts undermined the new-product development strategy.[1]

The participants below the top team suspected I had chosen this case deliberately because—they told me—SRSD had just the same problems. When I asked if their senior team had openly acknowledged these problems and had promoted a discussion, the answer was an emphatic no. Yet, in later interviews, Russ Eisenstat and I learned that everyone on the senior team knew about these problems. (We recommend that facilitators interview the senior team, because senior team members would not be as open with fitness task force members.) As I have said before, people often understand the issues confronting their company. They know what's wrong—or at least a good part of it—but have no way to talk about it and to be taken seriously. This virtual paralysis can afflict not just people at the lower levels, but also the senior team itself. Often, even the CEO or general manager has a good idea of what's wrong, but, fearing open conflict and even greater mistrust if they try to address the subject, they do not.

For its first step in the division's SFP, the senior team created a statement of direction. It clearly defined SRSD's dual strategies: develop three new technology systems platforms for the long run while protecting and growing its fourteen legacy businesses supplying custom products for needed profits. A task force was chosen and began interviews. At the same time, my colleagues and I interviewed senior team members about SRSD's strengths and weaknesses potentially affecting their intended strategy. We also asked them to assess their own effectiveness. Although task forces report on this issue generally, they cannot interview their own bosses or get complete openness about their perceptions of senior team effectiveness. For this reason, it is best to have a third-party facilitator (someone outside the division or an external consultant) make this assessment.

In brief, we learned that Wright had urged Sam Scott, head of the Custom Systems Group (the fourteen legacy products), to find some much-needed short-term profitable opportunities. Sam Scott went about this like a zealous and highly effective entrepreneur. His success convinced him that custom systems were a huge long-term opportunity: "I want us to be the guns for hire in the systems business," he told us. "CS isn't selling technology as much as it is selling a capability. I want to take that capability and use it for any customers that we can find whose systems needs are not being handled by SRSD's three business teams. This strategy represents a tremendous opportunity for SRSD's profitable growth objective."

Meanwhile, John Vink, who headed R&D, was equally motivated to achieve what he understood to be SRSD's primary mission:

> There is just such a confusion on priorities. I understand the mission of Custom Systems, but the problem is that it is too often at the expense of SRSD's future businesses. The projects of . . . the three R&D-led businesses are revolutionary. They are breaking new ground and establishing SRSD as the leader in new, high-growth systems technologies. The test and measurement systems business is practically brand-new to HP, and the purpose of R&D is to make sure that SRSD is positioned . . . as a new player, but one with long-term success potential. SRSD has to focus on new markets like radio-frequency integrated circuits and test and spectrum monitoring if it is to be a leader in the systems market.

R&D and Custom Systems found themselves in competition for limited engineering resources. R&D needed Custom Systems Group engineers to customize the standardized technology platforms (solutions) that were SRSD's long-term future, while Custom Systems needed R&D engineers to deliver the mission-critical custom products that ensured the divisions short-term survival. This was the cold war that Edwards had mentioned to me when we first met.

SRSD's marketing department, which was responsible for the strategic marketing critical to identifying needs and opportunities, lacked the budget and staff to simultaneously supply the market intelligence for both R&D and Custom Systems. Its budget might have been adequate for the traditional box businesses but was well below that of a competitor trying to establish a foothold in the systems business. Indeed, SRSD's senior managers had yet to fully understand the need for a shift in power from R&D to marketing, the latter being so critical to the solutions business. Steve Fossi, SRSD's marketing manager, told us: "Marketing's connection to the customer is so much more important in systems markets than it ever was in dealing with box instruments. But the marketing function in SRSD still does not share equal footing with R&D. We may bring them customer-partners and market research information, but R&D is still leading the business teams and having the final say on strategic matters."

The problems inside SRSD extended to its relationship with the sales organization for the test and measurement sector. This sales group, too, was confused by the lack of clear strategic priorities and clarity about who was responsible for selling what systems. One business team leader might tell the salespeople, "No, we can't do that kind of system," while Sam Scott or a Custom Systems engineer might say, "Sure, we can do that system." No wonder sales were lagging.

Fossi recalled the uncertainty then: "We were six months away from all getting reassigned . . . Our assumption was that we probably would not get fired, but that the division would go out of existence and we would all end up somewhere else, probably not at the same level."

In retrospect, it was George Mosby, the finance manager, who put his finger on the problem: the division's difficulty in developing teamwork and collaboration and its inability to resolve conflicts and change its culture. As he put it back then, "Most of the people within this organization are confused about how this division is really supposed to run. Unfortunately, they want to stay confused until they get what they want."

The lack of teamwork in this business unit was puzzling, given HP's strong and widely admired corporate culture. Why was this one part of HP falling short? The shared values of the "HP way," we learned, were undermined in SRSD by conflict caused by a system of management that did not fit the strategy *and which they did not discuss openly*, as so often happens. Fossi later recalled, "I think people did not know how to break through to it." As I will show next, honest, collective, and public conversation guided by SFP enabled the division to finally have that needed discussion.

Feedback and Diagnosis

SFP unfolded at SRSD much as described in previous chapters. The eight task force members interviewed eighty stakeholders: people in SRSD, sector salespeople, and executives in sector management, including Wright's own boss. Then, having organized their findings into themes, the task force presented them to the senior team in the familiar fishbowl arrangement. The eight members quoted the interviewees and gave examples of breakdowns in coordination, though, of course, always without attribution.

After a discussion of SRSD's strengths, they turned to a list of barriers to strategy execution that had been brought up by most of their interviewees. These barriers included conflicting strategies and priorities, ineffective leadership, lack of clarity on roles and responsibilities, poor teamwork, the cold war between R&D and Custom Systems, and the organizational shift from a box business model to a systems one. As we will see, these barriers can also be understood as the silent killers that we have found in nearly every organization we have worked with or studied.

But then the task force did something no other task force had ever done (having discussed their intention with Russ and me). With emotional intensity, the members told the senior team: "You have to do something about the problems quickly, or trust, morale, commitment, and performance will plummet. People are planning to transfer to other divisions." One of the members recalled: "I think the top team felt pretty beat up after the task force feedback. It's not that we were taking cheap shots at them, but straightforward, constructive comments can sometimes feel like an icy bucket of water over the head."

After five hours of fishbowl discussion only interrupted by a lunch break, the task force left so that the senior team could discuss the feedback they had just heard and develop an action plan for change. (The team does this alone, so it can have an open discussion of sensitive issues.) The senior team had indeed been riveted. The feedback was compelling. It revealed to Wright and his team the *whole truth*—tangible and intangible assumptions, mindsets, and feelings—about problems they all sensed existed and had told us about in our own interviews with them. They had not, however, understood the emotional intensity with which people regarded these problems. Nor had they heard these problems put together in the way they heard the task force do. As Wright later recalled, "When these problems were spelled out in detail to me and the staff by a group of employees, the situation took on a whole new light."

Russ and I followed the task force report with our own findings from interviewing the senior team. Of course, our report was anticlimactic, reflecting much of what the task force had already reported. Our feedback, however, included what senior team members themselves had told us about how they saw their collective ineffectiveness. The conversation took off when Sam Scott acknowledged that these problems were his own fault. He could see now that his commitment to deliver badly needed profits had caused him to lose sight of SRSD's long-term strategy and had thus contributed to the cold war.

A response like Sam Scott's has several important effects. By making himself vulnerable, Scott had demonstrated trust in his fellow senior team members. They reciprocated, responding to his mea culpa with a candid and productive discussion of the cold war and its tensions.

As the session broke for dinner, we asked each senior team member to come the next day prepared to share his or her diagnosis of the root causes of the organizational problems outlined by the task force. The next day, Mosby volunteered to start the discussion:

> SRSD suffers from the legacy of HP. We are not a box division, yet we manage and have structured SRSD as though we are. Although Custom Systems has taken on a much more expansive role in

creating systems than it ever did in past divisions, it is still run out of manufacturing. Although test and measurement systems have to be heavily marketing oriented, we still have R&D calling most of the shots. Although our product lines need to be grown and managed as businesses, we still treat them as projects. The systems market is so vastly different than anything that HP has done in the past with test and measurement that we need to start thinking of ourselves as a unique entity operating in circumstances that require a different strategy and structure than has been traditionally utilized in the past.

These insightful observations motivated the senior team to discuss SRSD's lack of fit with the new systems business it was trying to enter and the effects of that poor fit on strategy execution.

The Silent Killers: What Makes Organizations Unfit to Perform

As I said at the beginning of the chapter, I offer the case of SRSD not to reiterate what we have already learned about SFP, but to introduce one more dimension of what SFP uncovers and helps organizations resolve. It is, of course, no coincidence that a process designed to address organizational silence should find itself grappling with silent killers.

While not all businesses we worked with were as dramatically unaligned as SRSD, all had alignment problems that were a function of silent killers. At SRSD, a full day of discussions revealed all six silent killers (figure 4-1). Now, let's examine them as they manifested in that organization.

Silent killer 1: Unclear strategy, unclear values, and conflicting priorities

The task force's findings that SRSD had "two competing strategies battling each other for the same resources" and that "SRSD is still not sure

FIGURE 4-1

The silent killers of effectiveness and change

- Unclear strategy, unclear values, and conflicting priorities
- Ineffective senior team
- Leadership style: top-down or laissez-faire (hands-off)
- Poor coordination across businesses, functions, or geographic regions
- Inadequate leadership development
- Inadequate vertical communication: upward and downward

what kind of business it wants to be" reflected the executives' lack of agreement on strategy and priorities. This conflict infiltrated the lower levels as well. The senior team had agreed that the first priority was R&D's development of technology-based solutions platforms—not the customized offerings of Custom Systems Group. But Sam Scott's unexpected success with Custom Systems had persuaded him that customizing systems was, in fact, an equally important opportunity. We have seen this happen in other organizations: managers want to succeed and that can change their view of company strategy to one that gives their activity the importance they crave. Because the senior team did not get together regularly to discuss strategic issues and resource requirements (see silent killer 2), this shift in the Custom Systems manager's strategic perspective—and the implications of that shift for SRSD's overall strategy—were left unexamined, and the resulting conflicts unresolved. (Not that people didn't notice or complain about this shift. But it was never examined and resolved collectively by the senior team.)

In case after case, we have found that the lack of clarity about strategy and priorities resulted from the way strategy was formulated and reviewed—or not reviewed. The underlying problem was not this or that strategy, but rather the *process* by which strategy was formed—or the lack of any such process. In these troubled companies, strategy was usually developed by the leader along with the chief strategy or marketing executive, and only then was it communicated to the rest of the senior team for discussion. But this is not at all the same as developing a strategy jointly from the start, putting it on paper, and then reviewing it periodically to consider new information and develop agreement. As described earlier, Lynne Camp, general manager of the Systems Generation and Delivery Unit at Agilent Technologies, told us that SFP's requirement to agree on and write down a two-page statement of direction had brought to light different perspectives she had not realized existed and led to better clarity and agreement among her senior team. In fact, as the late Richard Hackman, an expert in team psychology, has shown, a compelling direction is the first step in developing a real team.[2]

A senior team might think its strategy is clear, but SFP might reveal either that it has not been clearly communicated throughout the company or that it actually isn't very clear and that the senior team's impression of clarity came from groupthink. Consistent with our findings that task forces almost always reported an unclear direction as a barrier to performance, recent research has established that clarity of direction and firm purpose are more powerful predictors of employee engagement—and, in turn, of business performance.[3] Clarity of direction is clearly important.

Unclear strategy and values and conflicting priorities underlie many conflicts and stalled-out strategies, qualifying them as silent killer number 1. But they themselves have an underlying cause, which we call silent killer 2.

Silent killer 2: Ineffective senior team

SRSD's task force also reported that members of the senior team "operate within their own silos. . . like fiefdoms that refuse to cooperate effectively for fear of losing power." This feedback reflected the widespread view at lower levels that the senior team was indecisive and ineffective. Wright's experience elsewhere, combined with his own personality, had taught him to avoid endless unproductive arguments that never led to a consensus. So instead, he used a hub-and-spoke approach to manage his senior team. Departmental goals, problems, and resources were decided in one-on-one meetings with each functional department head.

One senior team member referred to the hub-and-spoke process as "the godfather approach. All you needed was [Scott Wright's] permission, and you had complete control of the project." Another told us, "Whenever we sit down to discuss a strategic issue, I have this nagging feeling that Scott's decision concerning the matter has already been prewired. Chances are that he has already had a closed-door meeting with one of the other functional managers to make the decision."

But this approach prevented senior executives from having the honest and constructive dialogue they needed to arrive at the best strategic decisions, agree on priorities, and allocate resources accordingly. Everyone on the senior team was frustrated with Wright's management pattern, and the task force was clear that everyone else in SRSD saw the senior team as ineffective and was hugely frustrated—even angry—about it. Yet, it had never been discussed openly.

Top-team ineffectiveness was reported by almost all the task forces in the many organizations we studied, though the granular details and feelings in each case did not emerge until we interviewed senior team members. The consequences of this ineffectiveness were low trust, low commitment to strategic decisions, and different and sometimes conflicting understandings of what the strategy even was. To be fair, the finding that "SRSD is still not sure what kind of business it wants to be" may reflect the unique difficulty of developing a strategic identity in a new market, but an unclear business identity is also a problem revealed in many organizations having trouble implementing their strategies.

In all these cases, the leaders and their senior teams had not solved the fundamental problem of getting the right people in the room to talk about the right things in the right way—honestly and constructively. Wright's hub-and-spoke approach was only one of many forms of this fundamental mistake. Some senior teams, for example, were too large to have meaningful discussions, as Vince Forlenza of Becton Dickinson noted in chapter 3: "We couldn't have the right conversation with the right people, because the group was too large." Others mixed strategy reviews with financial or administrative reviews, usually driving out time for the deeper discussions needed for strategic choices—an example of the urgent driving out the important. Many senior teams had no clear process for conducting debates and for winding them up with a decision. When SRSD's senior team finally defined such a process for itself and put it on the wall of the conference room as a reminder, visitors from other divisions said, "Wow, we can use that," and took it back to their divisions.

Our finding on the near universality of senior team ineffectiveness is consistent with those of many other studies. My Harvard colleagues Ruth Wageman and the late Richard Hackman found that only 21 percent of senior teams were effective and that 71 percent were mediocre or poor.[4] A global survey of 175 CEOs and 675 top teams revealed that these executives perceived senior team ineffectiveness—in particular, poor team dynamics and lack of openness and constructive conflict—as a major barrier to strategy execution.[5] But these problems are hard for senior teams to confront without the mandate for change that honest, collective, and public conversation provides.

Silent killer 3: Ineffective leadership

The SRSD task force identified leadership as a barrier to effectiveness, but did not describe Wright's interpersonal behaviors, such as his aversion to conflict. The lower-level interviewees were typically not privy to what happened in senior team meetings and could not report on the details of Wright's leaderships style with any degree of confidence. The interviewees simply noted that Wright was not carrying out his role as division manager effectively. Why else was SRSD foundering as an organization?

Our analysis of feedback from two dozen task forces, like the ones we've described at Becton Dickinson and the SRSD, has found two styles of ineffective leadership: a top-down style that does not involve senior team members sufficiently and a laissez-faire, nonconfrontational style. Note that either way, the senior team is not being fully engaged in honest conversation. Thus, the leader doesn't learn about what's not working and why. The details of these two styles vary from organization to organization, but one or the other or both were always there when an organization was having trouble implementing strategy and when employees found their leader to be part of the problem.

The senior team typically attributes both styles to the leader's personal aversion to conflict or to the lack of a clearly defined process for opening a constructive debate and carrying it through to a decision (in other words, a decision-making process).* Wright combined both styles. Some senior team members viewed him as uncomfortable dealing directly with conflict. They reported that people who challenged an implicit consensus about a project found themselves playing the role of an unwanted messenger. Consequently, differences were never fully explored, and the quality of the decisions suffered. One team member described Scott Wright: "Scott is a very perceptive and intelligent manager, and if you disagree with him, he will ask about fifty questions until he finds a weakness . . . By that point, you are no longer in much of a mood to continue supporting your argument. So the issue gets pushed off to another day." The hub-and-spoke system reflected Wright's fear of constructive conflict. At the same time, HP headquarters had given him a special assignment that took him away for long periods, making him even less visible and necessarily more hands-off.

Problematic leadership behaviors, such as Wright's unhelpful hub-and-spoke approach, are often functions of the leader's interpersonal style. The behavior can become particularly problematic given the challenges the company is facing, as Wright's did when SRSD was trying make a place for itself in a highly fluid market. But that did not mean that Wright and other leaders with whom we worked could not change. They did—the urgency of the feedback impelled them to. As described earlier, SRSD's task force told Wright and his team that if they didn't become more effective, performance and morale would plummet further and people would leave.

Wright and his team changed the hub-and-spoke structure. The inability to confront conflict and resolve it in a timely way was changed

---

* This attribution came out in consultants' interviews with the senior team. The lower-level interviewees typically lack this inside look.

by introducing a new decision-making practice: The senior team starts by putting the problem up for consideration, discussing it for a specified time, then coming to an agreement. If the team cannot agree, then Wright decides. He announces his decision, and if further arguments do not persuade him otherwise, his decision is final and everyone must support it. Because this change (suggested by us, the consultants) was a team decision, members enthusiastically embraced the new ground rules for decision making. Without the team's support, it would have been difficult for Wright to change his ways.[†]

Silent killer 4: Poor coordination

Confirming Edwards' initial characterization, the task force reported: "There is a cold war going on between R&D and the Custom Systems Group located within manufacturing." Coordination across functional silos—business units or geographic regions at the corporate level—is always a challenge, as much research, including our own, has shown.[6] It requires an organizational design that overcomes these naturally occurring obstacles.[7] In many cases, the design of the mechanisms for integrating various functions is flawed and the lack of honest, collective, and public conversation prevents the organization from recognizing and correcting the flaws. Wright and his team had recognized the threat of silo mentality from the start. Understanding that coordination between marketing, R&D, and the Custom Systems Group was essential to the development and sale of solutions, they created three cross-functional business teams. However, the design of these teams and their organizational context were flawed, and the flaws had gone undiscussed and uncorrected.

The senior executives, reflecting on the feedback from the task force, identified the following organizational design flaws in addition

---

† Scott Wright was arguably the most courageous of the leaders we worked with. He embraced the honest conversation and the very difficult feedback that SFP made possible, and as Ned Barnholt's statement at the beginning of the chapter suggests, SRSD's transformation was the most successful of any he had seen at HP. SRSD's turnaround was the most successful of the twelve companies' transformations we studied.

to their own ineffectiveness: business teams were strategy discussion forums, not real decision-making bodies with strategy execution capability. R&D leaders had no experience outside of R&D and did not know how to run a business. Not that they could have, considering that the business teams were not designed to function as real business teams. They were not accountable for profit, which would have forced their leaders to prioritize initiatives and allocate resource accordingly. Moreover, because they lacked any authority to evaluate the performance of functional team members, the business teams could not ensure that their members came to meetings and worked as a team to achieve profitable growth.

Because of these organizational design flaws, the R&D managers focused business team meetings almost exclusively on the development of technology platforms within R&D. Thus, there was too little opportunity for the Custom Systems engineers to present their rich understanding of what solutions the customers needed—market knowledge that was essential in a solutions business. Not surprisingly, the engineers assigned to the team stopped coming to those meetings.

In short, the structure, the clarity of roles and responsibilities, the performance evaluation systems, reviews, and resource allocation—all the elements necessary for a matrix-like structure to function—had not been designed to ensure execution of SRSD's strategy. Indeed, as the senior team dug deeper into these problems, it realized that the whole system of organizing, managing, and leading they had created was not working. They began to redesign it, as we will see below.

Silent killer 5: Inadequate leadership development

SRSD's task force did not list leadership development as a problem per se, though many other task forces have reported it. Those organizations lacked a robust talent development program for high-potential managers to gain general-management and leadership skills through experience in various functions, businesses, or regions. Nor did SRSD have such a program. The shortcoming became obvious when the senior team members began designing a new matrix organization (in response to silent killer 4) and realized they had no managers with the skills to lead such business teams.

The causes of inadequate leadership development are directly tied to three silent killers already discussed. An ineffective senior team (silent killer 2) in a siloed organization with "fiefdoms" (number 4) does not have the perspective or capability to define the organizational values and behaviors it expects of leaders (number 1), nor to design a talent-management system that enables the cross-boundary developmental as-signments required to develop general management ability.

Here's an example: A CEO needed to figure out why the company was not developing managers. The executive first tried asking HR to create a program to develop them. Then the CEO initiated SFP to look into why managers were not being developed. But the SFP task force found a deeper problem: an ineffective senior team, each running its own siloed fiefdoms with no clear common strategy or shared values and behaviors that it expected of leaders. In fact, the same three silent killers at work at SRSD were also at work there.

Given this CEO's organizational situation, it is not surprising that when other groups asked the business and functional department heads for talent, the heads sent their least effective people, to protect their own units' performance. The organization's design failed to promote and reward coordination and collaboration to overcome silos or to pro-vide leadership development opportunities in general management. Research has shown that leaders usually develop not through training, but through challenging new assignments. Yet the silent killers prevent these opportunities.[8] Indeed, my colleagues and I have found that many HR-driven leadership programs are sabotaged by an organization beset with the first four silent killers—unclear direction, ineffective senior team, ineffective leader, and resulting poor coordination.[9]

Silent killer 6: Inadequate vertical communication

This book began with the problem of organizational silence. In every organization that used SFP, the fitness task force's interviewees said they had long known about the issues they were then reporting. Because it was the first time the interviewees had been given a chance to voice their concerns, many people were quite emotional in conveying their observations. This problem is the sixth of the silent killers. It strikes in two directions; it undermines both upward and downward communication (which we collectively refer to as vertical communication).

Upward communication: People in all organizations find it hard to speak truth to power. That is why a method like SFP that enables honest conversations across levels is necessary. Organizational silence allows the silent killers—in particular, the first five—to become so devasting in so many organizations. It allows individual failings to become organizational pathologies. Moreover, leaders and senior teams with top-down assumptions about how to lead (silent killer 3) typically communicate strategy down but do not promote a two-way conversation that might expose doubts or disagreements at the lower levels. Of course, these doubts and disagreements will impede implementation. Top managers won't be able to solve the problem, because they won't know where it's coming from.

Downward communication: A senior team that has not developed its strategy as a team will not be committed to it and will therefore be unable to speak with one voice about it. This failure of downward communication was one reason the lower levels in SRSD saw their leadership as divided into fiefdoms and observed such confusion about strategy and priorities.

Inadequate honest vertical communication is like a case of weak circulation of the blood. The necessary information about an organization's strategic direction and values does not circulate from the senior team to the lower levels, and the necessary information about the barriers to that direction and those values is not recirculated from the lower levels to the senior team. Rather than healing, there is increased poisoning and illness.

The Ubiquity of Silent Killers

That lower levels see the silent killers so clearly and are so frustrated with them tells us two very important things. First, employees know both the changes that senior management's strategy requires and the problems with the strategy itself. Second, because they typically have no way to talk honestly with the senior team about the silent killers, employees feel victimized by the organizational system in which they are embedded. They become demoralized, cynical, and less committed.

Most surprising to us was that the senior leaders at SRSD and at most other organizations were equally frustrated. Our interviews with them in advance of the honest conversation indicated that they knew about most of the problems later reported by the task force but had not mustered the courage or safe method to develop an open conversation among themselves and certainly not with the rest of the organization. George Mosby's insight about how poorly SRSD's organization fit the business model it was attempting to execute had not been discussed among the senior team, but even if it had, the discussion would not have gone anywhere without the motivation of the task force's feedback. Problems at SRSD would never have reached the crisis stage had there been a way to have an honest conversation. People were uncertain about how to break the barrier of silence.

The silent killers are challenging because they are what I call intangible human socioemotional issues. Eisenstat and I came to our own understanding of them by analyzing the feedback from twelve task forces. We later replicated our findings with an analysis of twelve additional task force reports (including that of SRSD). And we have seen the same silent killers in hundreds of organizations in which my colleagues at TruePoint and I have facilitated SFPs.

When I present the silent killer syndrome to management audiences, there is almost always immediate recognition. In fact, I was recently on a walk with a group of friends, one of whom had brought along his adult daughter. When my friend told her I was a professor of management, she described the nonprofit where she worked. She loved it for what it was trying to accomplish but was frustrated by its ineffectiveness. When I described the silent killers, she responded immediately, "That's us." In addition to our findings in hundreds of organizations that my colleagues and I have studied or worked with, such immediate personal responses support my argument that the silent killers are common barriers to effectiveness that undermine many organizations. To use a geologic metaphor, the silent killers are stress points. When the organization is faced with an earthquake—a significant change in its competitive environment requiring a major change in its system of organization, managing, and leading—these stress points become fault lines that can threaten survival.

The silent killers are consequently something worth knowing about for all organizations. By stress points, I mean that they are inherent weaknesses in all organizations because they demand socioemotional capabilities—sustained emotionally positive relationships—that are difficult for all human systems to develop and maintain over time. Remember how easily your own relationships can unravel because of unintentional things you or others do. If you would like to do a quick assessment of the silent killers in your own organization, complete the questionnaire in appendix C.

The silent killers will always reduce an organization's effectiveness to some extent. This continuous challenge alone is a reason for periodic honest, collective, and public conversation integrated into what I call strategic learning and governance (chapter 6). But it's when the organization faces a fundamental strategic change that the silent killers can really earn their name.

The Dynamics of an Organization Unfit to Compete

To succeed, an organization needs three strategic outcomes:

- **High-quality direction:** a clear strategy and clear values that everyone on the senior team is committed to and that lower levels
  understand and are also committed to

- **High-quality implementation:** a system of organizing, managing,
  and leading that is aligned with the strategic direction and values

- **High-quality learning:** the ability to learn the truth about barriers
  to execution so that the organization can adjust its strategy or
  its system

As we saw at SRSD, the silent killers prevent the development of all
three of these assets (figure 4-2). Silent killers 1, 2, and 3 prevent the
development of a high-quality direction. A leader who is averse to constructive discussions about strategy and values will be unable to develop
a clear direction and a senior team committed to that direction. The
resulting team ineffectiveness leads directly to silent killers 4 and 5:
lack of coordination and of leadership development, both needed for
implementation of the strategic direction.

SRSD's coordination problem—the cold war that was recognized
by all—was brought about by a system of organizing, managing, and
leading that did not fit the division's strategy. There was a functional
structure with an overlay of three business teams, but they were strategy discussion groups, not true business teams. They were not assigned
accountability for strategy execution and profitability and were led by
engineers who had no experience outside of engineering (they had not
developed a general-management perspective) and no authority to run
their businesses. Wright and his team did not initially understand why
that structure was hobbling implementation of their strategy, having
done well at HP up till then in functional structures that did not need

FIGURE 4-2

The dynamics of an organization unfit to compete

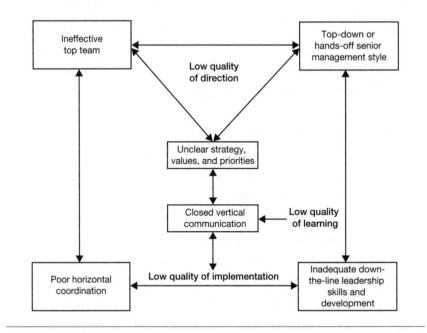

cross-functional business teams for success. Mosby hit the nail on the head when he observed, as quoted earlier, that the division carried the burden of HP's past. He described the problem of structuring SRSD like a box division when it no longer fit that form.

SRSD's lack of leaders with expertise in general management (silent killer 5) for its business teams was the other reason for its ineffectiveness and indicated that the senior team had not developed these talents in the organization. This shortcoming became even more obvious once the senior team deduced that SRSD needed a strong-matrix organization and then tried to identify people in SRSD to lead the necessary business teams.

Silent killer 6—poor vertical communication, both downward and upward—led to confusion about SRSD's direction. Although that confusion was largely due to an ineffective senior team (silent killer 2), it was poor upward communication (number 6)—that is, organizational silence—that kept the senior team from becoming fully and emotionally aware of this confusion and the other barriers to entering the solutions business.

Considering that so many organizations repeatedly describe these silent killers and their obvious damage to trust, commitment, and performance, we can better understand the core leadership and management capabilities that organizations must develop and continuously redevelop. Turning silent killers into core capabilities (sustained strengths) enables an organization to develop second-order business capabilities such as innovation, product development, and business development. SRSD's inability to develop new technology platforms and to identify new customer needs quicker was a casualty of the silent killers. As I will show below, when SRSD addressed the silent killers and thus became able to develop the corresponding core capabilities, it found itself able to do those things that it had been flailing at before.

As figure 4-2 shows, to enable continuous learning about silent killers, leaders will have to continue learning about the condition of their organization and keep improving it. Regular honest, collective, and public conversation through a structured process like SFP will facilitate this learning and adaptation. This discipline is missing in corporations because it is not widely acknowledged as being critical in enabling strategy implementation. As discussed in chapter 6, when institutionalized, it is a strategic learning and governance process (it gives key people a regular voice to which management responds with strategic changes) that should integrated into strategic planning.

In summary, organizations that cannot achieve or sustain three key outcomes—high-quality direction, implementation, and learning or adaptation—will fail in a changing competitive environment. The silent killers cause failures to achieve the three essential outcomes The organization is locked into a negative, self-reinforcing, vicious cycle until these problems finally produce a crisis of performance. Regular honest, collective, and public conversation would prevent this crisis.

Concrete Steps for Becoming Fit to Perform

At the end of SRSD's three-day fitness meeting, the senior team reaffirmed two things. First, its top strategic priority was developing solutions (technology platforms), with the development of custom systems second in importance. Second, improving SRSD's coordination would require stronger business team leaders who would be accountable for profit. We—the consultants—helped the team members understand that they were in fact creating a strong matrix and clarified for them the changes in the roles and responsibilities of the business and functional leaders that this change in organizational form required. We did not recommend their new direction. They had to decide on that and own the choice themselves. We did, however, use our expertise in organizational design to clarify for the team members the strengths and weaknesses of alternative organizational designs from which they had to choose. Had we lacked this expertise, we would have suggested they engage an expert in organizational design. (And if we hadn't even recognized that such expertise was needed, we wouldn't have been qualified to be consultants facilitating this SFP, given the complexity of the challenge.)

Because the honest conversation had made all six silent killers discussable, five were targeted for immediate action. (SRSD addressed inadequacies in its leadership development by giving its promising potential leaders new, challenging responsibilities over five years.) These responses are the sort of rapid simultaneous solutions that honest conversation makes possible because not only does the senior team find out what the real impediments are, but it also finds out how interrelated they are.

The senior team agreed to, and carried out, the following changes (the silent killers addressed are given in parentheses):

- The members agreed on strategy and priorities (clarity of direction).

- They reorganized SRSD from a functional organization with weak business teams to a business-by-function matrix strong in both dimensions (coordination, clarity of direction).

- All product lines were consolidated into four new business teams (coordination, clarity of direction).

- The team defined the new roles, accountabilities, and decision rights for each side of the matrix. Business leaders would decide what and when; functional leaders who and how (coordination, senior team effectiveness).

- Each of the four functional department heads would now wear two hats—as functional leaders and as business team leaders. Business team leaders were assigned accountability for profits. SRSD did not have lower-level leaders with the general-management perspective required of business team leaders (leadership development).

- R&D and Custom Systems were consolidated into a single engineering department (coordination, senior team effectiveness).

- The senior team shifted from its hub-and-spoke pattern to a new role as a strategic business council composed of all members responsible for ongoing review of strategy, prioritization, and allocation of resources as circumstances change (leader and senior team effectiveness).

- The administrative and financial review meetings would be separated from the strategic review meetings. Importantly, the team set new norms for behavior and a new decision-making process that would bring discussions to an actual decision that everyone was committed to (senior team effectiveness).

- The team agreed to conduct an SFP every year to learn about barriers to executing the annual update of the three-year strategic plan (open vertical communication).

Wright and his senior team emerged from the three-day fitness meeting not just with an action plan but also with greater mutual trust. They were energized and committed to execute their new system of organizing, managing, and leading—a system that would now be fit to perform.

Cementing a Partnership

Wright had one more hurdle to jump, however—one that revealed to us as researchers a critical missing link in SFP. Overcoming this hurdle has since become an important step in cementing a partnership between the senior team, the task force, and—by extension—the whole organization.

We asked the SRSD task force to meet alone to evaluate the senior team's action plan—something we had not done in earlier honest conversations. Previously, we had asked senior teams and the task forces to meet so that the senior executives could hear task force members' critique of the action plan. But in those meetings, the task forces rarely disagreed with the action plan. This time, we had the task force meet alone to discuss their the members' concerns, and the group came back with doubts about it. The action plan specified hard, tangible changes in structure, the members said, but did the senior team have the soft people skills to lead such changes and to manage the new organization that would emerge? Had the senior team truly developed such mutual trust after just one meeting? Was the plan prewired, or was it genuinely a response to their feedback? Finally, the task force disagreed with how the senior team had assigned SRSD's fourteen legacy products to the four business teams that represented one side of the matrix. All these concerns reflected a disbelief that the senior team had suddenly changed its stripes.

The task force did not realize that the senior team members' trust in each other and commitment to improve SRSD's organization had dramatically grown during the three-day fitness meeting. The executives had not explicitly told the task force about this change in their attitude.

If the executives had been fully transparent about what had happened during that meeting, the task force would have found their proposals—and their ability to carry them out (the soft skills)—much more credible. But to make such a disclosure, Wright and the senior team would have had to make themselves vulnerable by disclosing how their trust of each other had changed when they openly discussed feedback they had received about their leadership of the division and their ineffectiveness as a group. Taking that step would have alleviated concerns about how genuine and able the senior team was to carry out the action plan, thereby enabling a productive conversation about the action plan's strengths and weaknesses.

Wright later recalled the impact of the task force's negative reaction: "[Their] reaction to the business groupings literally felt like it took the wind out of the sails of my team. My staff and I worked for almost half a day on just those groupings alone and finally felt that we had come up with the best possible option." He and his senior team tried to convince the task force of the merits of their plan, but to no avail. As I noted earlier, rational communication and arguments do not overcome emotionally resonant doubts when there is distrust ("How could one meeting have changed trust among senior team members? How could it have changed their soft leadership skills?") or when there is doubt about the authenticity of the solutions—"Had they truly emerged from our feedback, or were they prewired?"

To Wright's great credit, he demonstrated his willingness to make himself and the senior team vulnerable—to share control of the outcome with the task force. He formed three subgroups composed of senior team *and* task force members and instructed them to arrive at an alternative action plan if they concluded that one was needed. Here was a response consistent with the overarching principle of honest and collaborative conversation—to create a partnership with the task force and, by symbolic extension, with the rest of the organization. A week later, the three groups came back with only minor changes to the plan. (The role of vulnerability in creating trust will be discussed in the next chapter.)

During those meetings, the task force had learned from senior team members in their subgroup about how the three-day fitness meeting had changed their trust in each other and their effectiveness. The task force heard, for example, how Sam Scott had openly admitted that his zeal to grow the Custom Systems Group had contributed to the problem. Now that the task force members were convinced, the only remaining concern was the grouping of products into businesses. Suggested changes were incorporated into the plan.

We, the consultants, learned a lot from SRSD's experience and changed the SFP process to include a meeting of the task force as a group so they can develop a joint critique of the senior team's action plan and then speak as a group about their doubts. If there are significant doubts, we now recommend that senior teams meet with task forces to discuss differences in viewpoints about the action plan and adapt it together. (This is an example of the iterative process my colleagues and I have employed to improve SFP and adapt our understanding of the underlying principles.)

The coming changes in SRSD's organizational design were then communicated to the whole organization. Within three months, the new design was in place and functioning. (Yes, it was *that* fast.) It was the first step in SRSD's rapid and highly successful transformation. Let's look even closer now at what made this transformation possible.

The Power of Self-Design and a Simultaneous Solution

The honest, collective, and public conversation that emerges from SFP encourages two useful approaches to strategic change. First, our research and that of others has shown the power of self-design—the involvement of all the stakeholders in the design of solutions—as opposed to top-down design or designs made by consultants.[10] Second, working on all the silent killers, or most of them, concurrently (some observers call this approach the simultaneous solve) makes a transformation systemic and more sustainable. Although so much change is intimidating, leaders know they must respond to what has been revealed or lose trust and their own legitimacy as leaders. Giving a voice to lower levels and involving them in developing the new solution encourages everyone's commitment to rapid change that might otherwise be intimidating and lead to resistance.

Simultaneously attacking issues sounds radical and is not, of course, the norm. Most organizational change is piecemeal and nonsystemic, an approach that seems prudent. But research has found that most organizational change doesn't work; the efforts lead to faltering and even failed transformations.[11] At SRSD, for example, a strategy consultant's recommendations for a new direction would not necessarily have changed Sam Scott's conviction that custom systems were an essential part of SRSD's future. Nor would a consultant's recommendations engender the commitment to change that he demonstrated. Team building alone—a common organizational fix—would not have solved the cold war in SRSD's organizational design. Had an external consultant recommended a new matrix organization, the new structure would not have been executed as successfully or as quickly without a simultaneous change in the way the senior team operated. The structure of meetings and the hub-and-spoke approach to decisions needed to change as well. If done separately, without additional solutions, the hiring of a management coach for Wright, for example, or a new leadership development program or the recruiting of more-experienced business team leaders would have failed to achieve the rapid change that occurred at SRSD (even though any of them might have helped to nudge change along slowly).

Nonsystemic, piecemeal changes over a long period lead people to lose hope that sufficient change will ever happen. At SRSD, such an approach might well have led to the replacement of Wright and his senior team, as they had indeed feared. It was the simultaneity of the changes—along with the trust and commitment that honest conversations had elicited—that made SRSD's rapid and effective change possible.

In a study of twelve organizations we worked with, my colleagues and I have confirmed that meaningful simultaneous change in the

TABLE 4-1

Extent of change in silent killers and overall change in twelve organizations after SFP

Industry and type of organization	Change in silent killers*	Extent of overall change[†]
Technology company A, business unit	4.67	7.00
Toy company	4.67	6.00
Pharmaceutical company, Mexico unit	3.83	5.90
Technology company B, business unit	4.23	5.50
Technology company C, business unit	4.33	5.20
Pharmaceutical company, Brazil unit	5.00	5.00
Hotel company	0.33	5.00
Technology company D, business unit	2.33	4.36
Banking business unit	2.17	3.50
Pharmaceutical company, Argentina unit	1.90	3.33
Medical technology company	2.67	3.09
Privatized government agency, Canada	1.33	2.55

* *Change in silent killers*: The mean difference between pre- and post-SFP assessments using a seven-point scale (where 1 = "strongly disagree" and 7 = "strongly agree") to rate how well twelve organizations addressed silent killers. The larger the number, the greater the change. See appendix B for details.

† *Extent of overall change*: The mean difference between pre- and post-SFP assessments of twelve organizations. The researchers rated questionnaire items describing organizational qualities such as effectiveness, commitment, and trust on a seven-point scale (where 1 = "strongly agree" and 7 = "strongly disagree"). Pre-scores were subtracted from post-scores so the higher the difference, the greater the change in overall quality of the organization. See appendix B for details.

silent killers is associated with successful rapid transformation and with greater improvement in the company's performance overall (table 4-1).[12]

SRSD Transformed

"I see them as one of our star divisions," HP's executive vice president of the Test and Measurement Sector told me. "Compared to other divisions, it probably is the most dramatic turnaround." Over the five years of our study of SRSD, its revenues grew by 60 percent and its profits grew by 702 percent, indicating much greater effectiveness in capitalization on revenues—and all this despite the Asian financial crisis of 1997–1999, the last two years of our study. Senior team members acknowledge that an improving economy during most of that five-year period contributed to their high growth, but also felt strongly that without honest, collective, and public conversation, they would not have been in any position to take advantage of that strong economy. They wouldn't have been fit enough had they not transformed silent killers into core leadership and organizational capabilities. Figure 4-3 shows the results of this transformation.

But it was not just the original SFP that made all that difference. As we will see, SRSD's persistent use of honest conversation enabled contin-

FIGURE 4-3

The dynamics of an organization fit to compete

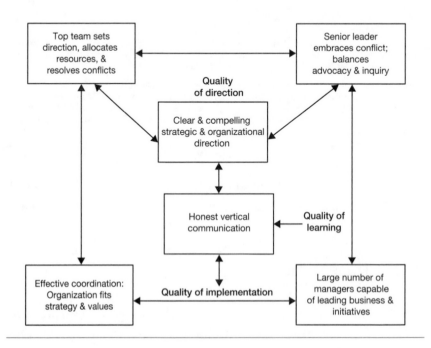

uous improvement. Repeated use of SFP transformed silent killers into core capabilities over time and firmly cemented a collaborative community. This success was borne out in interviews some three years after the transformation started. The group vice president who was Wright's immediate boss observed: "Scott was faced with a real challenge . . . [but] I think they did a remarkable job of striking the balance between functional and business with the matrix. They have made it work. I give them a lot of credit for that. They speak with a coherent voice, which a functional organization normally lets you do better . . . They have grown the business and gotten good profits and results."

Other participants in the process also described the success of the transformation. A midlevel SRSD production manager weighed in two years after the original SFP: "What was really important was that we really understood what the [SFP] was trying to do, that is, align the different parts of the organization. I think that the alignment we now have after the reorganization is both accurate and necessary to become an effective organization." A task force member noted: "Our top team has taken some big strides in becoming more effective. Scott looks to be taking more control of the reins and becoming the kind of leader the division needs. He and his staff will sit down as a group now and talk strategy, where before they would have only talked about administrative detail."

George Mosby later observed that the "honest conversation functioned as a powerful tool to communicate difficult issues" and that it demonstrated to the organization that the top team cared about what employees thought and was serious about improving. This same dynamic was what made honest conversations in many other organizations so powerful.

SRSD's human resource manager, Jody Edwards, also noted the improvement in morale, trust, and commitment: "We lost a lot of employee satisfaction and commitment as a result of our problems but regained it and more. People from other divisions now want to come to work here, and they cite that interesting process—honest conversation—that we now conduct annually as one of the reasons."

An honest, collective, and public conversation about the organization's ineffectiveness and its alignment with its purpose, values, and strategy had not only improved SRSD's performance but also created a partnership between senior management and lower levels and restored morale and people's sense of purpose. People were now engaged and unified around a clear strategy and purpose.

Summing Up

Using the lens of Hewlett-Packard's Santa Rosa Systems Division, I have shown that honest, collective, and public conversation allowed an organization to substantially improve its performance, as my colleagues and I have seen it do in many other organizations. I used the case to highlight the six silent killers that we have found in all organizations struggling with implementing necessary strategies.

Uncovering the silent killers as they manifest themselves in an organization allows it to address many or all of them at once. This simultaneous approach not only works better and faster than piecemeal, non-systemic organizational change, but also does much more to foster trust and commitment, which are themselves necessary for strategy implementation. Moreover, repeated use of SFP helps change silent killers into sustained strengths—core capabilities essential for organizational and leadership effectiveness and agility. Without institutionalizing honest, collective, and public conversations, these very human capabilities atrophy, like any other human relationships not strengthened regularly by open discussions about their condition. Chapter 6 will discuss this issue further and offer illustrations.

Chapter 5

Fit to Trust: Overcoming Hierarchy

The notion that power corrupts is not a new one. History and literature are replete with numerous examples of how the powerful go astray.

—David DeSteno, professor of psychology, Northeastern University

Trust is a psychological state comprising the intention to accept vulnerability based on positive expectations of the intentions of another.

—D. M. Rousseau, S. B. Sitkin, R. Burt, and C. Camerer,
   "Not So Different After All: A Cross-Discipline View of Trust"

Trust is in crisis around the world, according to the Edelman Trust Barometer, a respected and scientifically sound global survey developed by Richard Edelman.[1] "The general population's trust in . . . business, government, NGOs, and media . . . has declined broadly," he reports. A different survey of managers in thirty corporations showed that roughly half don't trust their own leaders.[2] If that is true for managers, imagine the low levels of trust between management and frontline employees. In this chapter, I will discuss mistrust and how to turn it into high trust and commitment through the lens of American Diner Corporation's Green Acres Restaurant.[3] Consider these disparate views of the restaurant's new strategic initiative. Max Lawson, American

Diner's restaurant manager, said, "'Faster, Better!' is a terrific program. It's already helping us to increase guest counts, size of check, and total profitability," while an American Diner employee said, "This stuff just gets thrown at us. Suddenly we're asked to do more and more. And what do we get in return? Nothing." Similar sentiments were expressed by managers at Hewlett-Packard's Santa Rosa Systems Division (SRSD) in the last chapter and by managers in many other organizations we have worked with and studied. What has caused the crisis in trust?

Hierarchy creates natural barriers to openness and that creates the vicious, unvirtuous cycle that prevents silent killers from changing, as discussed in chapter 4. They become fault lines during the earthquakes created by an ever-more-demanding competitive environment that requires frequent changes in strategy and new execution initiatives. Pressured leaders and senior teams take even less time to communicate these changes or to foster honest conversations—which many managers in authority are naturally disinclined to hold, anyway—to learn from people below about the barriers to execution.

This chapter provides a deeper exploration of why and how honest, collective, and public conversation allows employees at different levels to overcome the emotional distance created by their hierarchical separation. We will see how it made that restaurant fit to trust for its employees. Being fit for trust is one of the three forms of fitness addressed by the strategic fitness process. We will see that a unit manager under pressure to perform can use a process like SFP to quickly transform the performance, trust, and commitment of everyone in the unit.

The chain between hierarchy and emotional distance has several links. Hierarchy inevitably creates vulnerability. Vulnerability breeds fear, which breeds mistrust. Mistrust leads to a lack of open communication and a lack of commitment. As I pointed out early on—and as many others have noted—these deficiencies keep higher management in the dark about many serious, or at least growing, problems and lead to low trust and engagement further down in the hierarchy. But as long as people at lower levels can't fully trust those above them, they will be reluctant to point out problems, especially when the managers and executives above them *are* the problems. This is why so many useful strategies can't be implemented.

This mistrust of higher-ups is matched by top management's mistrust of those below them. Mistrust doesn't have to mean management thinks employees are stealing or breaking rules, although sometimes they do. More often, it means that top management doesn't trust those below them to have anything useful to contribute to the formulation of strategy or its implementation. (Employees' potential to contribute to innovation may never even have occurred to the senior team.) We'll go into this oversight in more detail later in this chapter. But failure to involve lower levels in strategic change problems leads to a fatal emotional distance. As we saw in the last chapter, management fails to understand just how frustrated their key employees are, not only with barriers to strategy execution but also with management's failure to acknowledge and solve them.

Even if top management is aware of some of the problems undermining its strategy, it has little or no idea—as we saw in the last chapter—of how frustrated the employees are, not simply with those problems, but also with management's failure to solve them.

Honest, collective, public conversation can reverse this rot. By sometimes sidestepping the hierarchy, it allows the front lines and the higher management to build up mutual trust and commitment—a *shared purpose* to improve the organization. Assuming that the trust and commitment are then properly maintained—a big task in itself that by no means is always carried out—the front lines will survive the return of the organization's everyday hierarchy. In part, that's because the nature of the hierarchy will have been changed.

Think of a surgical team shutting down your body's immune reactions to transplant a lifesaving organ. Afterward, you have to let the immune system resume its normal function and you have to take special precautions to keep the new organ healthy. Nevertheless, you have a chance to live that you wouldn't have had otherwise.

To bring this concept to life for you, this chapter presents the case of the Green Acres, a restaurant in the American Diner chain. It's a much smaller affair than Becton Dickinson or even the Santa Rosa Systems Division, but if offers a particularly clear view of the loss and restoration of trust and commitment.

American Diner Company: When the Top Misses What's Happening Below

American Diner was founded in 1952 in Jacksonville, Florida. It was famous for its barbecued beef, home fries, and root beer floats. It advertised high-quality food served on real china by friendly servers, an unusual level of service for the prices it charged. Demand grew rapidly, and the company added drive-through service. Joshua Duncan was recruited by American Diner's chair to lead the company to the next level of growth and profitability. Duncan had been a highly successful general manager in several consumer food businesses.

Within a few months of becoming CEO, Duncan was surprised to discover that American Diner's performance was not as strong as the board chair had assumed. While overall profits were growing through the addition of new restaurants, same-store sales and profitability had begun to slip. Duncan took action on several fronts.

He introduced honest, collective, and public conversations—guided by SFP—at the corporate and functional levels to enable people to make a difference and thereby develop the trust and commitment necessary to transform the company. He described the enormity of the task: "The challenge in transforming the company is that we must transform every restaurant, every regional area, and every corporate function. We are painting a whole bridge and every brick in it. That is the challenge in a world-class company. It is hard, but that is the work we must do."

Duncan also organized an offsite meeting with the chain's most successful restaurant managers and compiled their best practices into a new program called "Faster, Better!" Its goal was to increase sales in each restaurant by filling orders quicker and giving friendlier service. The program reemphasized the company's "Eight Secrets of Service" and detailed the actions each server should take. It also established an aggressive goal of serving food within eight minutes of a customer's sitting down (five minutes for drive-through).

The Green Acres Restaurant: A Small Attempt at SFP

Among the first restaurants to implement Faster, Better! was Green Acres, one of several American Diner facilities in Charlotte, North Carolina. Green Acres had approximately fifty employees, generally in their teens or twenties. Most were students, young mothers, or two-job workers who benefited from American Diner's flexible work hours, working ten to thirty hours per week for wages similar to those at competing restaurants and other low-wage employers. With annual employee turnover at 220 percent—similar to that in other restaurant chains—there were many opportunities for promotion and raises. It was not unusual for a new employee to become a trainer in his or her first year or for a high school graduate to become a manager within two years. Managers received a salary and were also eligible for an annual bonus. A significant portion of a manager's bonus was tied to reducing labor costs within his or her restaurant. Yet despite the opportunities for promotion, most employees did not view their work as a career.

Green Acres had been turned around in the previous two years by Max Lawson, an experienced restaurant manager in his fifties. He had dramatically improved operations and grew sales by more than 20 percent. Lawson was proud of his employees and was pleased to have his restaurant chosen as a pilot location for Faster, Better! and then as the first of American Diner's individual restaurants to use SFP. In the weeks before the fitness meetings, he posted a memo to his people about the importance of employee involvement in the upcoming SFP and the steps that would take place.

The Unvarnished Feedback

SFP proceeded rapidly at Green Acres. The management team—that is, Lawson and his two shift managers—received a day of training to help them hold effective management debates, then held an offsite meeting, facilitated by consultants, to create a two-page statement of direction. It outlined their goals for the next two to three years and the kind of organization they would need to reach those goals. The statement of direction was posted where employees—but not customers—could see it. The management team then selected the six-person task force to interview all employees and ask each one about the restaurant's strengths and weaknesses as they related to the posted goals. In the following week, the task force interviewed all fifty employees.

Once the interviews were completed, the task force analyzed their interviews, created themes, assembled them in the fishbowl arrangement, and reported to management the six themes they had developed with help from the consultants, providing pertinent quotes and incidents but never identifying who had said what. The feedback was polite, but it communicated honestly the front line's serious frustration, most vehemently with regard to inadequate communication, lack of recognition, selection of unqualified associates, and lack of training.* It also described numerous operational problems and how to solve them. Several employees, the task force reported, appreciated that Lawson was asking them for their opinions.

The task force ended by relaying both positive and negative feedback about individual managers. Naturally, the key figure in this feedback was Lawson, who was seen as a caring but very strict father figure. "It's good that he keeps us on our toes," one interviewee had said, "but sometimes I feel like a dog being screamed at." Many employees complained

---

* Like many service providers—including restaurants, banks, and department stores—American Diner referred to its frontline workers (the servers and kitchen staff) as "associates."

that Lawson often yelled at them rather than explaining to them what the problem was or why they needed to do something differently. The task force members feared that the management team might be hurt or angered by such individual feedback, but the managers listened calmly and later commented that they had actually hoped for "more brutally honest" feedback.

After the fishbowl discussion, the task force left for the day while the managers stayed to discuss what they had learned. The conversation quickly turned negative and made the consultants uncomfortable.

"They shouldn't complain about us," one manager said. "Their work's not that good. Especially you-know-who. I'm always having to keep after her to get her to do her cleaning work or pay attention to guests."

"They have no idea how difficult it is to be a manager," complained another. "They act like we just stand around and tell them what to do. How many times have I worked a ninety-hour week, just trying to get people to do their jobs and helping them during rush times? It's great that they want to be appreciated more. How about if once in a while they tried appreciating *us*?"

Another manager agreed. "They complain about the yelling, but why do they think we yell?" he said. "They're so irresponsible. They're constantly wasting food, throwing away silver, sneaking away for long smoke breaks, and not doing their cleaning side work.[†] If they just did their jobs, we wouldn't have to yell so much!"

Why Hierarchy Undermines Trust and Commitment

Numerous academic studies support the conclusion that differences in relative power undermine trust.[4] But what, in particular, explains the low trust and low commitment among the Green Acres front line?

[†] "Side work" refers to the various tasks, such as wiping down counters and making sure condiment containers are full, that servers have to squeeze in between serving customers.

Think about what makes you willing to trust another person. You have to believe that he or she is trustworthy. That means the person has already made himself or herself vulnerable or that you have tested his or her trustworthiness by making yourself vulnerable—by taking a risk, by being less guarded, or by taking an action that you would be afraid to take with a stranger. Consequently, you come to believe in this person's integrity—his or her continued willingness to fulfill a promise and to resist taking advantage of you. And you believe that this person has the competence to do whatever you have trusted him or her to do. For example, I trust a medical specialist whom I don't know to do things I wouldn't trust my wife to do. Indeed, a variety of researchers investigating trust have concluded that it is "a psychological state comprising the intention to accept vulnerability based upon positive intentions or behavior of another."[5] Only after we experience repeated cycles of making ourselves vulnerable can we really trust someone.

Frontline workers are already vulnerable by virtue of their position in the hierarchy. For that reason, managers at the top, like Lawson, must take the first step in developing a virtuous cycle of trust building and commitment building. The low trust and commitment at Green Acres reflected Lawson's failure to demonstrate vulnerability until the SFP gave him a way to do so. Lawson started Faster, Better! with a wrong step. He signaled his lack of trust in his people by not involving them in the implementation. Had he made himself vulnerable to their honest feedback and their own ideas on implementation, he could have initiated a virtuous cycle of trust building. The frontline associates would certainly have noticed that Lawson was asking for their help. The consultants saw the Green Acres management team's lack of trust in their frontline workers also reflected in their deprecating responses to the feedback: "Their work's not that good." "Why do they think we yell?" Little wonder that frontline employees did not trust managers and were uncommitted to implementing Faster, Better!

Top management groups are often surprised by the capability of task force members immediately. For example, although Green Acres top management didn't exhibit this until later in the process, a leader at another company said, "The work of the employee task force was impressive and was much like a professional consulting firm."[6] This sense of surprise betrays a lack of appreciation for the talent and the potential commitment that has been there all along. But employees know when their own talent and potential commitment is going unrecognized. They consider the lack of recognition as mistrust, which feeds the negative cycle of mutual mistrust.

The situation at Green Acres is not at all unusual. Nor can it be attributed to the inexperience and low emotional intelligence of Lawson and his management team. My colleagues and I have frequently observed emotional distance and mistrust between leaders and their reports, even at high levels—for example, between CEOs and key executives running major subunits. We discovered this emotional distance in many companies, when we observed that senior teams already knew much of what the fitness task force reported back to them but had not at all understood the emotional intensity of those concerns. Executives heard the cough, but they didn't feel the high fever. Their lack of emotional intelligence had kept them from acting quickly enough to change the organization and the way they led it. The managers at Green Acres had to be at least dimly aware that their employees didn't like being shouted at, but what management didn't know—until the honest, public conversation—was *how much* the employees didn't like it. Their lack of awareness, in turn, was related to something else the managers didn't know: *exactly why* the associates thought the yelling was unfair.

Why would those at the top, like Lawson, not make themselves vulnerable to gain the cooperation of those below them? David DeSteno, in his groundbreaking book, *The Truth about Trust*, explains that because those at the top have more resources—power, money, autonomy, and control—they feel "less need for the resources of others and correspondingly little motive to accept any vulnerability."[7] (They may be wrong about what they need, but if that's how they see it, that's how they'll act.) Thus, business leaders rarely make themselves vulnerable by asking employees for feedback or help in implementing strategy and, in particular, seldom engage employees in honest conversations. Lawson, though an exemplary manager in some respects, was more a typical manager in this respect.

While Green Acres managers had less power than did their own senior management at American Diner, they had plenty of power over their servers and kitchen staff. Trustworthy behavior, research shows, is affected by *relative* position in the hierarchy, not by *absolute* levels of power and authority.

Not all managers in all organizations are susceptible to the hierarchical effect I describe. Those with sufficient emotional intelligence and empathy are likely to overcome the effect, but such managers are uncommon. The scarcity of good managers is why companies spend millions on leadership development. Once the leaders in this book had been presented with the opportunity to use SFP, they began to see a companywide honest, collective, public conversation as a way to nullify the hierarchy effect. They saw SFP as a way to develop, as leadership expert Thomas Rice put it, a "workplace worthy of the human spirit." Lawson may not have had the emotional intelligence to seek out SFP on his own, but given the opportunity, he used the process to develop a high-trust, high-commitment, collaborative restaurant organization.

The Honest Conversation at Green Acres

When the managers of Green Acres began their second day of meetings to discuss the feedback the task force had presented to them, they started off with some more griping about their employees. Fortunately, however, they quickly got down to their real task—analyzing the root causes of the problems they had heard described. They settled on three underlying issues that they believed were causing all the other problems:

- **Training and development:** Lawson pointed out that American Diner had no budget for employee training. In fact, a big chunk of a manager's bonus was based on cutting labor costs. The managers thought that this focus on controlling labor cost, rather than on developing employees, was a major reason that employees believed they did not receive the training and appreciation they deserved.

- **Role of the managers:** The managers discussed complaints about their shouting at employees. They realized that a chief reason for this behavior was that they often worked eighty- to ninety-hour weeks and spent much of their time helping employees with food preparation and customer service. The managers were stressed and angry because they were trying to do everything in the restaurant on their own. They pointed out that they were actually doing much of the work that should have been done by trainers, who weren't pulling their weight.

- **Employees acting irresponsibly:** After some complaints about "irresponsible teenagers," the managers pointed out that most of their young employees had never held positions of leadership or responsibility. Not surprisingly, they didn't understand the importance of doing their side work or avoiding food waste, because they had never before experienced responsibility for these tasks.

The next morning, the management team turned to creating an action plan. They decided on two major changes to their management system:

- **The role of the trainers:** The managers would no longer directly manage all the employees. Instead, they would assign teams of employees to trainers, who would now be held responsible for training the employees in restaurant tasks and developing them as employees.

- **The shift leader system:** To let employees experience leadership and responsibility, two shift leaders would be designated for each shift (one for operations and one for the servers). Each shift leader would be responsible for making sure the employees did their work, including side work. All employees would have a chance to be shift leaders. The managers felt that this arrangement would increase commitment by letting employees experience leadership and responsibility and would give some of them recognition and development as future leaders. It would also free up the managers to manage the restaurant, rather than chasing after each employee to make sure the work got done.

The managers thought that their action planning meeting had been a real breakthrough. They had stopped blaming individual employees and focused instead on changing the Green Acres system of organizing, managing, and leading.

The following morning, the management team met back with the task force to report on the team's analysis and to ask for the task force's help in refining the action plan for change. One manager had baked muffins to show appreciation for the task force's work. The task force and the managers sat together at a table and talked openly about the problems at the restaurant and the disagreements between managers and employees.

The managers began by summarizing the key messages that they had heard from the task force. The task force agreed that the managers correctly understood their concerns.

The management team then presented its action plan. Some task force members were surprised at the emphasis on giving them more responsibility. After the presentation, the task force met separately so they could discuss the plan more openly.

"What's up with all this extra work for us?" one task force member complained. "They're paid to be managers—why are they asking us to do managers' work?"

Others disagreed. "This is actually a good thing," another person explained. "I've always had to tell people what to do. Now I'll have the authority to back it up."

"I think the new system will also teach people to be more responsible," another member said. "Once everybody gets a chance to be a shift leader, they'll understand how managers feel."

After much further discussion, the task force agreed to accept the managers' action plan.

After a break, the task force members met again with the management team to present a summary of their reaction to the action plan. Lawson reacted immediately. "What do you mean, 'We're paid to be managers'?" he asked angrily. "Do you people have any idea how hard we work to help you?" Two task force members responded defensively, pointing out how hard *they* worked, without getting the higher salary or bonuses that managers got. Concerned that these defensive responses could undermine a constructive conversation of the issues, the consultants intervened by highlighting the key actionable issues that were emerging, helping people share their views, synthesizing, and reframing the conversation. Other task force members also intervened, pointing out that the managers *were* paid to be managers and that the task force's emotional reaction was only an initial response and that, overall, they had accepted the managers' action plan.

The conversation soon calmed down, and the management team and task force worked together to refine the action plan. Each expressed appreciation for the other's ideas. The participants discussed how to communicate the action plan to the other employees and made plans to begin implementing it at an all-employee meeting later in the week.

After the meetings, the managers and task force members together discussed their feelings about the process they had been through. Several complained that the process hadn't been explained very well in advance. But both groups thought that it had worked well and that the fishbowl arrangement was particularly helpful for uncovering and discussing difficult issues. They also said that going through the process together had made a stronger team of them. The managers and task force thanked each other for their feedback and asked for more and even tougher feedback in the future so that they could continue to improve their performance.

As they left the meeting, the managers and task force teased each other and talked about the coming evening's work in the restaurant.

Several people discussed how the other employees would probably react to the new action plan. One manager predicted it would be successful, calling it a great breakthrough for Green Acres. "I wonder a little whether we'll really stick with these changes, though," she added. "We've started a lot of things in the past that didn't seem to last."

The Result of Honest Conversation: Increasing Trust

That manager was right to wonder. Many equally promising starts have gone nowhere or slid back to where they had started. Over the next six months, however, Green Acres enjoyed a 32 percent annualized reduction in turnover and a 7 percent increase in performance on the company's guest satisfaction survey. Frontline associates were now more likely to agree that managers develop and train associates to their full potential. They also felt more valued and recognized for their contributions and indicated more support for maintaining the financial health of the restaurant (figure 5-1). Green Acres was also scoring high among the American Diner chain on several important employee sentiments: feeling valued, willingness to recommend Green Acres as a place to work, trust in management, awareness of how the store was performing, and feeling able to exercise initiative and apply judgment (figures 5-2 and 5-3).

What explains the amazing changes in trust and commitment fostered by the honest, collective, and public conversation about the restaurant's effectiveness? Such changes are all the more amazing, given that the associates were young, inexperienced, and noncareer employees. That is, they had a far lower sense of obligation to the company than most of the management did and far less than the professional employees typically involved in corporate transformations. It would have been easy for the employees to blow the whole thing off and just do whatever they had to do but no more.

The performance improvements, which in fact continued well beyond the six-month period reported here, can be attributed to changes

FIGURE 5-1

Green Acres dramatically improved associate satisfaction after SFP

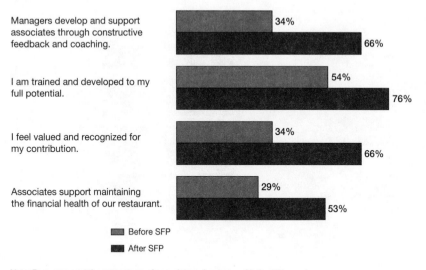

Managers develop and support associates through constructive feedback and coaching.
- 34%
- 66%

I am trained and developed to my full potential.
- 54%
- 76%

I feel valued and recognized for my contribution.
- 34%
- 66%

Associates support maintaining the financial health of our restaurant.
- 29%
- 53%

▨ Before SFP
▨ After SFP

Note: Bars represent the percentage of associates who agree with the statement.

FIGURE 5-2

Green Acres dramatically improved "associates feel valued" score after SFP

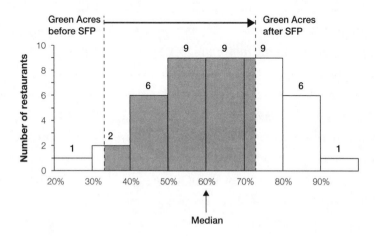

Note: Bars represent the percentage of restaurant associates who agree with the statement "I feel valued as an employee."

FIGURE 5-3

SFP helped Green Acres become a leader on many associate dimensions

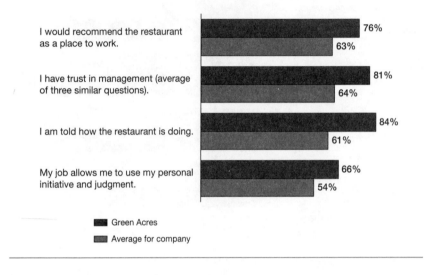

I would recommend the restaurant as a place to work. — 76% / 63%

I have trust in management (average of three similar questions). — 81% / 64%

I am told how the restaurant is doing. — 84% / 61%

My job allows me to use my personal initiative and judgment. — 66% / 54%

■ Green Acres
■ Average for company

in management's practices and behavior after the honest conversation. As one task force member said, "The best thing is that what came out is what the managers [now] do."

In effect, the collective conversation created changes in *collective behavior*—how managers and associates worked together. The change started, as it had to, with managers making themselves vulnerable by asking for feedback and not giving in to their initial anger that they were not being appreciated and that the associates were irresponsible. It was followed by concrete changes in how the restaurant was led and managed. The associates reciprocated with support for the proposed changes in responsibility (beefing up the trainer's role and creating shift managers) without succumbing to their first reaction that this was not their job—certainly not without more pay.

What enabled both sides to control their initial negative emotions was the honesty and hence the authenticity of the dialogue. Because the conversation was framed by the managers' statement of direction—

what the restaurant had to do to succeed—the energy released was immediately focused on working together to improve performance.

Note the sometimes necessary role of the consultants. Their interventions kept the conversation on track when people did become upset with one another, though anger and outbursts are rare. Such emotions are particularly rare at higher management levels, where years of experience have taught managers to control emotions and where those who cannot have been weeded out. But at Green Acres, even the consultants' intervention wouldn't have worked without the underlying understanding that managers and associates had no choice but to stand or fall together.

Before the SFP, frontline employees had seen their place in the organization as one of passively accepting top-down decisions but making little effort to contribute more than was required. The honest conversation, by bridging the emotional distance between the front line and management, helped Green Acres transform the associates' emotional stance and management's as well. It was a first step in making the employees and leaders true partners. The managers came to see the employees not as irresponsible and unhelpful but rather as collaborators to be trusted in the effort to improve service. The new psychological state of mutuality—based (as it must be) on trust—made all the other forms of operational and business success possible.

As explained earlier, after the hierarchy is temporarily suspended during SFP, it must be restored. But the hierarchy will also have been changed. Green Acres, for example, was transformed from a command-and-control hierarchy into the high-trust and high-commitment collaboration required for success in the twenty-first century. Of course, the hierarchy still mattered, but managers and associates no longer saw their roles solely in hierarchical terms, with bosses doing the bossing and everyone else doing what they're told. On the contrary, the honest, collective, and public conversation had made Lawson and his managers accountable to frontline workers to make the promised changes in their management practices and their own behavior, just as the associates had promised to reframe their roles and take on more responsibility. Green Acres was now an "organization worthy of the human spirit," in part because it was now fit to trust.

As explained earlier, the new levels of trust and commitment must be maintained after SFP. Leaders must not only carry out the promised changes in company practices and their own behavior but also continue the honest conversation, with the topic changing from "What do we need to do?" to "How much progress are we making?" Otherwise, the work of SFP is undone. Gains in trust, commitment, and performance that are not maintained will not be sustained. That is why most transformations fail to achieve their potential.

Because managers and executives have access to power and money and repeatedly face short-term pressures for performance, all but the most emotionally intelligent will slip back into the erroneous belief that they do not need to make themselves vulnerable to feedback and do not need to solicit help from those below them. This lack of trust in lower levels will be matched by a lack of trust in management, and we're right back where we started.

Yet our evidence from many companies shows that when honest, collective, and public conversation continues and becomes a habit resorted to whenever the organization is challenged, a culture high in trust and commitment develops. As I will discuss in detail in chapter 6, this practice was maintained at Becton Dickinson over a period of thirty years and at the Santa Rosa Systems Division in the five years of its existence.

Consider also the Belgian unit of a large Swedish company. The new country manager decided to use SFP, without the help of a consultant facilitator, to dispel and transform the distrust and low commitment created by his authoritarian predecessor. "The culture in the organization, strangely enough, changed . . . overnight," he explained. He said that the changes he had tried to initiate before SFP were perceived as top-down directives. "This strategic fitness process gave us a mandate from the organization. Now it was no longer the management team imposing some changes. It was the people clearly demanding some changes from us. And so, suddenly we got an enormous authority from the people to make a lot of changes that were desperately required in the organization. So that was a really, really big one."[8]

The manager described how trust had been institutionalized in the company's culture through two separate cycles of honest conversation. The persistence eventually enabled the employees to speak up even without the structure—and the safety net—of SFP. "Two years later," he said, "we had a lot of people spontaneously coming to us and saying, 'Hey, I want to be interviewed.' Because people now saw that they could be open. There were no consequences. That we actually tried to listen. So that was [the] most positive . . . for me . . . whereas, in the past, people were clearly afraid to speak up."

In the Belgian unit, the honest, collective, and public conversations eventually transformed a culture of antipathy, low trust, and low commitment into a culture of trust and commitment. Both the senior team and the lower levels have recalculated the risk associated with honesty. Leaders are more willing to accept unsolicited employee feedback about the ineffectiveness of the organization—possibly of their own leadership—and employees are much more willing to unilaterally make themselves vulnerable, even without the protective structure of SFP. Nevertheless, periodic use of the formal SFP is important when the organization is challenged. As described earlier, the best time to reinforce the leaders' belief that the lower levels are committed and have valuable help to offer is when the organization is in trouble.

My colleagues and I have seen trust and commitment rise in hundreds of organizations whose leaders used SFP—assuming, as they say in the pharmaceutical ads, it was "taken as directed." The implementation had to be consistent with the prescribed practice and underlying values. Authentic commitment to developing a partnership between the senior team and the employees matters. To accomplish this, prescribed best practices must be followed. The senior team must do informal check-ins with the task force about its progress. There must be regular communication with employees to tie the changes being made to the feedback received. And the senior team needs to hold open meetings to review the transformation's progress. And we have found that periodically having more disciplined conversations like SFP is valuable. We therefore feel justified in concluding that honest conversations are capable—perhaps uniquely so—of rapidly overcoming the low trust and low commitment found in most traditional, hierarchical, command-and-control organizations. Trust can, of course, be built through other forms of engagement over time, but not as rapidly and not in support of the immediate transformation at hand.

Transforming Mutual Expectations

Organizational transformations, as the previous chapters have illustrated, inevitably involve new roles, responsibilities, decision rights, and relationships. These changes require people at all levels to accept psychological losses of power, rewards, status, and identity as well as losses of reputation and self-esteem. (You lose self-esteem because you are likely to be less competent in a new role for a while than you were in your old role.)

For associates at Green Acres, the new shift leader and trainer roles demanded changes in their identities and in their perceptions of what they had to give management and what they would receive in return. Managers, too, had to change their identities and perceptions in a similar way. They had to give up some authority in return for a partnership that improved the restaurant's performance. Thus, on both sides, the transformation required a shift in the "psychological contract"—the implicit, unwritten understanding of the employment relationship—that had existed before the conversation.[9]

Becton Dickinson's transformation, too, demanded—just as its task force had indicated—a shift in power and decision rights from global business-unit managers and some corporate functions to regional leaders and other functions. Honest conversation made acceptance of these losses easier and accelerated the transformation. Business-unit leaders were understandably threatened at first by loss of control over results for which they were still accountable. Their participation in the honest, collective, and public conversation enabled them to accept this loss and sustain trust and commitment to the company, whereas the same changes made in a top-down manner—that is, shoved down their throats—would have undermined their trust in and commitment to BD. The open conversation about purpose, strategy, and barriers made clear to everyone what BD had to do to survive and prosper. Everyone, including senior management, had made himself or herself vulnerable, and everyone was ready to sacrifice. Put another way, BD's top management, by making itself vulnerable, made the organization fit to trust, just as Lawson and his managers did at Green Acres.

Summing Up

There is a disturbing decline in trust in all social institutions, including corporations and their leaders. Roughly half of all managers do not trust their leaders. The demands of an increasingly competitive environment are responsible for this trend. Under these circumstances, hierarchy makes it hard for higher levels to develop a new strategic direction and even harder for managers to craft a conversation to develop commitment to it. Competitive pressures also reduce the likelihood that senior managers will be inclined to overcome hierarchy with an honest conversation. The discipline of a structured honest conversation, as I have demonstrated, can overcome hierarchy and increase trust.

Trust is a psychological state of intention to accept vulnerability and is based on positive expectations of the intentions of another. This chapter has shown exactly how honest, collective, and public conversation guided by SFP enabled managers and their reports to make themselves vulnerable safely, thereby beginning a virtuous cycle of trust and commitment building on which can be founded a collaborative community "worthy of the human spirit" and capable of adaptive behavior.

Chapter 6

Fitness to Adapt: Overcoming Complacency

An institution can look strong on the outside but already be sick on the inside, dangerously on the cusp of a precipitous fall.

—Jim Collins, *How the Mighty Fall*

We have adopted the strategic fitness process for all the plans we've done here, and I have found it immensely useful. It's almost like cheating. All the places you would have screwed up, they [employees] give you the answers, so you don't have to screw up . . . It has rebalanced our focus . . . Amazing how far you can drift.

—Joshua Duncan, CEO, American Diner

As Charles Darwin noted, "It is not the strongest species, nor the most intelligent that survive, it is the most adaptive." To remain competitive, it must keep adapting. But adaptation always exacts a toll: it is exhausting, it is risky, and some people are bound to lose some of their decision rights, perceived status, and even their jobs. A company can therefore only keep adapting if their leadership teams and employees are willing to learn the truth and be trained in, and accustomed to, uncovering the company's weaknesses through honest, fact-based conversations that lead to solutions. Leaders and employees must also be confident in their ability to carry out this process. They need to trust the company to treat them fairly and be committed to executing the company's strategy and values. Finally, they must be committed to its long-term health and success. That is, a company can only keep changing if it possesses the *fitness to adapt*.

Strategic planning is the only widely accepted and institutionalized management practice that businesses use to insure their adaptiveness. It does not, however, provide any of the above capabilities. Henry Mintzberg, a renowned management scholar who has studied strategic planning, concluded that this top-down process does not develop an aligned and adaptive high-commitment organization. As he noted in his widely acclaimed *Harvard Business Review* article, "The Fall and Rise of Strategic Planning":

> When strategic planning arrived on the scene in the mid-1960s, corporate leaders embraced it as "the one best way" to devise and implement strategies that could enhance the competitiveness of the business unit. True to the scientific management pioneered by Frederick Taylor, this one best way involved separating thinking from doing. The problem accordingly is that planning represents a *calculating* style of management, not a *committing* style, one that engages people in a collective journey in which everyone on the journey helps shape [its] course.[1]

Another way to put it is that strategic planning engages heads (it is analytic), but only senior management's heads. It does not engage the heads of those below the senior management level. Nor does it engage their hearts and develop emotional commitment to the strategy nor their hands through involvement in the organizational change and improvement.[2] Strategic planning then, often excludes everyone besides senior management. But in fact, they are needed because they are the ones—the only ones—who can identify some of the hidden obstacles to senior management's strategy.

Five decades after the invention of strategic planning, the business world needs an innovation. The strategic fitness process is that innovation. It enables a discussion of the truth about the quality of the strategy and the organization's capacity to execute it. SFP also encourages action rather than precluding it. And the process promotes the commitment necessary to carry out whatever new strategy and organizational changes are needed—the very things Mintzberg advocated. This is why Joshua Duncan, CEO of American Diner, says in the chapter epigraph that he found SFP "immensely useful" and "almost like cheating."

As we have seen, the honest conversation enabled by SFP is the key to engaging heads, hearts, and hands—all necessary to developing fitness. It is the means to avoid denial and expose a company's weaknesses. Denial is the key reason for the fall of companies from grace, according to a study conducted by Jim Collins and reported in *How the Mighty Fall*.[3]

So far, we have looked in detail at onetime implementations of honest conversation in the form of SFP. Now we will look at organizations that have recycled SFP over years to avoid complacency. SFP becomes an ongoing practice that ensures honest conversations and promotes a company's fitness to adapt. I call it "strategic learning and governance" because it develops consent (not a vote) of the governed (its people), so essential for rapid and effective execution of strategies. It is missing in businesses and corporations around the world but, as I show here, it can become a regular part of a company's strategic planning process.

Below, I will discuss the benefits of integrating SFP with strategic planning, that is, institutionalizing honest conversation. When top management teams institutionalize SFP, they become able to continuously refine strategy, prioritize change initiatives, and prevent dangerous overload that is injurious to strategy execution and employee health and well-being. Further, institutionalized honest conversation offers a discipline for continuous improvement of core leadership and organizational capabilities (the opposites of the silent killers) essential for ongoing adaptions (see chapter 4).

These multiple outcomes occur simultaneously when a strategic learning and governance process like SFP is integrated with the discipline of strategic planning and review. I discuss these multiple outcomes separately and present examples to illustrate how they come about in practice.

Clarifying Strategy and Priorities and Preventing Dangerous Overload

Silent killer number 1—unclear strategy and conflicting priorities—is reported by virtually every SFP task force and in diverse companies and industries. The lack of clarity, it turns out, is not a onetime problem that, once fixed, is set for good. Quite the contrary. And given today's fluid competitive environment, it is, quite naturally, a recurring problem.

Duncan integrated SFP into his strategic planning at American Diner after witnessing the method's power to clarify strategy, prioritize strategic initiatives, and prevent dangerous overload.[4] For most of the decade and a half before Duncan's arrival as CEO, American Diner had been a top performer, consistently growing its sales, profits, and the number of restaurants it operated. Duncan understood that his job was to take the chain to the next level, but he quickly determined that its performance would be harder to sustain than he and the board had thought. Growth had already begun to slow, and there had been a four-quarter decline in same-store sales and a three-year decline in stock price. It seemed that the company's previous growth through opening new stores had masked some underlying problems—particularly in the area of same-restaurant performance—that were poised to get a lot worse. Duncan recalled, "I came in assuming that I had plenty of time to learn the business, that I could lie low and then slowly and quietly begin to move some pieces around. But soon I learned differently. The situation was much more challenging than I had realized."

He began by forming a senior team composed of his three immediate reports, but then added key functional managers below them to develop the collective comfort with interdependence and collaboration that he knew would be needed. Anxious to prevent further deterioration in American Diner's performance, the team got to work on understanding why growth was slowing. After launching some obvious change initiatives right away, they began developing the strategy, purpose, and values that they hoped would govern behavior in the company. They designed twelve initiatives to execute the strategy and then launched SFP to learn from key managers and professionals two to three levels below the top about barriers to the execution of these initiatives.

The task force came back with honest but bad news. One member reported how people felt:

> The first year of the [twelve-part] change effort was fast and furious. We had all these initiatives going on, and it seemed like everyone was working himself or herself to death. Everyone wanted to do well. They enjoyed the new atmosphere, the new energy, and the idea that we can make a difference and be a part of it, but it was a lot of work . . . It was like running a marathon and finding out when you got to the finish that there was another marathon to run after that. We were moving too fast. People felt overwhelmed, and you could not get hold of leadership when you needed to, because they were always in meetings.

In fact, many SFP task forces have come back with similar tales of overload. The senior team, anxious to make many things better quickly, typically puts too many strategic initiatives into its annual plan. With resources spread too thin, initiatives fall behind schedule and quality suffers. The more pressure there is, the more reluctant people become to tell senior management they can't deliver. For example, as described in the introduction, fear kept overloaded lower levels at Nokia from reporting problems and delays in key projects. Senior management was flying blind and lost the chance to reexamine its assumptions about the strategic plan and the resources the plan required.

Once Duncan got the factual observation that there were too many initiatives, he didn't take half-measures; he cut the number of initiatives down to five. "Going from twelve to five saved our bacon," he recalled, "because had we worked on twelve, we would have done all of them poorly. As it was, we were stretched at five."[5]

But Duncan wasn't done with SFP, because no company's bacon is ever saved once and for all. He then integrated honest, collective, public conversations—conducted through SFP—into American Diner's annual strategic planning process as the means to "slow things down" and get "unvarnished input," so that his team could make "fact-based assessments" and revise their plans accordingly. Each year's SFP brought to light new problems—or still-unsolved problems. But at the same time, it allowed people to "make a difference" and thus make their jobs meaningful—an integral part of Duncan's management philosophy.

Duncan believed that while listening to the feedback was painful—for himself and for his senior team—it was critical if they were to develop the right plan and carry it out successfully:

> We had all of these great initiatives to transform the company. We really felt, as top management, that we had figured this out. We had a direction and we wrote the strategic intent and I am thinking, "This is great stuff." Then the task force came back and said, "This is all very interesting, Joshua. We like the spirit of where you are trying to go, and for that we give you credit. But the truth is, until you fix some of the underlying problems that are going on in the restaurants, we do not really care about any of this." I felt I was getting hit again and again as they ran through their critique. They dished it up straight, but it was wonderful because it was exactly what we needed to hear.

This feedback also led to implementing SFP at the restaurant level to facilitate the execution of Faster, Better!, a program implemented to improve sales and service at the restaurants (see chapter 5). This example shows how SFP at the corporate level can and should trigger honest conversation in all relevant subunits to foster rapid and effective execution of corporate strategy.

Four years of using SFP as a strategic learning and governance process clearly helped Duncan pursue his strategic agenda. Management turnover was reduced from 48 to 25 percent, and frontline turnover declined from a horrific 220 percent to a manageable 158 percent. Comparable-store unit sales increased 11 percent, and there were strong earnings improvements.

Overload can be dangerous as well as inefficient. According to Jeffrey Pfeffer's *Dying for a Paycheck*, the stress of sustained long hours "hurts engagement, increases turnover, and potentially destroys physical and emotional health—while it is also inimical to company performance."[6] Stress can lead to heart disease and mental illness.[7] These are dangerous social and economic outcomes that responsible values-driven executives want to avoid for ethical reasons, not to mention for the potential legal liabilities.[8]

The American Diner story shows how institutionalizing SFP as a strategic learning and governance process gave managers at the corporate level and frontline employees at the restaurant level a voice that informed management at both those levels about overload. As an employee at Green Acres complained in chapter 5, "This stuff just gets thrown at us. Suddenly we're asked to do more and more." And the manager who complained, "They have no idea how difficult it is to be a manager . . . How many times have I worked a ninety-hour week, just trying to get people to do their jobs and helping them during rush times?" When managers used SFP to reorganize and reconceptualize their roles and that of the frontline employees, the efforts reduced overload and stress and improved performance. At Hewlett-Packard's Santa Rosa Systems Division, Scott Wright also realized that if one SFP was good, integrating SFP into the annual strategic planning process would be even better. After the first SFP, he announced, "We are going to do an SFP every year." SFP became the division's strategic learning and governance process. Each year, after the three-year strategic plan had been developed, a new fitness task force was formed and SFP was repeated in its entirety to learn what stood in the way of achieving the new plan. The division continued conducting an annual SFP for five years until the test and measurement business was reorganized after HP spun it off as a stand-alone corporation. Overload was a big issue there, too, particularly in the first year Wright used SFP. Five years later, Wright reflected on the issue and the role of SFP in dealing with it:

We are in a highly competitive industry, and all our salaries depend on beating the competition for our customers' money. And frankly, doing this is going to involve some stress and extended hours at times. However, we cannot rely on unsustainable heroic efforts by individuals as a way of doing business. Granted, for the longer term, it will only be through improved processes that we will be able to get an effective handle on our workloads. But the immediate steps [resulting from annual SFPs] are meant to bring some immediate relief and to show that we are doing something about it.

The Importance of Continuous Improvement

Just as quality management allows for continuous improvement of technical processes, institutionalized honest conversation allows—as we have seen—for continuous improvement in administrative, allocative, and collaborative decision making; in leadership; and in company culture. Honest conversation improves a company's decision making by pointing out who and what elements have been missing from that process. At SRSD, for example, honest conversation led to reorganization into a matrix that improved all these processes. It also encouraged Wright to acknowledge that, in his zeal to be decisive and not get bogged down in endless discussion, he had been by-passing people whose input was essential to the success he was trying to achieve. Annual SFPs led to continuous improvements to these solutions if they were found to be decaying or if changed circumstances required that they be adapted.

CEOs and unit heads such as Duncan of American Diner, Ed Ludwig of Becton Dickinson, and Wright recognized that SFP did for their organizations what Deming's quality principles have done for manufacturing production systems: ensure ongoing learning and a high-quality organization, which, in turn, is the source of high-quality solutions and products. As noted earlier, Deming believed that it is the system—"the interrelationships of all components of the system and everybody that works in it"—that must be changed to solve quality problems. "It is a mistake to assume," he said, "that if everybody does their job, it will be all right. The whole system may be in trouble."

Ludwig, CEO of Becton Dickinson, spoke to me about the appeal of SFP: "I had been a quality circle person in my prior life at BD. And I appreciated the power . . . of getting the people closest to the problem to solve the problem . . . And so, the idea of getting people engaged who were closest to [organizational] problems was intuitively attractive to me."

Duncan was also a committed disciple of Deming, and the CEO's attraction to SFP came from that earlier commitment:

The way that you lead is to have a fact-based assessment and then provide clear direction. You get unvarnished input from associates, you change your plans, you communicate and align, perform to plan, track results and optimize, and finally you learn and improve. The point is that anytime you do anything of significance, you go through these steps as a leader. You slow down long enough to get unvarnished input. This is a way of doing work that gives people a chance to make a difference. I adopted most of these steps from Deming, with the exception that we have added the listen and change steps [through SFP].

With any important change, nobody fully understands it from the start. That's why a continuous and effective feedback loop is so necessary. Institutionalized honest conversation provides just that, allowing senior teams to deepen their understanding of the changes they have already set in motion and to discover what further improvement is needed.

Wright's decision to carry out SFP every year reflected his commitment to continuous improvement in SRSD's organization and processes. Subsequent annual iterations of honest conversations are different from the first. Jeff Gould, a member of Wright's senior team, told me how the second SFP differed from the first:

Honestly, I did not think we would get that much out of this [second] iteration. The first time, we knew very clearly that there were things that needed to get done because . . . the strains and tensions were almost palpable. Well, this time the issues and tensions were much less apparent—comparatively. But even so, in this second SFP, we dug into the complexities of the system like we had never done before and really understood how different organizational levers affected the processes and culture. The first iteration was about how we wanted to set ourselves up as an organization. This time it was about how we wanted the organization to operate.

That second SFP enabled a focus on the problem of order fulfillment, an issue that had been voiced by the first SFP task force but did not get immediate attention. SRSD had needed to solve its larger problem: the conflict that was occurring between key functions and that was blocking strategy execution. The solution involved a much-needed reorganization into a matrix structure. The second SFP then brought a deeper understanding of flaws in order fulfillment and led to a yearlong successful effort to redefine that process.

Plans and organizations are never perfect and, even if a plan or an organization were perfect, it wouldn't stay this way for long, because circumstances change. Sometimes the very success of an activity changes the situation in a way that requires the activity itself to be revised. A perfectly good organizational solution that worked well for years may be challenged as a source of value creation, and a standard of effectiveness must often evolve to catalyze a company's next phase of growth. That is the situation that Vince Forlenza, Becton Dickinson's CEO, faced in 2018 after a seven-year successful transformation (see chapter 3).

Forlenza and Tom Polen, his president and COO, became concerned about coordination and speed of innovation, problems that had been solved by Forlenza's reorganization of BD into a strong three-dimensional matrix and the associated changes he made after the 2010 SFP (the one led jointly by Forlenza and then CEO Ludwig). BD was now twice the size and much more complex after eight years of growth catalyzed by two major acquisitions. It was time to learn why new versions of these same problems were resurfacing and if growth and complexity required further adaptation in BD's matrix organization, given the company's new complexity and how value creation was envisioned to evolve in the next phase of growth.

Forlenza and Polen now launched yet another honest, collective, and public conversation. They adapted the structure of SFP, consistent with its underlying principles, and commissioned three task forces to interview key people around the company. What those task forces reported set off a discussion of the underlying reasons for slow decisions and of potentially required changes in the matrix. By 2019, the conversation was taking place and SFP was enabling continuous improvement at Becton Dickinson.

Building Organizational and Leadership Capabilities

As discussed earlier, the six silent killers revealed by SFP in so many organizations are natural stress points—inevitable weaknesses. They weaken an organization's capacity to develop a strong direction, create a successful organization that fits that direction, and devise a suitable learning process to keep track of the direction and the organization.

These weaknesses must therefore be transformed into strengths—core adaptive capabilities—that must be maintained over time if the organization is to sustain its performance (see chapter 4).

The silent killers reflect underdeveloped organizational and leadership capabilities. These are not technical or administrative capabilities, such as franchising or robotics. Rather, they are socioemotional capabilities that take a long time to develop. People's collaborative capabilities—trust, attitudes, interpersonal skills, and feelings—do not change quickly or easily and are quite fragile unless continuously maintained and developed. Yet we know from the work of many management scholars that these soft capabilities are the source of sustained competitive advantage precisely because they are hard to develop quickly. Once you've done it, other companies can't catch up with you so quickly.[9]

The core capabilities whose weakness takes the form of the silent killers are not individual capabilities, which can be developed through leadership development programs. These capabilities depend on what Robert Gibbons and Rebecca Henderson have called *relational* capabilities and what I have been calling socioemotional capabilities.[10] Gibbons and Henderson show that these capabilities are crucial to long-term competitiveness. All relationships are subject to erosion, however. Just one mistake, such as keeping information from someone or blaming someone unfairly, damages trust and collaboration. It happens rapidly but takes a long time to restore.

The syndrome of silent killers—deficiencies in essential core leadership and organizational capabilities—is so pervasive and resistant to change because the killers are highly interdependent. When one capability—say, the senior team's trust and effectiveness—erodes, it causes all the others to degrade. Or when conflicts arise within the senior team, such as SRSD's cold war between functional departments, everyone else's trust in the senior team can quickly degrade. That is, while the core capabilities are mutually supportive, their deficiencies, or silent killers, are also perversely mutually supportive. These key deficiencies exacerbate each other, leading to an downward spiral—the silent killer syndrome. That syndrome damages the organization's socioemotional

health, its effectiveness, and its capacity to learn and adapt. Or, put another way, it undermines the organization's fitness, eventually render-
ing it unfit to compete.

If, however, the silent killers are turned into strong capabilities, as we
saw happen at SRSD and so many other organizations, they become mutually reinforcing and will sustain a virtuous cycle of trust building and
collaboration. In this way, the transformed capabilities will strengthen
the organization's fitness to execute strategy and to keep changing as
its competitive environment changes. The organization becomes and
remains fit to compete.

Addressing any single silent killer with a single program—such as
hiring a consultant to develop strategy, changing the organizational
structure to improve coordination, or providing team-building training
for the senior team—will probably do some good for a while. But that
capability will not be sustainable, because the other silent killers—the
ones you haven't fixed—will drag it down. Looking back on some of my
colleagues' and my earlier research on organizations trying to change,
I now recognize that their failure to address all the silent killers concurrently explains why "change programs do not produce change."[11]

The periodic discipline of a strategic learning and governance process like SFP will develop and sustain these decidedly human organizational capabilities. SFP—or any other repeated process of honest conversation—creates and renews accountability for monitoring the silent
killers and developing them into strengths, specifically, into the core
capabilities required to implement ever-changing strategies. Many of us
can say we've experienced something like this already in our marriages
or other personal relationships. Certain conflicts are resolved, but they
come back under a new set of circumstances and have to be resolved
again. Ideally, the two partners get better at it and the overall experience is one of improvement, not just of going around in circles.

Using cases discussed earlier, I illustrate in the following sections
how honest conversations transformed each of the silent killers into
strengths. In each case, the conversation also enabled the development
of other capabilities.

Clear strategy, priorities, and values (silent killer 1)

Duncan and his senior team clarified their strategy and priorities after the first SFP revealed they had set too many initiatives in motion. They conducted SFP every subsequent year as new initiatives were added and had to be reprioritized. This annual practice prevented the erosion of trust in management and of commitment to the changes that Duncan's new strategy called for, as well as improvement in effectiveness. At Becton Dickinson in the early 1990s, CEO Ray Gilmartin's second iteration of SFP revealed that BD's values were unclear and technocratic and that its culture could become more human. At SRSD, annual SFPs kept reminding the senior team, the task force members, and the key interviewees that technology platform solutions—not custom solutions, however profitable—were the primary strategy.

Better senior team functionality (silent killers 2 and 3)

Wright's leadership and that of his senior team improved in the year after the first SFP, causing the task force to report in the second SFP: "Our top team has taken some big strides in becoming more effective. Scott looks to be taking more control of the reins and becoming the kind of leader the division needs." But the task force also reminded Wright and his team that they had a ways to go and needed to work at it. A task force member put it this way: "They are still not where they want to be as a team. They still seem to be having a tough time getting together and really coming to agreement over some tough and pressing issues. I think people in SRSD wanted an overnight change in the top team's behavior. But, realistically, most good teams are not made in a day. They will have to work at it." These annual reminders led SRSD's executive team to keep developing its effectiveness. These habits in turn led to continued improvements in the other silent killers, like poor coordination.

Coordination and collaboration (silent killer 4)

Poor coordination and collaboration cannot be solved just once. Transforming this silent killer into a core capability is a multilayered and dynamic process.

Consider how repeated SFPs over three years extended and deepened the development of coordination at SRSD. As explained earlier in the chapter, the division addressed its order fulfillment problem on the second SFP go-around, because even though order fulfillment was a concern that first year, other challenges had taken priority. In the third year, with another SFP still finding some coordination problems, the senior team redesigned and improved a poorly defined and underresourced program-management function. They also learned that functional and business managers—two sides of the matrix put in place to improve coordination—were not participating in the performance evaluations critical to an effective matrix, so the team improved that process as well.

Of course, none of these improvements in coordination would have been possible without the continuous improvements in Scott Wright's leadership and that of the senior team. The next section looks at this capability.

Improved leadership (silent killer 5)

By institutionalizing SFP, the senior leaders at SRSD enabled not only their own development but also that of many managers below them. Because half the task force turned over every year, some fifty task force members over five years were given a chance to develop a general-management perspective in real time while helping to solve real problems. They gained an understanding of strategy and organizational effectiveness issues through their experience on the task force and then in leading the resulting change initiatives.

Working with the senior team gave task force members an overview of the reasons for an organization's inability to execute its strategy—including their own biases. Interviewing outside their own functional departments broadened their perspectives and eliminated biases that had been causing them to blame other units or functions, a practice that naturally fueled (or refueled) conflict. In one SFP that I facilitated, a task force member ran up to me just before taking her place in the fishbowl to tell me that while she had thought the marketing department was a major problem, she now believed that her own R&D department was part of the problem as well.

These experiences led SRSD task force members to report that participation in SFP had been the "best management development experience" in their entire careers at HP, a company already known for its excellent leadership development. These improvements in leadership development would not have been possible without the continued use of honest conversations, which, in turn, depended on the continued effectiveness of Wright and his senior team and their commitment to open and honest vertical communication.

By developing the leadership capabilities of these fifty potential leaders, SRSD increased its own capacity to execute ever-changing strategies. Thus, there was a simultaneous improvement in performance.

Honest vertical communication (silent killer 6)

Repeated use of SFP reduces people's fear of speaking truth to power. At SRSD, leaders became less remote and more human (see chapter 8), and the culture became more open. And as described earlier, the leader of the Belgian unit of a Swedish company organization said that after two SFPs, people came into his office wanting to talk about problems even without the structure of SFP. In many organizations, we observed that employees became more comfortable and courageous, given the change in the cultural context that repeated SFP brings about.

With repeated use of honest conversations at American Diner, the leaders became more accustomed to and skilled in receiving feedback about their own and the organization's effectiveness. They came to see the pain that honest conversation sometimes inflicts as important and useful. "I felt I was getting hit again and again as they ran through their critique," Duncan recalled. "They dished it up straight, but it was wonderful because it was exactly what we needed to hear."

The institutionalization of honest, collective, and public conversations serves as a continuous feedback loop and builds the missing collaborative leadership and organizational capabilities represented by the silent killer syndrome. These capabilities, in turn, develop and sustain a culture of trust. I repeat here what Jody Edwards, HR manager at SRSD, told my class at Harvard Business School: "SRSD has gained back the trust and openness it had lost—and then some." She said that people now wanted to join SRSD (rather than people in the division wanting to leave) because "they had heard about the tradition of annual SFPs and valued what it said about SRSD's leaders and their determination to give their people a voice and make a difference."

Enabling Simultaneous Improvements in Performance and Capabilities

As a leader, you know that pressure for short-term performance leads to cutting investments in most things required for long-term success, particularly in the development of soft, intangible human capabilities. How often have you seen budgets for leadership training, team building, coaching, and community building cut when they were most needed? Moreover, trusting, collaborative relationships are fragile and easily destroyed. It takes a long time to build them back up through these traditional means. In addition, managers under pressure to improve results quickly are less willing to "divert" time and attention to a search for the underlying causes of poor performance—such as the silent killers. Fires are fought, but the faulty wiring and dangerous sparks remain. Companies therefore continue to endure cycles of high and low performance, people are fired or leave, those who remain see that top management is not going to solve the real problems, and organizational silence increases.

Integrating an approach like SFP into strategic planning enables simultaneous improvements in performance and in capability development. It can avoid the up-and-down cycles too many companies

FIGURE 6-1

How honest conversation enables a forty-five-degree path to sustained success

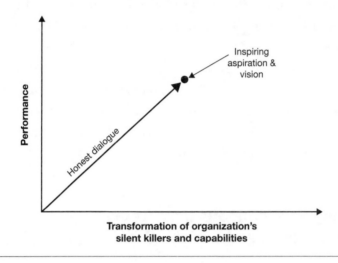

Transformation of organization's
silent killers and capabilities

go through. Although this integration takes a lot of effort—which, of course, costs money—it might nevertheless be seen as free. Faster strategy execution and a rapid turnaround in profits offset the costs of developing these capabilities in the same way that quality improvement on the shop floor not only raises quality but also reduces cost through improvements in manufacturing and the people who carry it out.

Figure 6-1 illustrates how SFP can improve performance and capability development simultaneously. Because performance and capability development are so often orthogonal—that is, independent of each other—I depict SFP and the honest dialogue it enables as a forty-five-degree diagonal that integrates them.

Institutionalizing Honest Conversations

A practice like SFP can become institutionalized, in a certain sense, through mere repetition: "This is what we do here because, as you can see, we keep doing it." A more effective form of institutionalization requires a much more deliberate effort over time. A practice is not only repeated, but also explained, improved, and adapted. In fact, institutionalizing a practice never ends, because practices do not last forever—or keep their intended form and purpose—if they are not carefully maintained.

Institutionalizing a strategic learning and governance process like SFP—that is, making it an ongoing practice repeated, maintained, and spread throughout a large multiunit organization—is difficult. The clearest threat is the ever-faster pace with which CEOs and key managers come and go. They are promoted or leave for a better position elsewhere. So, with the arrival of new leaders who do not know how to implement SFP or are not committed to its benefits, the practice devolves or erodes and ultimately dies.

To institutionalize a strategic learning and governance process like SFP and reap the benefits over time, CEOs need to have several practices in place in their organizations. Let's examine these requirements.

Leadership commitment

The most important requirement is commitment from top management. First, managers must be committed not simply to the process but also to its underlying principles. Second, they need a proactive plan—not just an intention—for embedding formal honest conversation as the company's strategic learning and governance process. There are no substitutes for leadership with these two qualities. Employee attitude surveys, leadership development programs, and speeches imploring leaders to lead with courage and openness will not teach leaders *how* to lead continuous improvement in the quality of their system of organizing, managing, and leading. Motivation is neither instruction nor transformation.

While starting at the top is clearly the best way, you can start below the CEO level. Honest conversation can be introduced first at the unit level, but the CEO must at least actively support it. And if the CEO's leadership clearly contradicts the principles underlying honest conversation, the experiment is unlikely to succeed.

Providing both support and consequences

The CEO and other leaders need to present formal honest conversation as part of people's jobs—as real strategic management work—not as a survey or a program taking place on the side and wasting people's time. The honest conversation must be used to solve a real performance problem, and leaders must be held accountable for reporting what they learned about the effectiveness of their organization and leadership. Subsequent success or failure in improving effectiveness must also have consequences for the leaders responsible for it.

The case of Merck Latin America offers a good example of these aspects of institutionalizing honest conversation.[12] When Grey Warner was appointed vice president of Merck Latin America in 1993, the region had long presented significant business challenges, not to mention an unstable political environment. Now that the region itself seemed to be changing and offering great opportunities, Warner had been asked to turn around Merck's business there. The company had just bought out and gained management control of the region's ten country organizations. Under their previous owners, they had been textbook cases of the reign of the silent killers. The companies were certainly not aligned with Merck's values and were prone to unethical practices.

Warner asked his ten country managers to conduct SFPs in their organizations. He positioned it as a process of learning and change by which they could develop their own leadership and their own organizations. He asked each leader to prepare for SFP by developing a strategy, but he provided them with corporate support for this task and reviewed the strategy with each manager. He also asked the managers and his team to use 360-degree feedback to create self-awareness and begin their personal development as leaders. Knowing that none of these leaders had ever received feedback from lower levels before—certainly not about their senior team and themselves—Warner thought this use of 360-degree feedback would prepare them somewhat for the potential shock of an SFP.

Two years after Warner's appointment, all ten Latin American country managers had implemented SFP as a governance and learning process. Warner asked them to present their findings to him directly as well as what they planned to do about their new knowledge. Sometimes he asked them to bring the whole task force with them so he could hear the feedback directly. This upward feedback about findings and plans for change gave Warner access to each country's leadership and organizational problems, which was particularly important since he was so far away in New Jersey. It created transparency and allowed Warner to evaluate the quality of each organization and its leaders. He could see how well the silent killers were being turned into core capabilities and could review progress in each organization's and manager's performance. Asking managers to repeat honest conversations on an agreed-on schedule is the best means to track progress.

Warner did all he could to help these managers succeed in this new endeavor, but he did not hesitate to replace someone after giving the person time and coaching to improve the organization. Given the imperative to turn around the region, this transition proceeded faster than might otherwise have been the case.

In the following years, the Latin American region achieved 20 percent compounded annual growth. It went from having the lowest survey results in the company with respect to attitude and morale to a much higher level of trust and commitment—well above Merck's average. Warner was promoted to senior vice president, as so many other SFP leaders and participants—both task force members and unit heads—have been promoted.

Warner institutionalized honest conversation in Merck Latin America not only by insisting that it take place—which any boss could do—but also in three other ways. First, he did his best to make sure SFP was successful and that his team wasn't overwhelmed by the process. Second, he ensured that his team members saw it as a path to their own success. And finally, he made it clear that there were consequences for not carrying out the endeavor successfully. Are not these the very qualities of good leadership?

Leaders who are attracted to and become committed to honest conversation begin with above-average leadership sensibilities and will themselves be changed by the productive dialogue they have led. Their success with this open communication leads others to adopt the practice and, in turn, helps institutionalize both the process and the spirit behind it. When employees see that a formal process is in line with how their leaders behave anyway, the process will seem legitimate. But top leadership must also be prepared to replace those who are unwilling or unable to learn—and learn from—honest conversation.

The point is not that people averse to honest conversation have to be punished, but rather that the company *needs* honest strategic conversation for its survival and therefore needs leaders who are adept at it. Thus, the institutionalization of SFP and similar practices is likely to sort out those who fit the new culture of honest conversation from those who do not.

Any new and unconventional process for learning and change has to be introduced in a way that is seen as fair and that builds commitment. Giving key leaders a chance to learn and supporting them in that process—as Warner did with his Latin American managers by helping them prepare the required strategy statements and by giving them a foretaste of SFP before the real thing—will be seen as fair. By allowing them a chance to make significant improvements in a timely manner, he avoided a mistake a Becton Dickinson senior manager had made in the early 1990s when the manager immediately replaced some subunit managers because of problems revealed by SFP, without allowing them an opportunity to make meaningful changes.

Spreading the practice

One way to institutionalize honest conversation is to make it the official company process by which new subunit managers take charge. New leaders (particularly those in their first general-management position) have found this an effective way to learn about the business quickly, build relationships with their key people, and create commitment to change. New leaders are particularly ready to use an unconventional approach like SFP because the problems that are surfaced cannot be attributed to their own leadership. You can let their early successes with SFP create a "demand pull" for more.

Top management can also create opportunities for managers who have used honest conversation to communicate their experiences and successes to other key managers in large public forums such as annual senior management meetings. But top management needs to make sure that as honest conversation spreads through the company, it is being carried out effectively. For each subunit undertaking an honest conversation, management should review the strategy and values that will drive it. Afterward, management needs to review what obstacles to organizational effectiveness the subunit's leaders uncovered and what they learned about their own leadership, preferably with a facilitator present as an honest broker for the conversation. At Becton Dickinson, this review brought accountability to expected improvements.

Building internal capacity

Honest conversations must be guided by leaders, not internal HR professionals or external consultants. To reiterate, implementing a strategic learning and governance process like SFP is real-time strategic management work in which senior teams must be the motivators and principal implementers.

For many tasks, however, senior leaders may want and require help from HR or consultants. Such tasks include organizing meetings and logistics, training the task force, facilitating the task force's rigorous analysis of the data it gathers, presenting and enforcing ground rules for engagement, facilitating a conversation by reframing it when it goes off track because of defensiveness (e.g., the Green Acres story in chapter 5), and serving as a knowledgeable resource on organizational diagnosis, design, and change.

Internal HR partners and consultants should be educated in these matters but often are not. That is when an external consultant may be needed to collaborate with internal consultants. For example, after a year of coaching and learning from us, Edwards, as HR manager at SRSD, took over facilitating the process from beginning to end, though she and her boss still asked me to be there when the task force presented its findings and to offer advice in the two following days of diagnosis and developing plans for change. Companies that want to institutional-ize SFP should develop these internal capabilities.

Lynne Camp, vice president of SGDU at Agilent (see chapter 1), de-scribed to me the value she received from the facilitation and advice of a third-party consultant. She said that whereas most consultants "think they know it all and tell you what to do," her SFP consultant came "alongside" her and "respected her position as the leader," using his knowledge of SFP "to help her make decisions." She also saw value in "being pushed"—that is, challenged on how she might go about lead-ing the honest conversation. Companies need to develop this type of internal capability if they want to institutionalize honest conversations.

Routinizing any practice can, of course, create form without func-tion. If a process like SFP is owned and motivated by HR, it will become a program with no benefit. Therefore, processes for honest conversa-tion should be used only when line leaders are motivated to close a gap in their own organization's performance. Of course, if they see no need to improve, their boss should be asking why. He or she should do what Warner did: ask them to lead an honest, collective, and public conversation to find out what does need improvement and why it is not improving.

Summing Up

Top-down strategic planning as practiced in the business world in the past seventy years separates thinking from doing. It fails to involve people below the top in discovering barriers to execution, facilitating the development of new organizational solutions that fit the strategy, and developing commitment to change. The cases in this chapter—and throughout the book—illustrate that SFP overcomes these failures. It promises to be the strategic learning and governance process that organizations require to learn and adapt. When companies make strategic learning and governance an institutionalized practice, they can continuously evaluate changes to their strategy and how they fit into the ever-changing business environment.

As illustrated by the cases in this chapter, institutionalizing SFP enables continuous development in three areas. It improves the quality of direction (e.g., more clarity on the strategy and reprioritization of initiatives at American Diner). It also raises organizational quality and improves a firm's ability to execute changing strategies (e.g., improved order fulfillment and program management at SRSD). Finally, making SFP a continuous, embedded process helps organizations better understand the silent killers that undermine strategy execution and performance and instead develop them into core capabilities. (e.g., Becton Dickinson and SRSD).

The six silent killers damage socioemotional capabilities. These highly interdependent capabilities underlie an organization's fitness— its learning and adaptive capability. The silent killers are therefore themselves highly mutually exacerbating, leading to an unvirtuous cycle of declining effectiveness. When honest conversations are routinized, repeated learning will transform the six silent killers into core adaptive capabilities and develop a mutually reinforcing, virtuous cycle of continuous improvement. This virtuous cycle occurs because ongoing honest conversations create accountability at all levels for improvement and keep reminding everyone—at every level—of their own accountability.

Institutionalizing a process like SFP requires more than intention. The CEO ideally legitimizes it by his or her own use of SFP and encourages—even requires—key business, regional, and functional leaders to use it and to report on what was learned and what will be changed. Most companies that use SFP have found that internal HR professionals can help leaders implement it by scheduling and facilitating the sequence of meetings that make up the process—but not by actually initiating or leading the process. Ideally these HR professionals have expertise in organizational diagnosis, design, and change that they can bring to the conversation while reframing interpersonal and organizational issues as needed to improve the insights and the plans for change. If HR professionals do not have these capabilities companies will have to develop them.

What If Honest Conversations Were the Norm?

PART THREE

Chapter 7

Corporate Stewardship

Every institution is vulnerable, no matter how great. No matter how much you've achieved, no matter how far you've gone, no matter how much power you've garnered, you are vulnerable to decline. There is no law of nature that the most powerful will inevitably remain at the top. Anyone can fall and most eventually do.

—Jim Collins, *How the Mighty Fall*

C orporate failures are in the news every day, as are CEOs who lose their jobs when their companies' fortunes decline. General Motors, perhaps the most iconic of these failures, took more than thirty years to die and could only be resurrected after bankruptcy. Many of the great and much-admired companies described in the books *Built to Last* and *Good to Great* are no longer high performers; nor have they sustained the cultural values of their founders.[1] Hewlett-Packard, a most respected company for its first five decades, is still alive but is no longer the venerated, high-commitment, high-performance company it used to be.[2]

Numerous explanations for corporate failures are offered: poor strategy, ineffective CEO leadership, bad culture, unethical behavior, low morale, rapidly changing technology or industry, wrong structure, poor customer service, and high prices, among others. While such explanations often do apply, they fail to identify the underlying root cause. I hope you have become convinced that the real root of corporate failure in many of its forms is the company's failure to overcome organizational silence through honest, collective, and public conversation.

Paradoxically, it is silence—the sixth silent killer—that prevents discussion of the five other silent killers that impede development and execution of strategy. Normal human defensiveness makes discussing the silent killers difficult. I hope you are convinced now that a strategic learning and governance process like SFP makes safe and productive discussion of silent killers possible and that it leads to timely and effective organizational transformation to which people are committed. (Transformations to which people are not committed are transformations that aren't going to transform much.)

Given this evidence, surprisingly few corporate boards of directors, CEOs, or unit executives make a serious attempt to engage their organizations in honest conversations about potential vulnerabilities—the kind that Jim Collins properly warns us about in the opening quote. As a consequence, most leaders forfeit the opportunity seized by the leaders in this book: the opportunity to be good stewards of their organization's future.

A Failure in Corporate Stewardship

The CEO of a privatized Canadian agency I will call Gov. Inc. called for help. His board of directors had asked him to engage a management consultant after hearing complaints from numerous key people about his leadership of Gov. Inc.'s transformation from a government agency to a private company. He agreed to move forward with SFP. He told me he planned to go to the board with what he learned from the honest conversation and present the action plan he and his senior team developed and asked me to accompany him when the time came.

SFP revealed deep problems of distrust of the CEO and numerous examples of the silent killers. In particular, people thought that the CEO was dishonoring them and the agency's proud, successful history when he publicly berated key people for not understanding how to lead and manage a for-profit enterprise. The change plan addressed both hard procedural issues—including a new project-management review process and improved resource allocation—and soft leadership and cultural issues, particularly changes in how the CEO and the senior team would lead and manage in the future.

At a dinner with the task force after the change plan had been agreed on, the senior executives were happy with what the honest conversation had achieved. They felt greater trust in each other and in the CEO. They looked forward to many positive changes. But I never received a phone call from the CEO asking me to accompany him when he briefed the board.

A year after my last contact with that CEO, I received a call from a member of his board. Once again, the board was hearing from frustrated key people who reported that the positive, honest conversation they had participated in had produced little or no change. (In a comparative study of the change accomplished in twelve organizations, Gov. Inc. ranked last [see table 2-1].) Could I help the board understand both the problems that had been uncovered by the honest conversation and the action plan for change that the conversation had produced? Moreover, could I give the board members *my* evaluation of the CEO's leadership? I explained that I could not share this information with them, because they had not been my clients. Further, I explained that if *they* had asked the CEO to implement SFP and had asked to review its outcomes, they would have had access to the very information they now sought. They could have had an honest conversation with the CEO about what changes they expected from him, followed up with progress reviews.

I later learned that five of the eight fitness task force members had left the company. I imagine (though I don't know for sure) that they had come to the pessimistic conclusion that nothing was going to change for the better. I also imagine that many others still there felt the same way.

Stewardship and Truthful Conversation

Virtually every type of institution—business, government, nonprofit, and nongovernmental organization—is vulnerable to deterioration in organizational health, and this vulnerability often goes unnoticed. This lack of awareness can be seen as a failure of stewardship. People responsible for protecting an organization's value and effectiveness are allowing these qualities to be lost. As my experience with Gov. Inc. illustrates, boards can become better stewards of a company's future when honest conversations become a norm. In that company's case, organizational silence prevented the board from learning in a timely and systemic way that the CEO's leadership was undermining the company's effectiveness.

A board must, of course, review a CEO's strategy and the projected economic outcomes such as growth in revenues, profits, and return on investment. But if a company is to have the culture and moral purpose (honesty and the will to do the right thing) required for long-term performance and for the sustainable commitment that—as I will show below—most employees desperately want, the board must also review the company's socioemotional health.[3] It is far easier for businesspeople to knowledgeably discuss hard business goals and outcomes than it is to similarly discuss socioemotional problems such as leadership, culture, and unethical or even illegal activities. Yet the latter group of problems can sink a company.

Attention to the system of organizing, managing, and leading was uppermost in the mind of David Packard, cofounder and then chairman of Hewlett-Packard. Asked by a journalist about the company's hottest product at the time—a small handheld engineering calculator—Packard surprised his interviewer by focusing not on the technology but on the careful design of HP's organization and the culture it created. Packard added that the system had required a "good deal of thought" and attention by senior management. The resulting headline for the article was "Hewlett-Packard Chairman Built Company by Design, Calculator by Chance."[4]

Unfortunately, Packard did not select and develop a board of directors who shared his view of how important HP's organization was to its success. The board later chose a CEO—Carly Fiorina—with a conventional top-down management philosophy and style. Lacking a discipline of honest conversation, the board failed to learn (that is, if they even wanted to learn) that her management approach was to liquidate human and cultural assets that had been developed over five decades by the founders.

Like most boards, the boards of Gov. Inc. and HP had not institutionalized a strategic learning and governance process that would regularly reveal a nonbiased evaluation of the three major outcomes essential for long-term success: fitness to perform, fit for trust and commitment, and fitness to learn and adapt. Few boards have valid data about the six silent killers, the deficiencies in the six core leadership and organizational capabilities that make these outcomes possible. Today, more than ever, responsible stewardship by a board requires that it adopt a perspective like Packard's and that it develop a strategic learning and governance process to prevent its own blindness. This is why I urge boards to require that CEOs enforce a discipline of honest conversation, and I urge CEOs to do the same with their unit leaders. Gov. Inc. and HP became more vulnerable because in both cases—and, unfortunately, as in most companies—the board was flying blind.

In the best companies, boards do receive employee survey results. Though standardized surveys provide valid comparative information that alerts boards to organizational problems, the data does not explain why the problems have arisen. Nor can it inform board members about matters they don't know enough to ask about, given their distance from what is really going on. Such matters are exactly what the board of Gov. Inc. wanted to know and what it and all boards need to know to be good stewards of their companies. Gov. Inc.'s board, like so many others, already knew there was some kind of problem, but the company lacked a learning and governance system like SFP to fully understand what was happening and why. Again, this shortcoming only made the board typical of corporate boards. How else can we explain the surprisingly

repetitive corporate scandals of the last several decades? Lower levels
know what's going on, and boards need a way to find out what the lower
levels know. (Not to mention that the lower levels generally wish someone upstairs *did* know and would do something about it.)

Consider the recent scandal at Wells Fargo. Employees knew well
before news broke in 2016 that some of their colleagues in the sales
function had opened checking and credit accounts without customer
authorization, an unintended consequence of a flawed cross-selling initiative and incentive system launched by senior management. The three
thousand or so salespeople who were eventually fired knew all along
that what they were doing was unethical and unsustainable, but they
were caught in an organizational hierarchy in which they had no routine safe way to inform the board about what they knew so that problems could be changed.

In the three years after the breaking news, the bank's stock price
declined by 8 percent while the Standard & Poor's 500 rose 12.7 percent and key competitors' stocks rose between 36 percent and 45 percent. The scandal cost Wells Fargo an estimated $100 billion in market
value—a loss for which its board is accountable. The episode led to the
board's public indictment, several resignations, and perhaps legal liabilities that will be playing out in court for years, not to speak of the
long-term damage to the bank's once-enviable reputation.[5] The same
story of organizational silence and its effects can be told about Volks-
wagen's emissions scandal in 2015 and the material, financial, and repu-
tational assets the incident cost the company. And it certainly applies to
the many scandals and failures in the 2007–2008 financial meltdown.[6]

These scandals—and, more importantly, the underlying failures of
boards to hold leaders accountable for developing an organization dedicated to the well-being of its employees, customers, community, and society—are responsible for a long-term, steady, worldwide decline of confidence in management and of trust in business and other institutions.
In the United States in 2018, trust among the general population suffered the largest ever-recorded drop in Richard Edelman's Global Trust
Barometer's history. Trust fell nine points to 43, placing it in the lower

quarter of this 28-market Trust Survey.[7] "The United States is enduring an unprecedented crisis in trust," Edelman concluded. He attributed the root cause to "the lack of objective facts and rational discourse." Within Gov. Inc. (and many other organizations, such as Wells Fargo), his conclusion could be restated as follows: we are enduring a crisis of trust caused by the lack of honest, collective, and public conversation.

Employees' desire for a better working world is reflected in their postings on Glassdoor, the public website that allows employees to speak up about their companies in ways they cannot do inside. Thirty percent of the complaints are about the company's culture and values, and 25 percent concern senior leadership—the intangible socioemotional assets embedded in the system of organizing, managing, and leading.[8] Granting that these are unsolicited posts from the most disaffected employees, we can still readily imagine that many other employees lack trust and commitment in their senior leaders but aren't moved to say so online. Compensation and benefits—the tangible assets about which boards have valid data and which they discuss regularly—are the least-discussed topic on Glassdoor, accounting for only 11 percent of the posts. It would appear that boards are rearranging deck chairs on the *Titanic* while employees are struggling with an iceberg. A learning and governance system like SFP is a way to turn that nonconversation into a real one.

Several recent studies, along with hundreds of others over several decades, confirm our own findings that employees are dissatisfied with their leaders' lack of intent and capacity to shape a purposeful, effective, and meaningful system of organizing, managing, and leading that goes well beyond the traditional goal of profits or shareholder value. Some of these studies have confirmed a relationship between intangible human assets and operational and financial performance.[9] Raj Sisodia, for example, found that firms with a higher purpose and human values showed profits nine times higher than those of conventional organizations in the same sector.[10] Business researchers Claudine Madras Gartenberg, Andrea Prat, and George Serafeim found a causal relationship between a clear shared purpose and financial performance.[11]

Consistent with these findings, Larry Fink, the CEO of BlackRock, the largest private equity firm in the world, legitimized the role of CEOs and boards as stewards of the company's intangible assets in a now widely publicized letter: "To prosper over time, every company must not only deliver financial performance, but also show how it makes a positive contribution to society. Companies must benefit all their stakeholders, including shareholders, employees, customers, and the communities in which they operate. Without a sense of purpose, no company, either public or private, can achieve its full potential."[12]

Fink does not, however, tell us how his lofty ambition might be achieved or monitored. While there are many ways that a healthy, purpose-driven organization can be developed and maintained, honest conversation, as I have shown, is a particularly powerful process that boards should ask CEOs to use and then review with them. Most corporate leaders have learned that companies must have a statement of values, but over time—if not immediately—these are viewed with cynicism by employees who see their company violating those values every day. If CEOs were held accountable by boards to periodically use a structured process like SFP, their public statements about the company's purpose and values would be more legitimate.

Imagine what might have happened if the board of Gov. Inc. had asked the CEO both to do exactly what he did on his own—lead a learning process like SFP—*and* to report on what he had learned and planned to change, bringing me along as an honest broker in that discussion. Or if they had asked the task force to repeat the fishbowl discussion in front of them so that they could learn directly. Such steps would have led to the honest discussions necessary to keep the CEO and company on the path to continued improvement. And if the CEO and the company did *not* improve, the CEO should have eventually been replaced.

In stark contrast to the CEO of Gov. Inc., Fred Lynch, CEO of Masonite International, was completely open with his board of directors. He invited three members of his board of directors to a meeting of his top one hundred leaders to share what he and his senior team had learned from SFP and the changes they planned to make, the final step in SFP that we recommend all leaders should take. But he decided to share what he learned in a radically different way that only a few leaders have chosen: Lynch asked the SFP task force to recreate a shortened version of the fishbowl in front of the leaders and board members so everyone could hear directly what Masonite's people had identified as the company's strengths and weaknesses.

The three board members had attended a strategy review meeting that preceded SFP. Lynch always invited board members to attend the first day of the meeting when the senior team reviews the prior year's people and organizational initiatives. Lynch explained why he chose to inform his leaders and board member in such a very open and public manner:

> We wanted our leaders to see that we were listening and being
> completely transparent. They were simply in awe that we managers
> were willing to expose our vulnerabilities in front of both this large
> group of leaders and board members and to commit to listening
> better and making changes the bulk of the organization believed
> would make us stronger. Many of the leaders came up to me after-
> wards and thanked me for having the courage to do this. To a
> person, they said we were tough in our comments (I didn't think
> so), but we also love the culture, working here, and just want to
> continue to make it better. Many told me they themselves needed
> to build up the courage to now go model this behavior with their
> organization.

At the meeting the following month, the three board members who had attended the leadership meeting described to the whole board what happened—the fishbowl and their reactions and those of the leaders. Lynch described that meeting:

> Board members expressed their gratitude for the transparency.
> It helped them to understand why I was so focused on investing
> in purpose and culture activities and, importantly, several board

members stated that they never felt they would be blindsided at Masonite because of the open and honest environment.

At my final board meeting in May [Lynch retired in 2018], the honesty we had displayed was one of the key things the chairman talked about. He told me, my senior leadership team, and the new CEO that he appreciated the open and transparent working relationship between the board and the management team. At the end of the day, you recruit smart and experienced board members who all want to contribute to the success of the company and help you avoid or solve potentially serious problems. If you sugarcoat the messages or are not transparent, you are actively making them less effective.[13]

This example demonstrates the power of involving a board of directors in an honest, collective, and public conversation like SFP: A partnership in stewarding the company develops. A CEO—or, for that matter, any key leader—who is uncomfortable with learning from an honest conversation and sharing it openly with the board or the CEO (for a unit leader) should ideally not be in a leadership role. That is why making honest conversations the norm and learning which leaders—including board members—are willing to lead and profit from them is the fastest way to develop an effective, high-trust, high-commitment organization. This willingness to be open and honest requires personal courage and mature leadership, but that is exactly what boards should expect from a CEO and what CEOs should expect from their key leaders who, in turn, should expect it from their key managers, and so on. The likes of Enron's Kenneth Lay and pharma fraudster Martin Shkreli simply need not apply.

Doing the Right Thing

Companies often use performance measures to decide on promotion and replacement. But given what we know about how leaders learn, isn't a manager's capacity to lead an honest conversation and to learn from it a better way to identify the most promising leaders? That's what Grey Warner of Merck Latin America meant when he said: "Get the best people that you can with the right values and . . . get rid of those who don't share those values."[14] Wouldn't the will to have an honest conversation and learn from it be a powerful means for a company to develop leaders—SFP requires key leadership capabilities—and replace those who cannot live to this higher leadership standard?

In every company, the CEO and the executives of major strategic activities face the same problems faced by the board of Gov. Inc.: How do they learn how closely their company and its subunits are aligned with its strategy, culture, and values? There is currently no widely institutionalized, disciplined management practice for learning the whole truth about the quality of leaders and organizations so they can be improved continuously. But good stewardship demands honest conversation that reveals the truth.

The combination of hierarchy and natural human defensiveness creates organizational silence at all levels. Even the best leaders in this book gained important strategic insights—things that had been largely kept silent about their own and their organizations' effectiveness—from SFP. As I have said before, SFP is not the only or even the best means for a strategic honest conversation. We have improved the approach over time, and more improvement is undoubtedly possible. I do, however, advocate for a disciplined way of holding honest conversations—by whatever method—regularly.

Given the deep human problems of trust and commitment that Edelman has documented and the increasing call, even by institutional investors like Fink, for organizations with a moral purpose, leaders at all levels must be held accountable for doing the right thing. And the right thing is whatever is good for both the business and its principal stakeholders, most especially its own employees.

The best purpose- and values-driven CEOs already do that, but they could do it even better if they made honest conversations the norm.

They could ask key unit leaders to conduct these conversations to learn not only about their organization's effectiveness but also how well the organization upholds its values and purpose. These leaders should then report back to everyone in their organization what they found and are planning to change. As we have seen all along, such conversations allow leaders to have more direct agency in the quality of the leadership, organization, and management below them. They typically gain this agency more remotely through information they get from their HR executives. Learning and governance processes like SFP are the most powerful way to gain agency simply because they are honest.

Direct, honest conversation allows senior leaders to humanize their leadership and legitimizes their expectation that key leaders below them will also lead with humanity—that is, with humbleness, authenticity, and a respect for the truth, however painful or embarrassing it might be. Lynne Camp observed that only through honest conversation did her people see her as a real human being and not just an "it" with more power than they had. Might it be the paucity of such conversations in organizations that underlies the two decades of decline in trust and commitment? Is the scarcity of honest conversations responsible for the increasingly transactional relationships between employees and their employers? For lower-level managers, the visible behavior of their successful higher-ups is a much more potent model than anything leadership training can offer.[15] The regularity of honest conversations is therefore the most powerful way—arguably the only way—to redefine what good leadership means in an organization. So why not make these conversations the norm at all levels?

Making Honest Conversations the Norm: A Thirty-Year Journey

Corporations are in a constant state of becoming better as they respond to continuous changes in the competitive and social environment. Each CEO must exercise strategic leadership to shape his or her strategic era, as Robert Burgelman, Webb McKinney, and Philip Meza remind us in their account of successive CEOs at Hewlett-Packard.[16] Responsible leaders lead change—sometimes dramatic change—while maintaining the continuity of the company's core capabilities. Honest conversation reminds leaders about the strengths they must preserve while legitimizing their agenda for change. Remember that of the two questions a fitness task force asks its interviewees, the first is what company strengths will help the company carry out its new strategy.

Becton Dickinson's development from 1988 to 2018 illustrates how SFP helped four successive CEOs—Ray Gilmartin, Clateo Castellini, Ed Ludwig, and Vince Forlenza—exercise responsible stewardship. The process enabled each CEO to manage the paradox of continuity and change and legitimize his change agenda by enlisting the necessary widespread commitment to that agenda. For each of these CEOs, SFP revealed barriers to his strategic intent and helped him overcome them.

1988: Executing a strategy

In 1988, Wall Street analysts advised BD's shareholders to hold (don't sell, but exercise caution about buying more stock) because they were uncertain about the firm's ability to deliver earnings in the near future. When Gilmartin took charge that year, he faced a major challenge: BD had to get better at executing its own strategy. Specifically, it had to grow overseas. Gilmartin began by asking business-unit leaders to use SFP to improve the effectiveness of their organizations. On the strength of a recommendation by Ludwig, then a business-unit leader who had already used SFP successfully in his own unit, Gilmartin launched a corporate SFP in 1990.

Here is how he saw the corporate transformation that was required: "We are trying to achieve multidivisional selling and supply chain management, which have to involve all our divisions. The transnational balance between global-scale economies and national responsiveness requires an organization philosophy and a way of operating that is not traditional. We also need the organizational mechanisms, commitment, and skill to manage technology."[17]

The fitness task force found numerous silent killers standing in the way of Gilmartin's strategic vision. The most pervasive was ineffective coordination—between US-based units and units based elsewhere in the world—concerning pricing, product development, manufacturing, and R&D resourcing. At the root of these problems were worldwide business teams that had been created to deal with these issues but that were perceived as ineffective. Several other issues were also reported: poor coordination between US business units in supply management, overly rigid and time-consuming corporate planning and budgeting, an HR function that didn't help business-unit leaders execute their strategies, an R&D function disconnected from the businesses, general overload, and an overemphasis on strategic planning at the expense of implementation. As if that weren't enough, the task force also reported a perception that BD lacked human values.

Gilmartin and his senior team had already observed some of these issues, particularly the tangible business issues, and had begun to deal with them. But SFP, like the genie in a bottle, gave them three gifts: a deeper understanding, a greater urgency, and a solid mandate for change. There were modifications in the way global business teams operated, as well as a number of other changes in response to feedback from the SFP task force. Ultimately, the company eliminated the International Division and created two worldwide businesses in its efforts to improve implementation even further. Many of BD's general managers went on to use SFP in their units. These were BD's first efforts to deal with the known but difficult to discuss silent killer of coordination. The effort was the beginning of BD's efforts to develop a worldwide system of organizing, managing, and leading that then kept evolving as each of Gilmartin's successors led change in his own strategic era.

1994: Becoming more human and less bureaucratic

Castellini became CEO in 1994, when Gilmartin left to become CEO of Merck. The new CEO felt strongly that BD was too bureaucratic; he complained about it whenever I saw him. He was also concerned about the impact of this pattern of management on innovation, people, and profits. Castellini wanted to de-bureaucratize, foster entrepreneur-ship, and create a more human organization. Even though BD's lack of human values had already been reported in the 1990 SFP, Castellini thought that little progress had been made.

In the first months of his tenure as CEO, he decided that the best way to start implementing his agenda was to use SFP again to initiate an-other honest conversation about BD's values, organization, and culture. He began with an offsite meeting of his senior team to develop BD's new values direction. A catalyst was the discussion of a case about Hewlett-Packard's human-centric organization. He then modified the process, but not its principles of engagement—that is, listening and change—to involve key people across the company in a discussion of the new values and cultural direction the senior team had developed. Each senior team leader was assigned to lead several honest conversations about the new direction in town meetings of key people in various locations around the globe. At each meeting, the executive presented the new direction, solicited feedback, and welcomed ideas for change. The senior team as a whole met regularly to discuss what the members had been hearing in their town meetings. From these internal meetings emerged a change agenda for making the company more human and entrepreneurial.

The team devolved decisions on strategy and resource allocation to business units. With less bureaucracy, BD rapidly increased its revenues and profits for several years, but profits and stock price declined pre-cipitously in Castellini's final year.

2000: Regaining performance and developing a higher purpose

To address the performance crisis, Ed Ludwig, Castellini's successor, de-cided to launch an SFP upon taking charge.[18] My colleagues and I have ob-served that in addition to identifying deeper systemic problems, SFP helps employees report urgent issues that must be tackled immediately. In this case, the task force reported two fires that needed to be put out quickly:

- A major enterprise resource planning upgrade, known as Gen-esis—begun under Ludwig's leadership when he was chief financial officer—was basically off the rails. The design was not robust, implementation was floundering, and there was a serious risk that the program would create major financial and operational difficulties.

- To inflate reported revenues, shipments of large volumes of products to distributers were made at the end of each quarter. BD had been employing this practice, known as channel stuffing, for several years. (It was legal at the time, though it no longer is.) But the resulting quarter-to-quarter volatility had led to hefty overtime, overload, and operational costs at the end of each quarter, which in turn resulted in low morale both inside the company and among dissatisfied distributers.

The fitness task force also reported several familiar silent killers that were busy undermining organizational effectiveness:

- Confusion or doubts about the company's strategic direction and its ability to achieve overall operational goals

- Coordination and collaboration problems due in part to decentralization

- Inadequate leadership development; significant underinvestment in retaining and developing talent

- A less than fully effective senior team

- Confusion about roles and responsibilities in BD's matrix organization, including who was responsible for strategy formulation and operational effectiveness

- The resultant slow decision making and gridlock because of the confusion about responsibility

After a sleepless night, Ludwig decided to take personal responsibility for immediately fixing the two most urgent problems. He stood up in front of the senior team and the task force and said, "I own the Genesis problem, and I will fix it." He promised that he would "stop further implementation of the Genesis project until problems with it have been fixed." He also promised that BD would "stop channel stuffing by the end of the year," even if it meant "missing the numbers." Looking back on those decisions, he told me that "if we hadn't addressed these two things, they could have shut the company down."

Ludwig then did something that is not a common practice in corporations but, as I argued earlier, should be. He reported to the board what he had learned and presented his ideas for fixing the two immediate problems that SFP had made discussible, thus gaining board support to do what needed to be done.

Implementation of Genesis was delayed for a year, at a cost of millions, but the results proved worth the expense and effort. "We got it right," Ludwig told me. "People are coming here to learn from us how we do this stuff." An independent analyst cited the BD Genesis project as one of the most successful SAP installations he had ever seen. And not only did BD end the inefficient distributer incentive program, it completely revamped its purchasing, sales, and distribution procedures. "Our supply chain now [is] just unbelievable," Ludwig said. "Order fill rates, efficiencies, back orders—any way you want to measure, it's much better."

Ludwig and his team also began what turned out to be an eleven-year effort to create a purpose- and values-driven company. In addition to offering great performance, BD would become a great place to work and would make a great contribution to society by helping people live healthier lives. BD University was created, in which senior executives taught managers how to lead in a way consistent with those three "greats." The conversion of silent killers into stronger core leadership and organizational capabilities facilitated many of these changes.

In 2006, Ludwig initiated another SFP, this time to check on progress and to further strengthen the capabilities he had begun to build. This honest conversation indicated that significant progress had been made but also led to a long-term effort to develop a new product-development process.

At the end of Ludwig's eleven-year tenure as CEO, an industry analyst on Wall Street sent him the following note: "Real leadership is getting [people] to do something they've never done or aren't even sure is possible. It is by this measure that we, the analyst community, hold the past decade at Becton [Dickinson] in such high regard."[19]

2010: Becoming a more innovative growth company

Vince Forlenza, soon to be Ludwig's successor, led yet another honest conversation through SFP with Ed Ludwig at Ludwig's suggestion. Both men reported to the board on what they had learned and on their transformation plans. Once Forlenza was CEO, he led the transformation of BD's capacity to innovate and grow faster (see chapter 3).

2018: Speeding up decision making and innovation

As Forlenza contemplated his own retirement in 2018, he and president and COO Tom Polen began to discuss Polen's concerns about the speed of decision making and innovation. BD was now a much larger and more complex global organization, and the strong three-dimensional matrix Forlenza had created required adaptation, as did other practices and processes. Polen assembled three task forces to collect data and begin an honest conversation (see chapter 6).

Honest conversations through SFP enabled four CEOs to steer Becton Dickinson on a thirty-year journey of continuous change. And now a potential fifth CEO is continuing that journey. These conversations legitimized change and sustained trust in, and commitment to, the company. Twice, the CEO brought the truths uncovered by SFP to the board.

By asking many unit leaders over those thirty years to implement SFP in their units, the four CEOs developed a bench of more-effective leaders, in part through what was learned but occasionally through replacement. Thus, honest conversations in various parts and levels of the organization improved BD's quality of leadership, its organization, and the execution of the CEOs' own strategic agendas. While BD did not fully institutionalize SFP in the sense of making it a regular strategic management discipline everywhere in the company, it does come very close to what I am advocating.

BD's board was fortunate in having two CEOs who understood the importance of collaborating with the board as stewards of the company, but that does not guarantee that future CEOs will do the same. As I have argued, wouldn't all boards be better stewards of their companies by asking CEOs to hold periodic strategic honest conversations and then hearing from the CEO what he or she had learned about the company's fitness to compete and the CEO's own leadership effectiveness?

Over those thirty years, Becton Dickinson has enjoyed great success. It acquired and successfully integrated many small and two large companies, and it continues to be a highly ethical, purpose- and values-driven company that achieves great performance, is a great place to work, and contributes to society. Between 1990 and 2018, its revenues grew by 694 percent—from $2 billion to $16 billion—a 7.68 percent compounded growth rate. Its net income grew by 70.64 percent, a three-year rolling-average compounded growth rate of 5.64 percent. And its stock price has outperformed the S&P 500 Composite Index by a large margin (figure 7-1).

I do not claim that these outcomes are all a direct result of SFP and the honest conversations it enabled. But the conversations did help the four CEOs and many key managers learn the full truth about BD's ability to execute its strategic agenda and accelerated the transformations these leaders led. It was, of course, the CEOs and the other key leaders involved in the conversations who have to be credited with BD's success. But the CEOs use of SFP in each era legitimized their change agenda, raised commitment to his agenda and the company, and enabled a partnership between top managers and their people. These benefits, in turn, sustained the continuity of BD's ethical and people-centric culture. In all, BD emerged from each honest conversation much more fit to compete.

FIGURE 7-1

Becton Dickinson stock performance versus the S&P 500, 1990–2018 (rebased to 100)

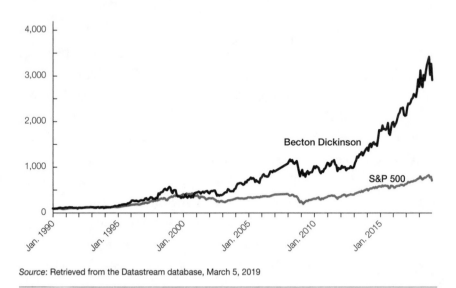

Source: Retrieved from the Datastream database, March 5, 2019

Summing Up

Is it inevitable that power will corrupt and that absolute power will corrupt absolutely? It's certainly the most likely outcome if leaders cannot overcome the organizational silence created by the power differentials that go with any hierarchy. Many management failures—including the many corporate scandals of the last twenty years and the concurrent growing mistrust of leaders and institutions—are rooted in the inability of corporate leaders to learn the truth and respond effectively.

Few corporate leaders would want to lead ineffectively or ruin their organization's reputation. But the leaders who manage to make these blunders have no way to find out that their assumptions about how to organize, manage, and lead are in fact undermining their intentions. Things will go astray in any organization, but power differentials—necessary though they may be—keep those things from being discussed and turned around.

The good news is that the honest conversations discussed throughout this book are by now a well-tested means for learning about failures well before the damage is irreversible. Just as important, the conversations encourage involvement by many stakeholders and their commitment to change. Yet such conversations are decidedly not the norm. Nor do those who follow and practice strategic management theory recognize that organizations must be disciplined enough to carry out such conversations to avoid the typical gyrations in performance and reputation.

Widespread adoption of this discipline must start with boards of directors. They must hold CEOs accountable for honest conversations and learning, not only to avoid Wells Fargo–level scandals but also, more importantly, to be long-term stewards of the organization. Good stewards value the capabilities embedded in the organization's people, assets, knowledge, and systems. Without such stewardship, the company cannot develop sustained commitment and performance. Instead, cycles of high and low performance destroy value for all stakeholders. And just as boards need to hold CEOs accountable for honest conversation, so must those CEOs hold their business-unit, functional, and regional leaders accountable.

Of course, honest conversations can be uncomfortable for the CEO, the board, and people in lower levels. But the stakes are too high not to do it. Without this dialogue, the six silent killers tend to take root and become greater and greater obstacles. Certainly, they will not be converted into the six core management and leadership capabilities that are rare in most organizations. These silent killers, or stress points, can become fault lines when the organization is challenged by an ever-more-competitive environment and they therefore require continual scrutiny.

Making honest conversations the norm demands courageous leaders with distinctive human sensibilities. That is the subject of the next and final chapter.

Chapter 8

The Need for Courage

Every leader will come face to face with his or her darkest doubts. In these moments, the way forward is to move directly into one's fear—to do the thing, address the person, or seek out the information that seems so terrifying.

—**Nancy Koehn,** *Forged in Crisis: The Power of Courageous Leadership in Turbulent Times*

Though the leaders my colleagues and I worked with and studied did not explicitly articulate to us what they considered their darkest doubts, they did—like all transformational leaders—have doubts and fears about how to lead change:

- Ed Ludwig, as an inexperienced business-unit leader who looked even younger than he was, learned that the business he had been assigned to lead faced strategic challenges no one at headquarters had told him about. All the managers who reported to him were older and more experienced and knew more about the business and technology than he did.

- Scott Wright and his senior team were convinced that they would be replaced within six months if they didn't turn their underperforming unit around. And there were deep conflicts that they had not confronted, because of their erroneous fear that confrontation would reduce trust levels even further.

- Lynne Camp had never managed a global business unit and had no experience in the business she was assigned to lead. She faced an all-male senior team of strong, opinionated leaders who thought her intention to reorganize into a matrix organization was wrongheaded, and she faced resistance to change from regional leaders wedded to the status quo.

- Joshua Duncan took over as CEO of American Diner thinking the company was in good shape and that he was there to take it to the next level. He soon learned differently: "The situation was much more challenging than I had realized."

- Ludwig, as Becton Dickinson's CEO, and his successor, Vince Forlenza, knew they had to transform the company but were uncertain about how to change an organization that, after all, was still successful, healthy, and 120 years old. Would transforming BD into a more innovative and faster-growing company wreck a good thing?

Embedded in the strategic fitness process is a demand for courage. The structure of the SFP process—its prescribed sequence of steps, behavioral guidelines, and guardrails—prevented defensiveness and counter-defensive reactions from erupting. That helped leaders and task force members to have the courage to be vulnerable. In all studies, senior teams heard the whole truth about their organization and their own leadership and management of it. There were differences, however, in the extent to which senior leaders embraced the authenticity and humility required to unleash the potential power of SFP to form a partnership with stakeholders. That is why depth of change and the extent of commitment to change varied from one organization to the next. (See table 2-1 for the amount of change in twelve organizations.)

Variations were a function of differences in assumptions about leadership. Consider one CEO, for example, who encouraged his key subunit leaders to employ SFP and had implemented it himself at the corporate level. Nevertheless, when we told him that some of the senior executives who had implemented SFP did not fully embrace the spirit of partnership that the method is intended to develop, he responded, "What do you mean, 'partnership'? Leaders decide." Differences in assumptions and beliefs then largely explain the variation in SFP's power to develop deep and sustained change in organizational effectiveness, leadership, and culture. Situational differences—the motivation for using SFP and the degree of change required—also affected relative success, but far less so than did differences in the leaders.

Nevertheless, the leaders in this chapter, and hundreds of others not mentioned in this book—had the courage to "move directly into their fear" when they decided to seek out the information that, if not terrifying, was at least anxiety-producing. (Several leaders mentioned sleepless nights just before or just after a report by the fitness task force.) Moreover, all the leaders were probably concerned about whether they would be seen as indecisive by their boards, their bosses (in some cases), and those below them.

Most leaders run away from these fears by hiring smart consultants to make recommendations and then selling those recommendations to their people. That is a much less threatening way to lead change than is fostering an honest conversation that might reveal to all the unwelcome truths, uncertainty, and disagreement about solutions. The leaders who used SFP rejected this conventional model of top-down, transformational leadership. They had the courage to let SFP make them vulnerable. Their humility went a long way toward creating a partnership with their senior team and those below the top.

In this chapter, I will describe seven courageous practices that my colleagues and I have observed in those leaders whose assumptions and beliefs were most aligned with those of SFP. These practices amplified the power of SFP to transform an organization deeply and sustainably, that is, its power to instigate systemic change in a way that develops trust and commitment. Each of these practices requires courage and authenticity. If you are convinced by now that the assumptions underlying

SFP are the best way to lead change, then the capabilities I describe below will define for you what transformational leaders must *do* and *be* to lead successful systemic change, regardless of the process they employ to do it.

The scarcity of leaders with these capabilities explains why so many companies fail to sustain high commitment and high performance. The lack of capable leaders is the biggest barrier to making honest conversations the norm.

Whatever outcome a leader's actions gets—good or bad—will change his or her assumptions and actions. Successful honest conversations changed leaders' views about the value of SFP and its underlying assumptions. Scott Wright was originally skeptical about SFP; he turned it down the first time his HR manager suggested it. But when he finally gave it a try and saw how dramatically it had improved SRSD and his leadership, he decided to use the process annually. Ed Ludwig's commitment to SFP as CEO of Becton Dickinson was grounded in his success using it to lead change as a division manager. Leaders who have good results with SFP find that they have learned not only how to carry out a useful process, but also how to behave in new ways as leaders. Both Lynne Camp and Wright, for example, learned about the counterintuitive power of vulnerability. Camp believed that SFP is a "training ground for becoming a humble leader." In the remainder of this chapter, several leaders who led SFP most effectively, particularly Camp, describe the varieties of courage that when amplified through things they said or did, increased the power of SFP.

Advocating and Inquiring

I hope you haven't gotten the idea that the leaders who showed the most humility were the least ambitious and the least interested in recognition and promotion. On the contrary, all the leaders who used SFP had ambitious goals and tremendous drive. They were ambitious, just as the great authentic historical figures Nancy Koehn studied were. In particular, though, they had strong conceptual capabilities that enabled them to advocate a new direction. Archie Norman, who led the transformation of the Asda grocery chain in the 1990s, made clear the importance of advocating a direction: "You start off with a company that's in disarray with low morale. They want direction and it's no good coming in and saying, 'Well, hey, guys, I'm here now. I'm going to listen.' They all think, 'Well, that's pretty disappointing. We want to know which way to march.' So, you tell the troops which way to march—in a broad direction—and then create some time for yourself to understand the steps you really need to make."[1]

All the leaders who led honest conversations possessed what Jim Collins calls a strong professional will or what Marvin Bower, the founder of McKinsey, called the will to manage.[2] These leaders cared deeply about creating a high-performance, winning enterprise. Camp's take-charge attitude, her rapid reevaluation of the business and its strategy, and her advocacy for transforming a functional organization into a business-by-function matrix are all examples of her will to lead. Ludwig and Forlenza had a similar commitment to lead when they decided that Becton Dickinson, successful as it already was, needed to become more innovative and to grow faster. Duncan of American Diner was motivated by a deep desire to create a people-centric, values-based organization: "I figured out over time that meaning should not be reserved for people who work in hospitals, that everybody deserves the right to find meaning for themselves at their work. And this work really does make a huge difference for all the people who touch it . . . Learning how to bring that meaning to people at work is worth my life."

Guided by SFP, the best leaders involved their senior team fully in developing the new strategic and values direction they were advocating. As I described in chapter 2, Duncan involved his senior team in developing not just a plan, but also the legacy they wanted to leave. Each team member, Duncan recalled, "brought important insights and perspectives" to the development of that legacy.

While the leaders in this book were strong advocates for change, they also had the will and courage to inquire into the quality of their organization and their direction. They believed that such inquiry would not frighten or confuse people but, rather, would empower them. Norman, having advocated change to his senior team and having asked for their help in his first meeting with them, then began an inquiry into why Asda was failing. Although he did not use SFP per se, his inquiry was definitely in the spirit of honest conversation. He traveled alone to numerous stores in his chain, arriving unannounced with clipboard in hand. There he began to ask employees and customers about how to improve their working and customer experiences. He then asked every store manager to hold regular honest conversations with employees and customers—listening circles—and to act on the results. If, over time, a store showed no improvements, he replaced the manager.[3]

Asking lower levels to define problems and involving them in developing solutions created a spirit of partnership in the organizations described in this book. Duncan, for example, believed that SFP "is powerful because it gives people the opportunity to make a difference."

Inspiring Trust by Revealing One's Humanity

One way some of the most successful leaders inspired trust was to share something about their life that revealed who they were as human beings. When Duncan told his senior team the new strategic and cultural direction in which he wanted to take American Diner, he found himself instinctively revealing his humanity by talking about his father: "I well up every time I do this," he told me, "so forgive me. But I talked about being with my father when he died . . . And he was an incredibly good guy . . . and had lived a really worthy life, and he's sort of my inspiration . . . Anyway, I decided to share that story. And I think it allowed people to connect with me in a way that they knew I was real."

Camp did something similar. With the task force seated in the fishbowl ready but apprehensive about delivering the straight truth, she stood up and said with considerable emotion: "My dad was a football coach, and I sort of grew up on a football field. My father would always tell me, 'When the going gets tough, the tough get going.' I was raised that way. In fact, I had a sign with that saying posted in my college room to remind me. That saying has inspired me my whole life."

Camp and Duncan revealed their human side instinctively for reasons they may not have fully understood at the time. It may have fortified them for the difficult transformational task ahead. It certainly communicated an authenticity that helped them develop commitment. Duncan believes that his authenticity comes from his ability to inspire himself:

> The ability to lead and energize and inspire others stems directly from the ability to lead and energize and inspire myself. In those moments when I am crystal clear about what I stand for and what I'm doing and why I'm doing it and why it matters, I can talk to anybody and get them fired up. Being authentic with people about the way I am and the way I work is absolutely essential for getting it to come out right. And what's been true for [my ability to persuade] the board, true for the investment community, true for my associates, is that I have to speak from the heart.

That kind of purpose inspires authenticity when leading honest, collective, and public conversations.

Embracing Feedback

Leaders who started with a readiness to see their employees as valued partners embraced the feedback they got despite the temporary embarrassment it may have caused. Camp was mortified by the criticism she received in the fishbowl—as any of us would be. But she also saw it as an opportunity to lead change more effectively, something she desired even more than she desired to be appreciated at any given moment:

I think the fishbowl was probably one of the most difficult days of my life. I walked in really excited about what I was going to hear that would support changing our functional structure to a matrix. I was completely humbled while I listened to ten of my second-level managers speak passionately about the issues and barriers to success we were facing. I was almost crawling inside myself, internalizing what I was hearing: "You know what? This isn't working." I thought it was working a lot better than it really was.

In a perfect example of how courage amplifies the effect of honest conversation, Camp describes how the honest conversation gave her new courage and how that, in turn, inspired her senior team to commit to change.

I took personal responsibility. I stood up and unhooked my name badge and put it on the table saying, "It's clear that this isn't working. It's also not clear whether I am the right leader to lead this organization going forward." I told them I was committed to spending the week trying to get to a solution to address these issues: "At the end of the week, if I am not the right leader, I will step down."

It was heartfelt and in the moment. I had never done anything like that in the past . . . My staff then each unpinned their name badges and put them on the table. We were all pretty touched by how bad it was and that we were responsible.

As I told you, each of my staff was very talented, with very strong opinions about the business and their individual functions. When they took off their badges, it was a signal to me that they were ready to become general managers alongside me and to put their agendas aside and make the right decisions. That was huge for me. I left that day feeling we have the starting of a real team because we are in it together and we are in it to serve the organization, instead of serving personal and political agendas.

Confronting Difficult Problems and Resolving Conflict

Ron Heifetz, my Harvard colleague, reminds us that instead of looking to strong saviors who will impose their strategic and organizational solutions, we should be calling for leadership that will challenge us to face problems for which there are no simple, painless solutions.[4] To do so, we must uncover and confront conflicts and help people resolve them collectively (although collective action needs leadership, the type I describe here). That is precisely what honest, collective, and public conversations allowed leaders like Camp to do:

> I was really clear with the task force that I wanted the truth. I wanted them to fully represent their interviews and not hold back. I had been waiting, pretty excited, to hear back on what we needed to do to get this matrix structure—in retrospect, I was pretty biased—so I entered that day highly energized and pretty excited to get the matrix kicked off. It didn't end that way . . . After hearing the fishbowl feedback, my staff and I went to work identifying the root causes of the issues and the actions we collectively needed to take to turn the situation around.
>
> The biggest takeaway for me in this whole process was that barriers to successful execution of a strategy are always in play, and you're ignorant at the top if you don't use a process like this to tap into it and to surface them. It's going on and it's stopping you from being effective. You can either put your head in the sand and pretend it isn't there, or you can go after it and find it. Then, when you find it, you can act on it.
>
> We were spending our time trying to figure out how to manage the business. I think what we overlooked—or what I overlooked—was how much these "silent killers" were killing us and stopping us in terms of being effective.

Basing Systemic Change on Facts

When confronted with fundamental problems in how the business was organized, managed, and led, the best leaders had the courage to reorganize and specify new roles, responsibilities, and decision rights. For some key people and in some value-creating activities, these changes would lead to losses in authority or status.

Based on feedback from the fitness task force, Becton Dickinson CEO Vince Forlenza had the courage to create a strong worldwide matrix organization. It took away responsibilities, decision rights, and status that the global business-unit leaders had had for years and assigned them to regional managers.

Camp had the courage to essentially take decision-making power away from herself. She let go of her conviction that a matrix organization was the solution to the many organizational problems she faced. Instead, she and her senior team agreed to reorganize SGDU into a decentralized product organization. The arrangement took away some decision rights from her strong and opinionated functional leaders. The businesses themselves would be responsible for R&D, product planning, marketing, and delivery. Functional leaders would now play a supporting role rather than their traditional driving roles. Camp described the systemic, detailed, and politically sensitive redesign process: "We specified roles and responsibilities and decision authority. Who made what decisions? Decision authority previously was all over the map. There were decisions being made about deals that we were going to bid on and how to price them at multiple levels of the organization. We clarified the decision process. We tested ourselves in scenarios: 'Well, if this were to happen, who owns it? Who makes the call?' That was a major outcome of SFP."

Few senior leaders have the courage to make such rapid and clear changes in power and decision rights early in the change process. Typically, they hope to ease their key leaders into it over time. Of course, this gradual approach slows down the transformation because it generates confusion and encourages underground efforts to save what's going to be taken away. It also corrodes trust. Most senior executives can clearly see who is going to lose what, even though their CEO is unwilling to say so directly.

In Camp's case, the courage to redesign the system openly came from her courage to inquire into and learn about the whole organization—the system. To less courageous leaders, such a broad exploration can seem too much to cope with. That openness, in turn, allowed the change to proceed much faster than one might expect. According to Camp, "We agreed to have the whole organization in place in six weeks." And they did.

Replacing Heroic Leadership with Collective Leadership

Camp discovered that redesigning an organization has to be collective work; it cannot be driven from the top by one or a few leaders, however committed they are to it. A major change is made up of many uncomfortable and unwanted smaller changes, each of which is a point of friction. Without real commitment, there will generally be enough passive resistance to undermine or sink the effort.

Camp's decision to let go of her commitment to a matrix organization is an example of collective leadership. She embraced feedback from the fitness task force and allowed their truths to shape her and her senior team's solution. Her attitude solidified the collective commitment that had already inspired her senior team to take off their badges—that is, their collective commitment to *earn* their positions by making their division more effective. According to Camp,

"We ended up *not* going with a matrix organizational design. Once the facts were all on the table and everyone had had their say, it was very clear to me that matrix was not the right answer. Instead, we designed SGDU's organization into business segments with a dotted line into functions that would support each of the businesses . . . We debated it pretty heavily over those three days, but ultimately that's the design that we went with. Some people won and some people lost, but it was agreed to. Everyone said, "Yes, this is the right organization."

When Scott Wright's task force vehemently objected to organizational changes to which he and his senior team were committed, having spent two intensive days developing them, he did not try to push them through, as so many managers would have been tempted to do. Instead, Wright created three subgroups composed of senior team and task force members to reexamine the proposed changes. His action led to one important change and commitment to the rest of the action plan. It may seem like the effort of those three subgroups outweighed the results, but the real result was *commitment* to a better solution. The alternative would have been resentment and resistance.

Camp also noted that what seems like a technical debate over a strategy can mask an emotional debate over trust and commitment:

> The fundamental strategy, which everyone was fighting, wasn't the real issue. The strategy can often be right on. It's all these silent killers and it's all the barriers that are boiling up and not allowing the organization to execute the strategy that's the key . . . It's been my experience multiple times . . . that when you put a strategy in front of folks, they'll argue and debate it and discuss it, but when you really engage them and get underneath it, they really do support the strategy. It's about the rest of the stuff that's so important to get out onto the table so that the organization can be successful.

Forlenza began his transformation effort convinced that BD needed stronger functions. SFP and the honest conversation it brought out broadened his thinking and enabled him to see that a more comprehensive change—the strong three-dimensional matrix—was the right solution. "I didn't have the whole thing scoped out in my head," he said.

"It was information from SFP that enabled me to refine my thinking." Letting that refinement happen took courage.

The leadership platform of SFP did not itself guide Wright, Camp, or Forlenza to let go of their particular convictions about this or that organizational solution. The honest conversation spurred respect for the differing views and the capabilities of lower levels. But it was all three leaders' human sensibilities that led them to instinctively commit to collective leadership, a predisposition uncommon in senior leaders. One of the long-term benefits of making honest conversations the norm will be to make a commitment to collective leadership the norm as well. Businesses will be much the better for it.

Suppressing One's Ego, Becoming Vulnerable, and Learning

When I asked Wright what he had learned from leading annual honest conversations using SFP, he said, "I learned that making yourself vulnerable is powerful." What he meant was that vulnerability gave him credibility and influence. The most successful transformational leaders, like Wright and Camp, went beyond the requirements of the process to suppress their egos and listen. They either learned to accept the vulnerability imposed by their decision to use SFP as their transformational leadership platform or were already predisposed to do so. You might imagine that Camp's offer to resign if she and her team could not fashion a good action plan for change would have put her at a disadvantage, weakening her ability to negotiate with her team. Instead, it was powerful precisely because she couldn't really back down from it. She had to be as dedicated to saving the organization as she was claiming to be:

> In that moment, all the dirty laundry was out on the table. I heard it. Running from it or pretending it wasn't there was just not an option . . . I was also transparent about how I felt. The level of

vulnerability that I showed in that meeting is probably more than they had ever seen me demonstrate before, and it was heartfelt.

. . . When I reported out to the organization about the plans to reorganize, I was trying to prepare my thoughts. You and I were on the phone. [Camp was referring to a conversation she had with me after I consulted with her on SFP.] And you said, "Use some negative quotes about you." I think you were encouraging me to allow the truth that I had heard to become more public and also to allow my vulnerability to be seen by the organization. It was one of the more powerful things that I did on that conference call.

What I heard later from folks was that everyone was shocked that I would be on a global call with five hundred people talking specifically about things that I had heard about myself and the changes I needed to make in myself to be a more effective leader.

When you are in a power position, you are exposed to a lot of things. You have to move fast. But I think the lesson here is don't forget that you're a human who has flaws and to keep an ear to the ground so that you can get feedback and course-correct. None of us is perfect, and we all need to continue to learn and grow. When that truth can be open in the organization and acknowledged by the leader, it makes leaders better because they're now human.

. . . One of the challenges you face when you're at the top of an organization is people see you as an object. They stop seeing you as a human. You wield too much power over them. One of the frustrations I always had at being at the top of an organization is people thought I was an it, as opposed to Lynne Camp, who actually is human. And yet, until you show that whole part of you—your vulnerability and who you really are—they are going to keep you at an it level. It's when they see you being human that you become someone that they can trust and follow because they can relate to you.

Camp described the corporate norm of discouraging the open display of vulnerability—a norm that makes organizations less human:

In none of the leaders I ever worked for did I ever see personal weakness expressed or that willingness to be vulnerable. I never saw it role-modeled. It's rare. But I will tell you, my own experience is that people trusted me more. They believed in me more because they saw that I was willing to listen to the ugly truth about what was already being said about me. I just didn't know it.

The ability and the willingness to listen and to act quadrupled my credibility with the organization. And that credibility allowed us to execute the plan extremely fast. That was our intent, given that one of our pieces of feedback was that we are slow making decisions.

Summing Up

The human sensibilities of the leaders featured in this chapter were not projected as powerfully by leaders who were less successful in their implementation of SFP. The courage to advocate *and* listen, to inspire trust and lead collectively, and to suppress ego and become vulnerable are not typical in corporate leaders. As Camp noted, most leaders remain an object—an "it" who is hard to trust and hard to follow with commitment. The human capabilities highlighted in this chapter are the scarce resource that organizations will need for honest and powerful conversations. But such capabilities are also a renewable resource, because humane and effective leadership will attract and keep young, idealistic people who can carry it on.

These capabilities will benefit any company, of course. As described earlier, the discipline of annual SFPs at Wright's Santa Rosa Systems Division attracted recruits to the division and restored the Hewlett-Packard culture that the division had lost. But over time, an increase in the number of business leaders with the types of courage described here will also restore a more widespread trust in business leaders and organizations. The test will be that someday, we read about an Enron or a Wells Fargo and think of it as a weird exception rather than as the tip of the iceberg.

Leaders can no longer be given a choice. Just as professional sports teams require athletes to develop well-above-average physical capabilities, corporations must require leaders to develop the well-above-average human leadership capabilities I describe in this chapter or be replaced. SFP and similar leadership platforms demand these leadership capabilities, but also develop them. The leaders discussed in this chapter had some natural inclination for the principles of honest conversation, but then, as they saw that the conversation accelerated their sought-after organizational transformations, they let it transform them as well. Making honest conversations the norm is thus a powerful way to develop humane leadership capabilities if leaders at all levels are held accountable for changing not only their organizations but also themselves.

A Final Word

Honest, collective, and public conversation. When you began reading this book, did that seem like "a consummation devoutly to be wished" but unlikely to be achieved? I hope you are now convinced that this kind of conversation is achievable—though it will never be easy—and that the institutionalized use of a learning and governance process like the strategic fitness process is at least one good way to achieve it.

More importantly, I hope you are convinced that it is worth achieving for the long-term health of your organization. A seemingly long-standing fact of life has been that companies—even the giants—come and go. Corporate evanescence may well be a fact of life, but the churn that we have become used to need not be. Companies can truly make themselves fitter. In a human sense, physical fitness means strengthening oneself against poor health through a fitness routine. Companies can also strengthen themselves against bad leadership and bad decisions by using honest conversation routinely to restore trust in their leaders.

Human nature will not go away, but the six silent killers do not have to take firm root in your organization and sap its ability to solve its own problems and adapt to changes in the world around it. They can, instead, be converted into the six core capabilities that make an organization fit to perform, fit to trust, and with fitness to adapt and learn—that is, fit to compete.

For me, what is "devoutly to be wished" is that you will bring all this to pass in your own organization.

Appendix A

Nine Steps of the Strategic Fitness Process

The strategic fitness process is vital strategic management work, not a human resource program. Over our thirty years of applying SFP, we have refined and developed SFP through an action learning process, evaluating results and making changes iteratively over time. Implementation revealed what aspects of the process worked as planned and what aspects did not. The result is a nine-step process facilitated by one or more third-party consultants or facilitators (internal or external, or both) (see figure 1-1).[1] At a minimum, the facilitators know how to implement SFP, including the nine sequential steps and how to conduct each meeting in the process. Ideally, they also have knowledge in the fields of strategy, organizational behavior, organizational design, and organizational change and development. With that knowledge, the facilitators can be a resource to senior teams when they analyze feedback provided by the fitness task force and make their plans for change.

SFP can be implemented in six to eight weeks, depending on the size and complexity of the organization. It requires four to five days of work time for senior management and six to seven for the task force. Task force members (eight to ten key people two or three levels below the senior team) are selected and commissioned by the senior team—not by the HR department. Task force membership is not a temporary full-time assignment; the members are expected to continue their usual work.

SFP is embedded in the following *six facilitated* meetings. These are scheduled once the senior team commits to implementing SFP. The length of each meeting can be adapted at that time, depending on the situation.

Step 1: Statement of Direction (1 day)

- The senior team (all the members must be there) develops a two- or three-page statement of direction. It articulates why the team is implementing SFP; the business's purpose, goals, and strategic direction; and the values the members would like to see guiding behavior in the organization.

- Each senior team member nominates two high-potential and highly credible task force members from his or her own organization. Senior teams have to agree on the final membership of the task force. Each member has one veto, though it is rarely used.

- Before the start of the process, the senior team communicates to the larger organization that SFP will be employed and why.

Step 2: Task Force Training (1 day)

- The head of the organization presents the statement of direction to the task force in person and asks it to bring back the unvarnished truth as seen by those they will be interviewing one to three levels below the senior team. The interview questions are as follows:

- Does the statement of direction make sense?

- What already-existing organizational strengths will contribute to execution of the direction?

- What barriers will undermine execution?

• Introductions are made, and task force members are asked how they feel about their assignment.

• The facilitator presents an overview of SFP and its underlying rationale and principles.

• The facilitator outlines the role and responsibilities of the task force: why, what, and when.

• The facilitator presents the fundamentals of conducting interviews, such as building trust and assuring confidentiality.

• Working as a group, the task force members adapt the interview protocol as may be required by the situation.

• The task force members interview each other using the same questions they will use in their interviews that follow.

• Task force selects one hundred or so interviewees in all parts of the organization. We have typically found this number sufficient, even in large global companies. Each member of the task force is assigned to interview a subset of the interviewees—usually ten to twelve. To ensure the objectivity of an honest conversation, the members do not interview people in their own function, business, or geographic region. This arrangement also gives task force members exposure to parts of the organization they may not know.

• The members are briefed about the data analysis they will be making in their next meeting and are instructed in how to prepare that data.

Step 3a: Data Collection (2–3 weeks)

Task force interviews

- Members of the task force call the interviewees and explain what SFP is about.

- They schedule a 1½-hour interview and send the statement of direction in advance of the interview. The interviews are ideally conducted in person. To that end, each task force member is assigned interviewees based as geographically close as possible without violating the rule that they interview people outside their department.

- The interviewers explain to the interviewees that the findings will be presented directly to the senior team and discussed with this team.

- The interviewers explain that the senior team has committed to share with the organization what it heard, its diagnosis of the root causes of problems the task force had reported, and the senior executives' action plan (what the executives plan to change).

- Throughout the interview, the task force members will follow the agreed-on interview protocol.

Third-party consultants or facilitators interviews

- Consultants or other facilitators will interview senior team members with the same protocol, but will also ask about the senior team's effectiveness.

Step 3b: Task Force Preparation for the Fitness Meeting (1 day)

- Each task force member comes prepared with three organizational strengths and three barriers he or she heard about from each interviewee.

- These are written onto sticky tags and posted on a wall. They are then grouped into themes for the feedback that will be given to the senior team.

- The themes are developed and assigned to task force members who will lead a discussion of their theme when they present their findings to the senior team.

- The discussion is rehearsed.

Steps 4–6: Three-Day Fitness Meeting (3 days)

Step 4: Task Force Feedback in the Fishbowl Format (1 day)

- The following rules for engagement are posted on the wall and presented by the facilitator:

  - Perceptions are fact.

  - The task force cannot be challenged about the validity of its findings.

  - The senior team can ask questions for clarification at the end of each theme discussion and at the end of the feedback.

- The task force reports its findings sitting in a fishbowl arrangement (see figure 1-2). Each theme discussion is led by one team member. This presentation of all themes typically takes between three and five hours, depending on the situation.

- Task force members leave the meeting after their presentation and are instructed to call their interviewees to tell them that their message has been delivered and that the senior team received it nondefensively.

- The consultants or facilitators present their findings.

Step 5: Discussion of Feedback and Root Causes (1 day)

- The senior team discusses the feedback and comes up with root causes for the problems uncovered by the task force's interviews.

Step 6: Development of an Action Plan for Change (1 day)

- Now that the senior team has identified the root causes for the barriers to the company's desired direction, the group prepares an action plan to address these barriers.

Step 7: Meeting of Senior Team and Task Force (1 day)

- The senior team members present to the task force what they heard, their diagnosis, and their action plan.

- The task force meets separately to discuss and critique the action plan, asking the following questions:

- Did the senior team hear the feedback correctly, and is the action plan responsive?

- What barriers does the task force see to implementing the action plan?

• The members of the task force give back to the senior team their evaluation of the action plan.

• If the task force sees deficiencies in the plan, it and the senior executives collaborate to reach a resolution.

Step 8: Implementation

Mobilizing the whole organization (1 day)

• A meeting of the senior team, the task force, the hundred interviewees, and other key people not interviewed takes place to inform this larger group about what was learned from SFP and what will change.

• The senior executives describe what they have heard and their action plan. Some companies have used a planned management meeting to do this.

- The organization's head—the CEO or general manager—communicates what he or she and the senior team heard.

- Some senior teams have asked the task force to re-create the fishbowl discussion in front of a large audience of key corporate leaders. The executives' willingness to expose raw feedback, as opposed to simply summarizing in a presentation, is perceived as a very powerful gesture that demonstrates the senior team's openness and courage (see chapter 7 for an example).

- The one hundred key leaders meet in small groups to discuss what they have heard and provide the senior team with their reactions—both positive and negative.

- In large companies, senior team members travel to multiple geographic or business units to present the results of SFP following the mobilization meeting. There too these small-group discussions are repeated to develop ownership and to work out what each unit can do to support execution of the corporate strategy.

Implementation of change (1 year or more)

Implementation

- Implementation teams headed by task force members or other key people are created to drive initiatives for change as required. They include members of the functional departments affected, who provide technical background and integrate with their departments but who do not lead the teams.

Follow-up

- The senior team regularly reviews the progress of each initiative. This responsibility is ideally not delegated, for example, to HR. A senior team member is appointed to coordinate the execution phase.

- The senior team meets with the fitness task force quarterly to hear its evaluation of progress. The evaluation is based on informal discussions with the people the task force interviewed and with others.

- SFP is repeated:

  - It can be integrated into strategic planning (see chapter 4) or simply done periodically.

– In large companies, the business units, corporate functions, geographic regions, or country organizations can be asked to apply SFP in their units with respect to that unit's strategy, framed in a way that supports the corporate strategy.

Step 9: Institutionalization

• Key heads of business units, geographic areas, and functions are encouraged or required to use SFP in their organization. SFP should not, however, become an HR program—an employee commitment building exercise—unconnected to the general manager's strategic and performance imperatives. SFP is not an employee survey. It must be motivated by the senior team's express desire to improve the organization's effectiveness. How frequently SFP is repeated should be governed by this criterion.

Specific circumstances may call for modification of these steps, but such changes should be evaluated carefully to assess how they may detract from SFP's objectives of improving organizational effectiveness and performance, developing high trust and commitment and building the organization's capacity to learn and adapt continuously

Appendix B

Research Purpose and Methods

The research that led to the insights reported in this book was motivated by a request for help from the CEO of Becton Dickinson in 1988. He and his senior strategy and HR officer were concerned about the company's inability to execute its strategy at the corporate and business-unit levels. They asked for help in developing Becton Dickinson into a company capable of executing its strategies.

The strategic fitness process (SFP), a structured leadership platform, was invented to help a leadership team execute its strategies at the corporate and business-unit levels. Implementation of SFP began at Becton Dickinson but quickly spread to other companies in diverse industries, where it was implemented at multiple levels: corporate, business unit, function, country organization, and operating unit.

My colleagues and I conducted our research using multiple qualitative and quantitative methods. Our research into the efficacy of SFP yielded many insights that were then used to improve the process. We were able to confirm or disconfirm the assumptions about organizational effectiveness, change, and development underlying SFP, and we gained new insights. In sum, the research and resulting insights have led to the development of a grounded, normative, actionable theory of organizational change and development.

Primary Purposes of the Research

1. We elected to evaluate the effectiveness of the strategic fitness process (SFP) in helping achieve the following outcomes:[1]

   a. Improve the organization's effectiveness: its capability to execute the senior team's stated strategy and values.

   b. Achieve outcome 1a in a way that builds trust and commitment.

   c. Improve people's collective capacity to continue learning about the organization's effectiveness.

2. We also aimed to learn about the principal conditions that moderate the ability of SFP to achieve the preceding three outcomes.

Normative Assumptions Underlying the Design of SFP

- Organizations are socioemotional as well as technical systems composed of many interdependent features, including strategy, structure, leadership behavior, processes, information systems, performance measurement, reward systems, and shared values or culture developed over years of organizational success and failure. The fit or alignment of these organizational features with each other and with the senior team's strategic and values direction determines the organization's effectiveness in executing that direction.[2]

- Realigning the organization's system of organizing, managing, and leading—the context—is therefore essential if the organization is to achieve the three outcomes listed above.

- The inability of the senior team and those below them to have a completely open and honest conversation about the organization's fit or alignment keeps the senior team from timely learning about organizational and leadership barriers to alignment.[3]

- An honest, collective, and public conversation about the system's effectiveness will enable the senior team to realign the organization with its strategy and values.

- This kind of conversation will also create trust, commitment, and partnership between leaders and their reports. These outcomes are essential in developing and sustaining a healthy and effective organization.

- An organization unable to have an honest conversation nondefensively needs a structured process that discourages defensiveness and enables learning.

Research Methods

The following methods informed the narrative and conclusions in this book:

- The fitness task force's feedback about strengths and barriers to implementing strategy and values in all organizations that implemented SFP

- In each organization that implemented SFP, consultant interviews with the senior team about its own and the organization's effectiveness

- The scholar-consultants' observations and insights are recorded in memoranda

- Meetings of a broader network of consultants in which they presented successful and less successful cases of SFP and the discussion of conclusions that could be drawn

- Interviews and questionnaire surveys

- Written cases about organizations that implemented SFP

- Selected interviews with managers who led SFP

- Analysis of performance outcomes when data was available

Because the consultants often had long-term relationships with the organizations we studied, they could observe the implementation of the changes over time and the factors that affected the effort's ultimate success or failure. The longitudinal nature of these relationships enabled insights about causes of success or failure.

Focused Studies

Beyond the observations and data collected through repeated implementation of SFP in approximately one hundred corporations and eight hundred subunits in North and Latin America, Europe, India, China, Japan, and Korea, my colleagues and I conducted the following focused research studies:

1. A study of twelve organizations, all subunits of Becton Dickinson, that had used SFP in the early 1990s.[4] The study had two stages:

   a. Post hoc interviews by an independent research assistant in each subunit at three levels—senior team, task force members, and a sample of those interviewed by the task force.

   b. A questionnaire survey of perceptions about SFP and its perceived outcomes on effectiveness. In each subunit, respondents were general managers, senior team members, task force members, and a sample of key interviewees.

2. An interpretive content analysis of feedback from twelve task forces in the same Becton Dickinson units as in study 1. We identified a syndrome of six barriers we call the silent killers (see chapter 4).

3. A post hoc comparative analysis of twelve organizations that had used SFP and the cases that had been written about them (see table 2-1).

   a. The analysis was conducted by a team of five scholar-consultants (three of whom had never facilitated SFP nor had any consulting relationships with the twelve organizations.

   b. A questionnaire was developed to evaluate the twelve organizations before and after SFP. Each team member was asked to agree or disagree with behavioral descriptions regarding effectiveness, trust, commitment, and openness, and the extent to which each of the silent killers existed in that organization before SFP and a year or more later when the time frame of the case allowed.

   c. Each member of the group read the cases and independently rated items on a seven-point scale ("strongly agree" to "strongly disagree").

   d. The group then met to discuss each of their pre- and post ratings. If there were differences in how group members rated an item, the case was reread and underlying reasons for disagreement were discussed, and a consensus was developed.

   e. The pre- and post-mean ratings were used to calculate the extent of change in each organization.

4. A wider group of consultants at TruePoint Partners held periodic case discussions of SFP implementations. These improved our collective understanding of SFP's effectiveness and the conditions that moderate its effectiveness.

5. I conducted in-depth interviews with a small group of CEOs and general managers who had led highly successful SFPs. Their retrospective impressions of their experience provided deeper

insights into their thoughts and feelings during SFP and how
and why the process helped them transform their organizations.

Limitations and Strengths of the Research

The research was not intended to be normal scientific positivistic research. Therefore, no conclusions can be reached about whether SFP
is more effective than any other intervention that leaders might use
to develop the three outcomes listed in item 1 of "Primary Purposes
of the Research." Nor can we conclude that SFP will be effective in all
organizations.

We can, however, conclude that SFP was effective in a variety of
settings and cultures when two important conditions—leadership and
corporate culture—were or became consistent with the underlying values of SFP. Insights gained from research and thirty years of helping
leaders implement SFP has helped my colleagues and me develop the
grounded, normative, and actionable theory of organizational change
and development reflected in this book.

Appendix C

Questionnaire for Assessing Your Own Organization's Silent Killers

The questionnaire in this appendix is divided into six categories, each a silent killer. If you have placed check marks in each or most of the six silent killer categories, your organization is probably struggling to enact change as a whole. If most of the items in any given silent killer category are checked, that particular silent killer is playing a strong role in undermining the effectiveness and agility of your organization.

You may use this assessment to evaluate the organization you lead or to ask your key people to assess your organization. The only way to improve your organization's effectiveness is to enable an honest conversation with your people to discuss the barriers. In such a conversation, they can give you examples of why and how these barriers are creating ineffective organizational behavior. As discussed throughout this book, the strategic fitness process is one way to enable such safe conversations.

If you are assessing your organization but are not leading it, this survey will give you a qualitative way to evaluate its overall effectiveness.

If it is struggling, the leaders must initiate an honest conversation with those below them to learn about the root sources of the problems, including how they themselves lead. If they are unwilling to support such an honest conversation, then the organization needs new leaders. But of course, the new leaders would need to engage in such a conversation as well, for the same reasons.

Silent Killers Checklist

Please check all that apply to your own organization.

Unclear strategy and values, too many priorities,
and conflicting priorities

- ☐ Our strategy may be well developed on paper but hasn't been translated into a simple, logical, and broadly understood story for how the business will win and the values that should govern behavior.

- ☐ We have a lack of clearly defined and articulated values to guide organizational behavior.

- ☐ Because functions and businesses each champion their own priorities, we face conflicting priorities, conflicts over resources, and poor execution of our strategy.

- ☐ People feel overloaded with everything being labeled a priority.

Ineffective senior team

- ☐ The senior team is ineffective and not really a team.

- ☐ Our senior team operates a hub-and-spoke model. Our leader meets with team members individually to review the results of their function, business, or region. The whole team rarely meets to review the business.

☐ Most of meeting time is spent on information sharing and updates on short-term operational details, rather than confronting and resolving tough strategic issues: "Death by PowerPoint."

☐ We have little constructive conflict in meetings. The real decisions get made outside the room.

☐ The senior team members don't speak with a common voice about our strategy and priorities.

Ineffective leader

☐ Our leader tends to get lost in the operational details and works "one level below his or her pay grade."

☐ Our leader is not visible. He or she spends relatively little time communicating overall strategy or direction or forcing constructive debate to resolve contesting views.

☐ Our leader does not confront issues or people directly to resolve festering conflicts.

Poor coordination or teamwork across silos

☐ The organization we have does not work effectively.

☐ It is painfully hard to execute on cross-functional, business, or geographic initiatives, often even despite good personal relationships.

☐ Work on horizontal cross-boundary teams is seen as secondary to meeting the goals for one's own unit (e.g., function, business, or region).

☐ The roles, responsibilities, and decision rights of functions, business units, or regions are unclear.

☐ There is conflict between different activities that need to coordinate and collaborate.

Inadequate leadership skills and development

☐ Too few managers can lead cross-business initiatives or take a general-management, business-wide perspective.

☐ We keep coming back to the same usual suspects when something important needs to get done.

☐ Too few opportunities are provided for leadership and management development.

☐ Our senior team does not review leadership talent regularly or offer career paths that enable the development of general-management capabilities.

Poor vertical communication

☐ There are few forums for downward communication of our purpose, strategy, and goals.

☐ Once purpose, strategy, and goals are communicated, little time is given to discussing them.

☐ People do not feel safe speaking out, especially to their leaders, about problems in organization and management.

☐ There are few forums for upward communication where managers and associates can openly and publicly communicate with senior management in a low-risk environment.

☐ Open, public discussion of difficult issues goes against the cultural grain.

☐ Our senior leaders rarely if ever ask lower levels to tell them about problems that stand in the way of our effectiveness as an organization or how they can be improved.

Notes

Introduction

1. Gary Cohen, quoted by Ed Ludwig, interview with author, 2012.

2. See McKinsey and Company, "How to Beat the Transformation Odds," April 2015, www.mckinsey.com/business-functions/organization/our-insights/how-to-beat-the-transformation-odds.

3. The Nokia, British Petroleum, Johnson & Johnson, and Toyota cases and quotes in this section and the next two sections come from Richard Lepsinger, "The 2010 Execution Round-Up: Six Companies That Couldn't 'Get It Done' This Year (and Two That Did)," *StrategyDriven*, January 24, 2011, www.strategy driven.com/2011/01/24. See also Yves L. Doz and Keeley Wilson, *Ringtone: Exploring the Rise and Fall of Nokia in Mobile Phones* (Oxford, UK: Oxford University Press, 2018).

4. Lepsinger, "The 2010 Execution Round-Up."

5. G. Colvin, "What the Hell Happened at GE?," *Fortune*, May 24, 2018, http://fortune.com/longform/ge-decline-what-the-hell-happened.

6. My use of the phrase *speak truth to power* does not have the political meaning it had in the early 1950s through 1960s. I do not mean to portray senior management as oppressors. But they do have the power to discourage criticism, intentionally or not.

7. I refer here to my colleagues in TruePoint, a consulting firm founded in 2002 to offer strategic change consulting services, among them helping companies implement the strategic fitness process.

8. M. Beer, *High Commitment, High Performance: How to Build a Resilient Organization for Sustained Advantage* (San Francisco: Jossey-Bass, 2009).

9. M. Beer et al., *Higher Ambition: How Great Leaders Create Economic and Social Value* (Boston: Harvard Business Publishing, 2011).

10. Paul Adler, Charles Heckscher, and Lawrence Prusak, "Building a Collaborative Enterprise," *Harvard Business Review*, July–August 2011.

11. Tonia E. Ries et al., *2018 Edelman Trust Barometer: Global Report*, Daniel J. Edelman Holdings, 2018, www.edelman.com/sites/g/files/aatuss191/files/2018-10/2018_Edelman_Trust_Barometer_Global_Report_FEB.pdf.

12. See C. G. Worley, T. Williams, and E. E. Lawler III, *The Agility Factor: Building Adaptable Organizations for Superior Performance* (San Francisco: Jossey-Bass, 2014). See also A. McGahn, "Competition, Strategy, and Performance," *California Management Review* 41, no. 3 (1999): 74–101.

13. The widely accepted concept that organizations are systems has a long history in the field of organizational behavior and development and has been written about by academics and practitioners such as Kurt Lewin, Michael Beer, Jay Galbraith, Michael Tushman, and Barry Oshry.

14. These three areas of fitness are from Beer, *High Commitment, High Performance*.

15. P. R. Lawrence and N. Nohria, *Driven: How Human Nature Shapes Our Choices* (San Francisco: Jossey-Bass, 2002).

16. R. Eisenstat, B. Spector, and M. Beer, "Why Change Programs Do Not Produce Change," *Harvard Business Review*, November–December 1990.

17. Beer, Eisenstat, and Spector, "Why Change Programs."

18. M. Beer, M. Finnström, and D. Schrader, "Why Leadership Training Fails and What to Do about It," *Harvard Business Review*, October 2016.

19. M. Beer, R. Eisenstat, and B. Spector, *The Critical Path to Corporate Renewal* (Boston: Harvard Business School Press, 1990).

20. M. Beer, *Organization Change and Development: A Systems Perspective* (Santa Monica, CA: Goodyear, 1980); J. R. Galbraith, *Designing Organizations: An Executive Guide to Strategy, Structure and Process* (San Francisco: Jossey-Bass, 2002); M. L. Tushman and P. Anderson, *Managing Strategic Innovation and Change* (New York: Oxford University Press, 1997).

21. H. Quy, "Emotional Capability, Emotional Intelligence, and Radical Change," *Academy of Management Review* 24, no. 2 (1999): 325–345.

22. R. F. Baumeister and K. D. Vohs, *Encyclopedia of Social Psychology* (Thousand Oaks, CA: Sage, 2007).

23. Steve Fossi, interview with author, 2004.

24. O. V. Timo and Q. Huy, "Distributed Attention and Shared Emotions in the Innovative Process: How Nokia Lost the Smart Phone Battle," *Administrative Science Quarterly* 61 (March 2016): 9–51.

25. I am indebted to my colleague Malcolm Wolfe for these insights and for this visual representation of why transformation is so hard.

26. C. Argyris, *Strategy Change and Defensive Routines* (Marshfield, MA: Pitman Publishing, 1985).

27. B. Oshry, *Seeing Systems: Unlocking Mysteries of Organizational Life* (San Francisco: Barrett Koehler, 2007).

28. I am indebted to Chris Argyris for the concept that information about how an organization is or is not working or is only valid when it includes intangible socioemotional facts that are typically not discussable. See C. Argyris,

Intervention Theory and Method: A Behavioral Science View (Reading, MA: Addison-Wesley, 1970).

29. The term *dynamic capabilities* has been incorporated into scholarly conversations about how capabilities need to be dynamic to be responsive to change in the competitive environment. For an overview of this idea, see: G. Dosi, R. R. Nelson, and G. Winter, *The Nature and Dynamics of Organizational Capabilities* (Oxford, UK: Oxford University Press, 2000).

30. C. Argyris, *Overcoming Organizational Defenses* (Needham Heights, MA: Allyn Bacon, 1990); E. W. Morrison and F. Milliken, "Organizational Silence: A Barrier to Change and Development in a Pluralistic Society," *Academy of Management Review* 25, no. 4 (2000): 706–725.

31. J. Detert and A. Edmondson, "Implicit Voice Theories: Taken-for-Granted Rules of Self-Censorship at Work," *Academy of Management Journal* 54, no. 3 (2011): 461–488.

32. Ibid.

33. C. Argyris, *Organizational Traps: Leadership, Culture, Organizational Design* (New York: Oxford University Press, 2010).

34. D. Heath and C. Heath, "You Can Change Anyone's Mind—If You Help Them Trip over the Truth," *LinkedIn Weekend Essays*, October 6, 2017, www.linkedin.com/pulse/you-can-change-anyones-mindif-help-them-trip-over-truth-dan-heath.

35. W. George and P. Sims, *True North: Discover Authentic Leadership* (San Francisco: Jossey-Bass, 2007).

Chapter 1

1. Information on SGDU and how Lynne Camp led its transformation through the strategic fitness process comes principally from my participation in the strategic fitness process as Camp's consultant, notes about what the task force reported, and interviews I conducted with Camp, the senior team, and other key people a year after the change process began.

2. L. Gerstner, *Who Says Elephants Can't Dance: Inside IBM's Historic Turn-around* (New York: HarperCollins Publishers, 2002).

3. American Diner is a disguised name I use at the request of the company. Joshua Duncan is a disguished name as well.

4. W. E. Deming, Address at Western Connecticut State University, 1990, https://quotes.deming.org/authors/W._Edwards_Deming/quote/10221.

5. For a discussion of the key ideas regarding organizational learning and a description of one organization's change journey in which the company conducted six SFPs over the years, see T. Fredberg, F. Norrgren, and A. B. Shani, "Developing and Sustaining Change Capability via Learning Mechanism: A

Longitudinal Perspective on Transformation," in *Research in Organizational Change and Development*, vol. 19, ed. A. B. Shani, R. W. Woodman, and W. A. Pasmore (Bingley, UK: Emerald, 2011), 117–161.

6. Quote from Kevin McVey, from a talk he gave to participants in a leadership development program at the Higher Ambition Leadership Institute, 2019.

7. Lynne Camp, interview with author, 2005.

8. The idea of bringing a large number of people, sometimes as many as a hundred or more, into one room to put issues on the table, sort out the key themes, and develop action plans has a long history in the field of organization development. See, for example, M. R. Weisbord, *Productive Work Places: Organizing and Managing for Dignity, Meaning and Community* (San Francisco: Jossey-Bass, 1987).

9. This approach was developed by my colleagues Russ Eisenstat and Kathy MacDonald at TruePoint in collaboration with leaders at Becton Dickinson and Waste Management.

10. For the whole story of change at Asda, see M. Beer and N. Nohria, "Asda (A)," case 498-005; "Asda (A1)," case 498-006; "Asda (B)," case 498-007; and "Asda (C)," case 498-008 (Boston: Harvard Business School, 1997).

Chapter 2

1. Jonathan Haidt, *The Righteous Mind: Why Good People Are Divided by Politics and Religion* (New York: Vintage, 2012).

2. B. Schneider et al., "Work Force Engagement: What Is It, What Drives It, and Why It Matters for Organizational Performance," *Journal of Organizational Behavior* 39, no. 4 (2017): 462–480; C. M. Gartenberg, A. Prat, and G. Serafeim, "Corporate Purpose and Financial Performance," *Organization Science* (in press, last revised October 18, 2018), https://papers.ssrn.com/sol3/papers.cfm?abstract_id=2840005.

3. C. Argyris, *Intervention Theory and Method: A Behavioral Science View* (Reading, MA: Addison-Wesley, 1970).

4. Len Hirschi, production manager in Hewlett Packard's SRSD as quoted in "Hewlett Packard's Santa Rosa Systems Division (A3): The Effects of Reorganization," case 498-014 (Boston: Harvard Business School, 1997).

5. Quote from an anonymous task force member at Whitbread PLC, 2002.

6. J. R. Galbraith, *Designing Organizations: An Executive Guide to Strategy, Structure and Process* (San Francisco: Jossey-Bass, 2002).

7. M. Beer and N. Nohria, eds., *Breaking the Code of Change* (Boston: Harvard Business School Press, 2000); McKinsey and Company, "How to Beat the Transformation Odds," April 2015, www.mckinsey.com/business-functions/organization/our-insights/how-to-beat-the-transformation-odds.

8. R. Lesser et al., "Algorithms for Successful 21st Century CEO Tenure," Boston Consulting Group Report, 2018.

9. M. Beer, "Leading Change," note 488-037 (Harvard Business School, Boston, 1991).

10. Haidt, *The Righteous Mind*.

11. P. E. Tetlock, "Social Functionalist Frameworks for Judgement and Choice: Intuitive Politicians, Theologians, and Prosecutors," *Psychological Review* 109 (2001): 451–457, as described and cited in Haidt, *The Righteous Mind*.

12. Ed Ludwig, interview with author, 2012.

13. Viktor Frankl, *Man's Search for Meaning* (Boston: Beacon Press, 2006), 74–75.

14. M. Beer, R. Eisenstat and B. Spector, *The Critical Path to Corporate Renewal* (Boston: Harvard Business School Press, 1990); M. Beer, R. Eisenstat, and B. Spector, "Why Change Programs Do Not Produce Change," *Harvard Business Review*, November–December 1990.

15. M. Seligman, *Learned Optimism: How to Change Your Mind and Your Life* (New York: Vintage, 2006).

16. M. Beer, M. Finnström, and D. Schrader, "Why Leadership Training Does Not Work: And What to Do about It," *Harvard Business Review*, October 2016.

17. D. McGregor, *The Human Side of Enterprise*, annotated ed. (New York: Random House, 2006).

Chapter 3

1. The story of Becton Dickinson's transformation is based on several Harvard Business School cases—M. Beer and R. Eisenstat, "Becton Dickinson: Opportunities and Challenges on the Road to the Envisioned Future," case 912-408 (Boston: Harvard Business School, 2012) and R. Sadun, R. Henderson, M. Beer, and J. Weber, "Becton Dickinson: Innovation and Growth (A)," case 717-419 (A) and "Becton Dickinson: Innovation and Growth (B)," case 717-504 (Boston: Harvard Business School, 2017)—and on many real-time observations of SFP and events that occurred later, and on conversations I had with people across the company.

2. My colleague Russ Eisenstat and I facilitated the SFP that launched the transformation in 2010, and we followed it between 2010 and 2016 through numerous visits and interviews with key people at multiple levels. Our relationship with BD continues to the present, though less intensively.

3. Ed Ludwig, interview with author, 2012.

4. Vince Forlenza, interview with author, 2016. All Forlenza quotes in this chapter are from this interview.

5. Psychological safety is a shared belief that it is safe to be open and honest. It can be defined as "being able to show and employ one's self without fear of negative consequences for self-image, status or career" and has been extensively researched by Amy Edmondson, my colleague at Harvard Business School. See A. C. Edmondson, *The Fearless Organization: Creating Psychological Safety in the Workplace for Learning, Innovation and Growth* (San Francisco: John Wiley & Sons, 2018).

6. N. Koehn, *Forged in Crisis: The Power of Courageous Leadership in Turbulent Times* (New York: Scribner 2017).

Chapter 4

1. Our original intervention as consultants grew into a five-year research and consultation engagement involving at various times Russ Eisenstat, then my colleague on the Harvard Business School faculty; Greg Rogers, my research assistant; and me. I will sometimes refer to this group collectively as "my colleagues and I." Chapter 6 will tell more about how SRSD integrated SFP into its strategic planning for five years as a means of continuous strategic learning and improvement.

2. R. Hackman, *Leading Teams: Setting the Stage for Great Performances* (Boston: Harvard Business School Press, 2002).

3. B. Schneider et al., "Work Force Engagement: What Is It, What Drives It, and Why It Matters for Organizational Performance," *Journal of Organizational Behavior* 39, no. 4 (2017): 462–480; C. M. Gartenberg, A. Prat, and G. Serafeim, "Corporate Purpose and Financial Performance," *Organization Science* (in press, last revised October 18, 2018), https://papers.ssrn.com/sol3/papers.cfm?abstract_id=2840005.

4. Hackman, *Leading Teams.*

5. J. McCarthy, "Executive Team Effectiveness," presentation at TruePoint practice meeting of unpublished survey results, Boston, 2015.

6. P. Lawrence and J. Lorsch, *Organization and Environment: Managing Differentiation and Integration* (Homewood, IL: Richard D. Irwin, 1967).

7. J. R. Galbraith, *Designing Complex Organizations: An Executive Guide to Strategy, Structure and Process* (San Francisco: Jossey-Bass, 2002).

8. M. McCall and M. Lombardo, *Lessons of Experience: How Successful Executives Learn on the Job* (New York: Free Press, 1988); M. Beer, M. Finnström and D. Schrader, "Why Leadership Training Fails: And What to Do about It," *Harvard Business Review*, October 2016, 2–9.

9. Beer, Finnström, and Schrader, "Why Leadership Training Fails."

10. S. A. Mohrman and T. G. Cummings, *Self-Designing Organizations: Learning How to Create High Performance* (Reading, MA: Addison-Wesley, 1989).

11. M. Beer, R. Eisenstat and B. Spector, *The Critical Path to Corporate Renewal* (Boston: Harvard Business School Press, 1990); M. Beer, R. Eisenstat, and B. Spector, "Why Change Programs Do Not Produce Change," *Harvard Business Review*, December 1990; P. H. Mirvis and D. N. Berg, *Failures in Organization Development and Change* (New York: Wiley, 1978).

12. By the standards of positivistic "normal" science, these findings are not conclusive. The ratings of the amount of change in the organizations and in the silent killers are made after the fact. Moreover, they are subject to the common rater problem as the before and after ratings were made by the same team of five raters. Action science is clinical research that cannot be held to positivistic standards for several reasons. Practice-based development of change methods rarely allows clean before and after research. The success of such new practices is affected by many unplanned and unanticipated exogenous factors, making claims of validity interpretative. Our claims of external validity are strong since we observe cause and effect relationships and could link action to result. Moreover, validity problems were offset by several factors. The ratings were based on facts in written research cases that contained pre-SFP information from the fitness task force feedback and post-SFP information based on action research or consultant knowledge. The ratings were made independently by each member of the research team, and the differences were adjudicated according to information from the cases or from the consultant team member who had in-depth knowledge of the situation. Finally, each consultant was in the organization throughout the SFP; had themselves conducted interviews of the senior team in parallel with task force findings, offering reassurance that their report was valid; and usually had followed the change in the organization, thus strengthening claims of causality.

Chapter 5

1. See "2017 Edelman Trust Barometer," Edelman Holdings, Inc., January 21, 2017, www.edelman.com/research/2017-edelman-trust-barometer.

2. R. Hurley, "The Decision to Trust," *Harvard Business Review*, September 2006, 55–62.

3. The Green Acres example is from a case written by the late Derek Schrader of TruePoint and is based on real events. Schrader was the SFP facilitator and consultant at this company, but its name and location and the names of individuals have been disguised to protect confidentiality.

4. David DeSteno, *The Truth about Trust: How It Determines Success in Life, Love, Learning, and More* (New York: Hudson Street Press, 2014).

5. D. M. Rousseau et al., "Not So Different After All: A Cross-Discipline View of Trust," *Academy of Management Review* 23, no. 3 (1998): 393–404.

6. M. Beer and G. Rogers, "Hewlett Packard's Santa Rosa Systems Division: Assessing Organizational Fitness Profiling (B3), case 498-019 (Boston: Harvard Business School, 1997).

7. D. M. DeSteno, *The Truth About Trust* (New York: Hudson Street, 2014), 133.

8. From my interview with the country manager, who wanted to remain anonymous, 2015.

9. D. Rousseau, *Psychological Contracts in Organizations: Understanding Written and Unwritten Agreements* (Thousand Oaks, CA: Sage Publications, 1995). Employers' and employees' understanding of their mutual relationships can also be more explicit and written with regard to wages and working conditions specified in union contracts, for example. See H. Behrend, "The Effort Bargain," *Industrial and Labor Relations Review* 10, no. 4 (1957): 503–515.

Chapter 6

1. H. Mintzberg, "The Fall and Rise of Strategic Planning," *Harvard Business Review*, January–February 1994.

2. I am indebted to Doug Conant, former CEO of Campbell Soup Company, and to Mette Norgaard for this formulation. See D. Conant and M. Norgaard, *Touch Points: Creating Powerful Leadership Connections in the Smallest of Moments* (San Francisco: Jossey-Bass, 2011).

3. J. Collins, *How the Mighty Fall: And Why Companies Never Give In* (New York: Harper Collins, 2009).

4. American Diner is a disguise for a company that my colleagues and I worked with and studied.

5. M. Beer, L. M. Roberts, and J. Weber, "Steak n Shake (B)," case 405–035 (Boston: Harvard Business School, 2005), 6.

6. J. Pfeffer, *Dying for a Paycheck: How Modern Management Harms Employee Health and Company Performance—and What We Can Do about It* (New York: Harper Collins, 2018).

7. L. C. Cooper and J. Marshall, "Occupational Sources of Stress: A Review of the Literature Relating to Coronary Heart Disease and Mental Ill Health," *Organizational and Occupational Psychology* 49, no. 1 (1976): 11–28.

8. See also S. Gupta, "One Nation under Stress," documentary, HBO Special, directed and produced by M. Levin and D. Pinkerson, 2019 (trailer available at www.hbo.com/documentaries/one-nation-under-stress).

9. See M. Beer *High Commitment, High Performance: How to Build a Resilient Organization for Sustained Advantage* (San Francisco: Jossey-Bass, 2009); J. Pfeffer, *The Human Equation: Building Profits by Putting People First* (Boston: Harvard Business School Press, 1988).

10. R. Gibbons and R. Henderson, "Relational contracts and organizational capabilities," *Organization Science* 23, no. 5 (2012): 1350–1364.

11. M. Beer, R. Eisenstat, and B. Spector, "Why Change Programs Do Not Produce Change," *Harvard Business Review*, November–December 1990.

12. M. Beer, and J. Weber, "Merck Latin America (A–D)," case 401-029 (Boston: Harvard Business School, 2001).

Chapter 7

1. J. Collins and J. I. Porras, *Built to Last: Successful Habits of Visionary Companies* (New York: Harper Collins, 1994); J. Collins, *Good to Great: Why Some Companies Make the Leap and Others Don't* (New York: HarperBusiness, 2001); J. Collins, *How the Mighty Fall—and Why Some Companies Never Give In* (New York: Harper Collins, 2009).

2. M. Beer, R. Khurana, and J. Weber, "Hewlett-Packard: Culture in Changing Times," case 404-087 (Boston: Harvard Business School, 2003).

3. For a rich and excellent discussion about managing a complex corporate system and its many tradeoffs and challenges, see J. Bowers, "The Purpose of Change: A Commentary on Jensen and Senge," in *Breaking the Code of Change*, ed. M. Beer and N. Nohria (Boston: Harvard Business School Press, 2000).

4. "Hewlett-Packard Chairman Built Company by Design, Calculator by Chance," *AMBA Executive*, September 1977, pp. 6–7.

5. J. Maxfield, "Chart: The Cost of Wells Fargo's Sales Scandal," *Motley Fool*, September 6, 2017, www.fool.com/investing/2017/09/06/chart-the-cost-of -wells-fargos-sales-scandal.aspx.

6. M. Beer, *High Commitment, High Performance: How to Build a Resilient Organization for Sustained Advantage* (San Francisco: Jossey-Bass, 2009), 327–332.

7. "2018 Edelman Trust Barometer Reveals Record-Breaking Drop in Trust in the U.S.," Daniel J. Edelman Holdings, Inc., January 22, 2018, https:// www.edelman.com/news-awards/2018-edelman-trust-barometer-reveals-record -breaking-drop-trust-in-the-us.

8. R. Warren, *The Purpose Driven Life* (Grand Rapids, MI: Sondervan, 2012).

9. Beer, *High Commitment*.

10. R. S. Sisodia and J. N. Sheth, *Terms of Endearment* (Saddle River, NJ: Pearson Education, 2007).

11. C. Gartenberg, A. Prat, and G. Serafeim, "Corporate Purpose and Financial Performance," *Organization Science* 30, no. 1 (2019): 231–245.

12. L. Fink, "Larry Fink's 2018 Letter to CEOs: A Sense of Purpose," Black-Rock, 2018, www.blackrock.com/corporate/investor-relations/larry-fink-ceo -letter?cid=synd%3ASA%3ALarrysFinks2018LetterToCEOsASenseOfPurpose.

13. Fred Lynch, personal communication with the author, 2019.

14. M. Beer, and J. Weber, "Merck Latin America (A–D)," case 401-029 (Boston: Harvard Business School, 2001).

15. G. Petrieglieri and J. Petrieglieri, "Can Business Schools Humanize Leadership?" *Academy of Management Learning & Education* 14, no. 4 (2015): 625–647.

16. R. A. Burgelman, W. McKinney, and P. E. Meza, *Becoming Hewlett Packard: Why Strategic Leadership Matters* (New York: Oxford University Press, 2017).

17. M. Beer and A. D. Williamson, "Becton Dickinson (A): Corporate Strategy," case 491-151 (Boston: Harvard Business School, 1995).

18. Ed Ludwig, interview with author, 2013.

19. Mike Weinstein, Managing Director, L. P. Morgan Chase's equity research health care team, email message to Ed Ludwig, 2010.

Chapter 8

1. Archie Norman, CEO of Asda, interview with author, 2008. Asda is a leading grocery store chain in the United Kingdom (2008).

2. J. Collins, *Good to Great: Why Some Companies Make the Leap and Others Don't* (New York: Harper Collins, 2001); M. Bower, *The Will to Lead: Running a Business with a Network of Leaders* (Boston: Harvard Business School Press, 1997).

3. M. Beer and N. Nohria, "Asda (A)," case 498-005; "Asda (A1)," case 498-006; "Asda (B)," case 498-007; and "Asda (C)," case 498-008 (Boston: Harvard Business School, 1997).

4. R. A. Heifetz, cited in M. Fullan, *Leading in a Culture of Change* (San Francisco: Jossey-Bass, 2001), 3.

Appendix A

1. A detailed SFP manual is available from TruePoint Partners at www.truepoint.com.

Appendix B

1. M. Beer, *High Commitment, High Performance: How to Build a Resilient Organization for Sustained Advantage* (San Francisco: Jossey-Bass, 2009).

2. The importance of alignment to effectiveness has been show in scholarly research and theorizing by Paul Lawrence and Jay Lorsch, Jay Galbraith, and Michael Tushman, among others.

3. C. Argyris, *Overcoming Organizational Defenses: Facilitating Organizational Learning* (Needham Heights, MA: Allyn Bacon, 1990).

4. See M. Beer and P. J. Maus, "Becton Dickinson: An Assessment of Strategic Human Resource Management Profiling," case 496-007 (Boston: Harvard Business School, 1995).

Index

Acknowledgments

The findings in this book can be credited to the collaboration between leaders who employed SFP, their people, and scholar-consultants. The leaders pioneered by employing SFP, a counterconventional method. The scholar-consultants brought knowledge and principles for solving the problem and facilitated implementation of SFP. The conclusions in this book about the role of honest conversations in changing an organizational system came from this collaboration. This book is therefore the product of a collaboration of many people in a variety of organizations. I am deeply grateful to all of them; I could not have written it without their help.

The collaborative inquiry began in 1988, when Ray Gilmartin, CEO of Becton Dickinson (BD), and the late Ralph Biggadike, his chief strategy and HR officer—an unusual combination of responsibilities—asked for help in developing BD into a company capable of executing its strategy. It was their intellectual curiosity and pioneering spirit that began the action research process of learning and change that, for me, has culminated in this book. Without them, SFP would not have been developed and the insights in this book would not have been possible.

Ed Ludwig, then a division manager at BD, was the first business-unit leader to successfully implement SFP, which made him, as he likes to put it, the first successful clinical trial in a long series of clinical trials that has followed for over thirty years at BD and many other companies around the globe. Many courageous senior managers at Becton Dickinson—too many to acknowledge individually—and an even greater number of managers around the world all contributed to the development of SFP and the underlying principles that emerged.

They not only used SFP but also collaborated with my colleagues and me in the writing of many research and teaching cases, some used in this book. Of the many courageous managers who implemented SFP in the 1990s (most of them no longer affiliated with their companies), a few stand out: Becton Dickinson's former CEO Ed Ludwig and current CEO Vince Forlenza; the late Scott Wright and his senior team at Hewlett-Packard, particularly Jody Edwards and Steve Fossi; Grey Warner at Merck; Peter Dunn, former CEO who employed SFP multiple times; and Lynne Camp at Agilent Technologies.

The research and theories of Paul Lawrence and Jay Lorsch on organizations as adaptive systems and of Chris Argyris on organizational defensive routines, along with the work of many early thought leaders in the field of organization development, influenced me and helped shape the thinking underlying the development of SFP as a means for fostering sustainable, high-commitment, high-performance organizations.

In addition to Russ Eisenstat, whom I already acknowledged in the author's note, I am deeply grateful to Nathaniel Foote, managing director of TruePoint, who cofounded the firm with Russ and me. He helped numerous CEOs implement SFP, collaborated in the research, and added many insights that have found their way into the book. Elise Walton, a scholar-practitioner who helped us execute the first few SFPs, played an important role in developing the fishbowl method as a means for safely delivering honest and rich feedback. My partners and the directors of TruePoint implemented SFP around the globe and were part of ongoing discussions that helped us refine the process and understand the conditions for its effective execution. They also read and provided feedback on a number of chapters. In the United States, these helpful individuals included Nathaniel Foote, Julian McCarthy, Kathy McDonald, Sean Quigley, the late Derek Schrader, and Chris Richmond. In Europe, the people who helped me included Magnus Finnström, Tobias Fredberg, Bjorn Frossevi, Flemming Norrgren (who introduced SFP to Northern Europe), and Malcolm Wolf. The late Derek Schrader—my student at Harvard Business School and the first

TruePoint employee—was an especially enthusiastic supporter of SFP and deserves special recognition for two cases he wrote, one of which is the basis of chapter 5, and for his enthusiastic support of SFP.

The Division of Research at the Harvard Business School funded a number of research associates who developed the cases that were the basis for a formal cross-case analysis. Special thanks to Jim Weber, who wrote the majority of the cases, and to Greg Rogers, who researched and wrote the case series about Hewlett-Packard's Santa Rosa Systems Division. A big thank you to David Delong, Russ Eisenstat, Nathaniel Foote, and Barry Sugarman, the research team who with me conducted the cross-case analysis. They generously gave their interest and time.

I received help in writing the book from many individuals. Russ Eisenstat and Nathaniel Foote gave me invaluable feedback about two earlier drafts and offered many helpful ideas that found their way into the manuscript. Teresa Amabile, my colleague at Harvard, provided encouragement and wrote a detailed and helpful critique of the book manuscript. Robert Bauman, former CEO of SmithKline Beecham (now Glaxo SmithKline), and Dick Walton, my former colleague at Harvard, provided feedback on an early draft. Mette Norgaard, my colleague at the Center for Higher Ambition, reviewed an early chapter and gave me valuable feedback. Ravi Venkatesan, who implemented SFP in India, reviewed the book and provided helpful criticism.

Last, but by no means least, John Elder became my partner in shaping the narrative in the book. He made it clearer and more powerful and provided detailed editing of the final manuscript. A special thank you to John.

About the Author

MICHAEL BEER is the Cahners-Rabb Professor of Business Administration, Emeritus at Harvard Business School. He is a cofounder and Director of TruePoint, a management consultancy, as well as cofounder and Chairman of the Center for Higher Ambition Leadership, a nonprofit whose mission is to help companies and their leaders do well by doing good. He is a well-known authority in the areas of organizational effectiveness, organizational change, leadership, and human resource management. Beer is the author of eleven books, including the award-winning *The Critical Path to Corporate Renewal* (1990), *High Commitment, High Performance* (2009), and *Higher Ambition* (2011). He is the recipient of numerous professional and academic honors, among them the Academy of Management's Distinguished Scholar-Practitioner Award and the Society for Human Resource Management's Michael R. Losey Excellence in Human Resource Research Award.